D0285412

THE
HOME
BREWER'S
ANSWER BOOK

THE
HOME
BREWER'S
ANSWER BOOK

Solutions to Every Problem,
Answers to Every Question

Ashton Lewis

Columnist for

Storey Publishing

2/11

*The mission of Storey Publishing is to serve our customers by
publishing practical information that encourages
personal independence in harmony with the environment.*

Edited by Margaret Sutherland and Dianne M. Cutillo
Art direction by Mary Winkelman Velgos
Cover and text design by Vicky Vaughn Design
Text production by Jennie Jepson Smith

Front cover photograph by © Jeff Shaffer/Shaffer Smith Photography
Back cover and page 2 photograph by © Suto Norbert Zsolt/Shutterstock
Illustrations by Randy Mosher, except for pages 12, 109, 307, and 357 by Mary Rich

Indexed by Susan Olason, Indexes & Knowledge Maps

© 2007 by *Brew Your Own* magazine

The information in this book is true and complete to the best of our knowledge.
All recommendations are made without guarantee on the part of the author or Storey
Publishing. The author and publisher disclaim any liability in connection with the
use of this information. For additional information please contact Storey Publishing,
210 MASS MoCA Way, North Adams, MA 01247.

Storey books are available for special premium and promotional uses and for custom-
ized editions. For further information, please call 1-800-793-9396.

Printed in China by Regent Publishing Services
10 9 8 7 6 5 4 3 2

Library of Congress Cataloging-in-Publication Data

Lewis, Ashton.
    The homebrewer's answer book / Ashton Lewis.
       p. cm.
    Includes index.
    ISBN 978-1-58017-675-0 (pbk. : alk. paper)
    1. Brewing—Amateurs' manuals. 2. Beer—Amateurs' manuals. 3. Brewing—Miscellanea.
    4. Beer—Miscellanea. I. Title. II. Title: Home brewer's answer book.
TP570.L469 2007
641.8'73—dc22

                                         2007022269

DEDICATION

To my parents,
Diane and Greg,
who have always encouraged me in my pursuits.

Looking back, it would have been pretty easy for them
to discourage me from exploring beer and brewing
during the three years preceding my 21st birthday.
Thank you for understanding that I was serious about
pursuing brewing as a career.

ACKNOWLEDGMENTS

I would like to thank the *Brew Your Own* editorial staff I have worked with over the years who helped make my column possible: Craig Bystrynski, Chris Colby, Garrett Heaney, Gailen Jacobs, Carl Landau, Kathleen James, Betsy Shaw, and Susan Walton. A special word of gratitude goes to Brad Ring, who successfully pitched the idea of this book to Storey Publishing, compiled all of these questions into chapters, and edited the questions and answers into manageable sizes from the originals.

None of this would be possible without a referral from Scott Ungermann back in 1995, when Carl Landau phoned the brewing lab at UC Davis looking for a technical editor for a new magazine he was looking to launch. I also must thank Dr. Michael J. Lewis, my friend, brewing mentor, and former business partner, for admitting me into his graduate program in 1991 and giving me the opportunity to do so much while at Davis.

Thanks go to Bob Maslar, father of my friends Andy, David, and Patrick, who loaned his homebrewing equipment to Tommy Flores and me. Tommy's parents, Janice and Dr. Felix Flores, were patient enough to allow Tommy, his cousin Billy Kelly, and me to commandeer their kitchen for some of our early brewing adventures.

CONTENTS

Foreword 8

Introduction 10

Chapter 1   The Basics of the Brewing Process 12

Chapter 2   Choosing and Using Brewing
            Equipment 41

Chapter 3   Cleaning and Sanitizing 83

Chapter 4   Hops, Grain, and Ingredients............. 109

Chapter 5   Choosing and Using the Right Yeast....... 167

Chapter 6   Fermentation and Lagering............... 213

Chapter 7   Bottling, Kegging, and Carbonation....... 257

Chapter 8   Homebrew Troubleshooting 307

Chapter 9   Extract Brewing 335

Chapter 10 All-Grain Brewing....................... 357

Glossary   From Adjunct to Zapap 407

Index   419

The one thing I can count on as publisher of *Brew Your Own* magazine is that my e-mail in-box will have questions each day from homebrewers asking for help and looking for answers. Brewing beer is an incredibly fun and fulfilling hobby, but it definitely comes with a host of questions. Some questions are obvious ones we all face in our brewing pursuits; others pop up only when something has gone horribly wrong with our latest batch. Then there are the questions that are just plain strange, such as the one about making beer from acorns. But all of these questions are important to ask — and answer — because they help build a greater base of knowledge among brewers, which results in a more successful and more satisfying hobby for each of us.

When *Brew Your Own* magazine launched in 1995, we realized the value and importance of seeking out reader questions and answering them in each issue. We were lucky to bring Ashton Lewis on board for that first issue as our "Mr. Wizard" and technical editor. Fresh out of the University of California–Davis's renowned graduate brewing science program, Ashton brought a wealth of wisdom and a sense of humor to his answers. He has since answered literally hundreds of questions spanning the world of brewing. Homebrewers can't get enough of his Q & A department. Every year, we send out a reader survey. Every year, readers tell us their favorite department in the magazine is Mr. Wizard, because of the variety of questions and the depth of the answers it provides. The "Brew Wizard Question of the

Week" section of byo.com is among the most visited areas of our Web site. Simply put, homebrewers have lots of questions and love reading Ashton's answers.

The funny thing is that few people knew Ashton was Mr. Wizard. We decided it would be fun to keep Ashton's identity as Mr. Wizard a secret, as with superheroes whose real names remain mysteries. So for 10 years, Ashton shared his wisdom anonymously with readers, on top of his daily duties as a professional brewer in Missouri. Not even many of his coworkers and friends in the craft beer industry knew of his double life as brewer by day and wizard by night. Now the secret is out, and Ashton's best work over the years has been collected here in this book for you.

More than 11 years of the best questions from small-scale hobby brewers follow in these pages. These are real questions from real brewers like you, many of whom made mistakes I hope you will learn from. Ashton's answers will help your understanding of beer and brewing, whether you are a first-time brewer or a knowledgeable veteran.

So, enjoy as the "Master of Mash," the "Sultan of Suds," the "Hero of Hops," the one and only "Mr. Wizard" answers common — and some not-so-common — brewing questions. You will definitely learn more about making super beer from this superhero.

— **Brad Ring,** Publisher, *Brew Your Own* magazine

INTRODUCTION

This book is a compilation of the many questions about brewing and the answers I have given over the last 11 years and counting. As a youngster, I was labeled the "question guy," and I have been thrilled to be the "answer guy" for *Brew Your Own* magazine in my adult years. Brewing is an avocation spanning thousands of years and brewers must look back to move forward.

In the United States, brewing companies shrank in number during most of the 1900s for a number of social and economic reasons. The result was a small number of really large breweries. Fortunately for the consumer, the craft brewing movement started to really take off in the early 1980s and has been strong ever since. Today, newcomers to brewing, both as hobbyists and professionals, seek information from those who know from hands-on experience. In days of old, wisdom may have come only from brewer-mentors. Today, that advice is supplemented by magazines, books, and Web sites.

I began brewing in 1986 as a homebrewer and had lots of questions. After all, I was a senior in high school and asking questions was par for my course! I prowled the stacks at the University of Maryland, College Park library, but came up short for the type of information I wanted. After earning my bachelor's in Food Science at Virginia Tech and master's in Food/Brewing Science at UC Davis, some of my questions were answered.

My brewing career began when the microbrewing movement in the United States was still quite young and good information about small-scale brewing somewhat scarce. Through a number of fortuitous moves in my career path, I became a conduit of information that homebrewers found useful. My colleagues in commercial brewing, both small and large, have given me insight into the inner workings of commercial brewing, and it is with this knowledge that I have answered many questions over the years.

The relevance of brewing practice really is blind when it comes to size, because the homebrewer and the largest commercial brewer have much in common. I often reference the practices of commercial breweries in this book because the homebrewer can learn a lot from peering over the fence, as can the wise commercial brewer. I also write about my own experiences with brewing on a small scale. I hope my mixture of personal experience, knowledge of the other side of brewing, and understanding of brewing science offer you some of the take-home advice about brewing I felt deprived of when I began this marvelous pursuit of brewing beer.

CHAPTER 1

The Basics of the Brewing Process

Q Is it difficult to make beer at home?

A Brewing beer at home can be a daunting task if you dive headfirst into advanced, all-grain brewing. Most brewers start brewing beer from kits containing liquid or dry *extracts,* pellet *hops,* and dried *yeast.* The first step of brewing is making the *wort.* This step is really easy when using kits, because there is no need for mashing. All you need is a large pot for boiling liquid, a fermenter, some plastic hoses, a bottling bucket, beer bottles, caps, and a capper.

I suggest finding a homebrew shop or club where you can talk to homebrewers and perhaps seek out a more experienced brewer to learn the basics. Most homebrew shops have equipment packages that contain everything needed for basic brewing methods.

While cleaning and sanitizing are not difficult, their importance cannot be stressed enough. Good beer requires close attention to detail when it comes to cleaning; some beginners struggle with this because they approach brewing like cooking. There are many similarities, but good beer requires that cleaning be kicked up a notch!

My suggestion for first-time brewers and beginners is to be patient and take one step at a time. Focus on the task at hand and worry about the next step after successfully finishing the first. Some of my early homebrews were really awful because I tried to get too fancy too quickly. As with most things, practice makes perfect, and adding complexity only makes sense after mastering the basics.

BASIC BREWING PROCESS

The process of making beer is the same whether brewing small batches at home or commercial batches in a large brewery. Here are the basic steps.

1. The first step is to produce wort, or the sweet fermentable liquid made from malted barley, specialty grains, hops, and water, that yeast will ferment. When hot water and milled malted barley are mixed together, the resulting mixture is known as a *mash.* Mashing allows *enzymes* naturally present in the malted barley to convert starches into fermentable sugars. Other grains are usually added to the mash for color, flavor, or a flavor-neutral starch source. These grains include specialty barley *malts,* wheat, oats, corn, and rice.

2. After mashing is complete, the wort is separated from the mash in a step known as *lautering* and the wort is collected in a large *kettle.* Hot water, called *sparge* water, is gently sprinkled on top of the grains in a step called *sparging* that helps rinse the wort from the grain bed. Extracts are made in this way, except they are concentrated and sometimes dried into a powder before packing. Extract brewers rely on the extract producer to take care of mashing and lautering.

3. Once the wort has been collected or the extract diluted with water, it is heated to boiling in the kettle and hops are added. Some extracts are prehopped

and not all recipes require hops to be added during boiling. Boiling usually lasts from 60 to 90 minutes. Boiling is important because it removes some unwanted aromas from the malt, sterilizes wort, and transforms insoluble bitter components in hops into water-soluble compounds that balance the flavor of beer. Hop aroma compounds are also extracted during boiling, so it is typical to add hops to wort toward the end of boiling, solely for aroma.

Chilling the wort

4. After the boil is complete, the wort is cooled and aerated and yeast is added. After about 12 hours, a little bubbling from the *airlock* is observed and thin white foam is seen on the surface of the wort. In 24 hours, the rate of bubbling will increase and the foam will be several inches thick. It will have a creamy color often speckled with little pieces of protein called *trub*, which is carried over from the *boil.* This is *fermentation* and lasts anywhere from 3 to 14 days, depending

on wort density or gravity, yeast strain, and fermentation temperature. Toward the end of fermentation, the rate of bubbling slows and the beer density approaches its final gravity. The change in beer density is a result of the yeast converting sugars into alcohol, carbon dioxide, and beer-flavor compounds.

5. After fermentation, the young beer is *racked,* or moved into another container known as a secondary fermenter. Racking moves the beer off the yeast *sediment* that falls to the bottom of the fermenter.

6. Following racking, most beers are allowed to mature for 2 to 4 weeks prior to packaging. Maturation gives the suspended yeast time to alter some aromas associated with young beer, as well as time to settle to the bottom of the fermenter, resulting in a clearer beer.

7. Most homebrew is not filtered and is racked to a bottling bucket after aging. A small amount of sugar is added and mixed with the beer. Called *priming,* this process provides *carbonation* through a refermentation in the bottle. This process requires 1 to 2 weeks; bottles are typically stored at room temperature during refermentation. It is now time to move the beer into a refrigerator and enjoy.

Q Can you make any kind of beer at home?

A Almost any beer you can find on the shelves of your favorite beer store can be made at home, provided that the right ingredients and brewing techniques are used. Many homebrewers start homebrewing to brew flavorful beers, and often mock commercial beers with very little flavor, such as light beers. As it turns out, these are some of the most difficult beers to brew because they have so little flavor and flaws stick out like a coffee stain on a white shirt!

Some beer styles use special yeast strains and/or *bacteria;* these beers can also be a little tricky to brew, and they sometimes take a very long time to fully develop. Many Belgian styles, especially the sour beers, fall into this group. *Lagers* can also be a challenge to brew at home because cooler fermentation and aging temperatures are used and temperature-controlled environments, such as converted refrigerators, are required.

Perhaps the single largest difference between commercial beer and homebrewed beer is that most beers you buy at the store have been filtered. *Filtration* is used by some homebrewers but is certainly not very common. Filtration produces a bright and visually appealing beer and removes flavor associated with yeast in suspension. Some craft brewers do not like filtration, because some flavors that are removed are desirable in certain styles.

Along the same lines, this means that most homebrew is carbonated by refermentation in the bottle or force-carbonated in kegs, as compared to commercial beers that are usually carbonated during aging and then bottled or kegged using counterpressure filling. These are differences in technique, yet the same array of styles can be made at home using different methods.

Q Do homebrewers make beer the same way as large commercial brewers?

A In a very generalized sense, all beer is made using the same basic steps. All beer begins as wort that is then fermented, aged, clarified to some extent, and packaged. The biggest difference between what is done at home and in a big brewery is the equipment used. Commercial brewers use multiroll or wet *milling* to crush their grains. Many breweries use *adjuncts,* such as rice and corn, that are milled with special mills.

Mashing is basically the same process, except most commercial breweries use steam-heated mash mixers with special agitators that help keep the mash at a uniform temperature while at the same time don't beat up the malt and keep wort separation running smoothly. Brewers who use adjuncts have to boil them to gelatinize the starch and commonly have a cereal cooker and a mash mixer. In fact, this setup is basically the same as a decoction brewhouse that has a decoction kettle and a mash mixer.

Most American breweries use *lauter tuns* to separate wort from malt solids; others use mash filters. The lauter tuns gently cut through the grain bed with slow-moving rakes to facilitate wort separation. The device is then used to move the spent grains into a pump that takes the grain to a spent-grain storage area.

Some smaller breweries, especially pub brewers, use infusion *mash tuns* for mashing and wort separation. This is more akin to what is done at home. It is common for the brewer to use a mash paddle when mashing-in and use some sort of hoe to remove the spent grains from a door in the side of the mash tun after mashing is complete. Then the plates are removed, and the mash tun is given a good cleaning. A lot of brewpub equipment, such as this infusion mash tun, actually grew out of homebrew equipment.

Wort boiling also uses different equipment, because of the much larger batch sizes. Small pub operations use steam-heated or flame-heated kettles that are not much different from big pots with an external heating jacket. As kettles get larger than about 1,000 gallons, more heating surface is needed than that available on the exterior of the kettle. Internal or external *heat exchangers* called *calandrias* are used to increase the heating area, and the boiling wort exiting the calandria is directed to a wort spreader that fans wort over the surface of the boiling volume. This helps knock down foam as well as create a large surface area for dimethyl sulfide (DMS) to evaporate and exit through the kettle stack. Some kettles are pressurized.

Hop separation is also different for commercial brewers because of the larger batch sizes. These days, most beer is made using hop pellets that can be separated in large whirlpool vessels. Homebrewers can also use the whirlpool method to help separate hop pellets and trub from yeast. Breweries that use whole hops typically use a hop separator that strains the hops from the wort and continuously augers the spent hops out of the device. Smaller brewers use hopbacks that look very similar to a mash tun.

Finally, in commercial breweries, the wort is cooled using a plate heat exchanger with enough surface area to cool the batch in 30 to 60 minutes. This means that the hot wort sits in the whirlpool vessel for a fairly long time. After cooling, wort is aerated in-line with filtered air or oxygen and then flows into the fermenter. Many brewers inject yeast in-line after *aeration;* others put the yeast in the bottom of the fermenter, where it mixes with the wort.

I would say that wort production in a commercial brewery is pretty darned different from the way most homebrewed wort is made, either with extracts or all-grain mashing. When it comes to fermentation and aging, however, the process is fairly similar. One big difference is that larger brewers typically ferment 4 to 6 batches in the same fermenter. Various techniques of yeast pitching and aeration are used when a tank is filled over the course of 12 to 18 hours.

Another notable difference between the largest breweries and the homebrewer is the use of a technique called high-gravity brewing. This means that high-gravity wort, usually between 14 and 18° Plato (1.056–1.072 SG), is fermented and later diluted with deaerated, carbonated water. The reason big breweries do this is to reduce their fermentation tank requirements by up to about 33 percent. Craft brewers typically do not use this method.

Aging is not much different at home, unless we are talking about the King of Beers and the use of beechwood chips. Anheuser-Busch is the only brewery I know of that still uses this once not-uncommon technique.

Next comes filtration. Commercial brewers use all sorts of methods to clarify beer, including diatomaceous earth (DE) pressure leaf filters, DE plate and frame filters, centrifuges, and sheet filters. The most modern method is cross-flow membrane filtration; its aim is to eliminate the use of DE in beer filtration.

The last step is packaging beer into bottles, cans, or kegs. Most large breweries pasteurize their bottles and cans in a tunnel pasteurizer after filling to kill any spoilage organisms that may be in the beer. Some *draft* beer is flash pasteurized like milk before *kegging*. As a general rule, craft-brewed beer made in the United States is not pasteurized. There are a few craft brewers out there who do have *pasteurization* equipment, but these are the exceptions. Pasteurization prevents beers from being bottle-conditioned because it kills the yeast.

Simply put, homebrewed beer and commercially brewed beer start with the same basic ingredients and may taste similar when poured into a glass, but they arrive at that point by very different paths.

THE FLAVORS BARLEY, HOPS, AND YEAST GIVE TO BEER

◆ **Barley.** The backbone of beer flavor in my opinion comes from the grain. In all-malt brewing, that means barley or wheat malt. Beers made solely from pale malts have a sweet, grainy flavor with a touch of toastiness from the light kilning used to dry the malt after germination. Beers that have special malts in their *grist,* such as crystal, Munich, and roasted malts, take on richer flavors of caramel, nuts, chocolate, and coffee from these darker malts. The caramel flavor from *crystal malt* also adds sweetness.

◆ **Hops** are the spice of beer and balance the sweetness of the malt. Hops contain *alpha acids* that are isomerized and made more soluble during boiling; these compounds give beer its pleasant bitterness. Hops also contain a whole multitude of aromatic oils that impart floral, citrus, piney, and perfumelike aromas to beer.

◆ **Yeast** transforms the syrupy sweet, hopped wort into beer. Alcohol, carbon dioxide, fruity *esters,* spicy higher alcohols, sulfur compounds, applelike acetaldehyde, and buttery *diacetyl* are all compounds created by yeast during fermentation. The clove, banana, and bubble gum aromas associated with hefe-weizens are also from yeast, as is the wet-horse-blanket aroma in certain Belgian *ales.* And in unfiltered beers, the yeast itself contributes a nice breadlike aroma and flavor.

Q How is brewing with *malt extract* different from just using grain?

A The main difference between brewing with extracts versus all grain is the omission of the mashing step. In *extract brewing,* the extract is diluted with water to make wort and is then boiled. Some extracts contain hops, and the addition of bittering hops is not required. These brews may be hopped later in the boil for aroma. Also, some extract kits do not require a full boil, since they have been boiled where they were made; a short boil is used to kill any stray organisms introduced at home.

Another practice used by some extract brewers is to boil a smaller extract volume at a higher gravity and then add additional cold water after boiling to dilute the wort to the proper gravity and to help bring the temperature down for yeast pitching, making wort cooling easier.

Extract brewers frequently augment their brews with specialty grains, a technique frequently referred to as steeping. The grains are typically added to hot water at around 158°F (70°C) and steeped much like making tea. Steeping bags make it easy to simply remove the grains from the grain tea before adding liquid or dry malt extract. This method is not a mash, as the grains used do not require enzymatic conversion of starch to be used. The most common grains used in this fashion are crystal and roasted grains, such as chocolate and roasted malt or barley.

Q What is the difference between ale and lager?

A Ale is made with one of the two types of yeasts: the so-called top-fermenting strains, which form a dense crop of yeast at the top of the fermenter. The yeast stays on top even after vigorous fermentation has subsided.

Lagers are made with the other type of yeast, bottom-fermenting, which tends to collect on the bottom of the fermenter, or bottom crop, after vigorous fermentation.

In addition to these differences, ales tend to be fermented at room temperatures (65–70°F/18–21°C) and lagers tend to be fermented at cooler temperatures (50–55°F/10–13°C). In general, ales have short, warm maturation periods and lagers have long, cold maturation periods. The generalizations, however, end here.

Ales can be any color from very, very pale yellow to jet black; the same is true of lagers. Some lagers tend to be quite bitter with pronounced hop aromas, while others have very subtle hopping. Again, the same is true of some ales. Regarding carbonation, cask-conditioned ales are the least carbonated beers in the world, while some of the German and Belgian wheat ales are the most carbonated beers in the world. Lagers tend to have a narrower range of carbonation.

Q Why is boiling wort important?

A The wort-boiling step is extremely important, whether brewing all-grain, partial-grain, or extract-only. With the exception of extracts specifically designed and marketed as "no-boil," brewers must boil their wort. The most significant thing accomplished by wort boiling is sterilization. This step allows brewers to determine what sorts of organisms are in the wort, because boiling kills nearly everything (spores can survive short boiling periods, but that is a technicality that you are not concerned with at this time) and gives us a clean slate with which to work. Of course, if we contaminate that clean slate with dirty equipment or bad yeast, that is our fault, and it's the job of the brewer to keep the wort in a clean and sanitary environment after boiling. Wort boiling also precipitates protein, isomerizes hop acids, and drives off certain undesirable malt volatiles such as dimethyl sulfide (DMS). (See wort boiling, page 14.)

Q What is the big deal about chilling wort quickly?

A The bottom line is that getting your wort cooled quickly is important because it preserves flavor and produces a good cold *break*. The flavor-preservation argument goes something like this: Hot wort can pick up bacteria, even though the wort is sterile before splashing it into the *carboy*. When the wort reaches about 140°F (60°C), some of these bacteria will start growing. Since bacteria grow rapidly, bacterial populations can become high enough to cause flavor problems before you ever pitch your yeast.

If you are able to cool the wort quickly, the chance of wort spoilage is decreased because of yeast. Yeasts are handy, because they quickly reduce the wort *pH,* produce alcohol, and inhibit the growth of many bacteria. Those bacteria that can still grow are in competition with yeasts for food. Since there are far more yeasts than bacteria cruising around in the wort looking for food, the yeasts tend to gobble it up before the bacteria have much of a chance. Of course, this is only true if your pitching yeast is clean. If you pitch contaminated yeast, all bets are off — but then again, so is your beer!

Assuming you have cooled the wort relatively quickly, you may notice an increased amount of cold break, the protein that comes out of solution when wort is cooled. Cold break explains why clear, hot wort turns cloudy when chilled. In any case, fast cooling produces more cold break than slow cooling. Some brewers, especially those from Germany, firmly believe that cold break left in the wort contributes to harsh flavors. These brewers want to maximize its formation during cooling and remove it. So, if you want to buy into that idea, there are then two valid reasons to cool your wort rapidly.

(See wort chillers, page 52.)

Q **Is it necessary to strain hops from the wort before it goes into the fermenter?**

A Commercial brewers always separate hops, be they cone or pellet, before fermentation. This practice is needed for wort cooling using plate heat exchangers that will become clogged with hop pellets or cones. And the yeast harvest is free of hop debris as a result of the practice, which is a good thing!

But is hop separation really necessary? My guess is that very good beer could be made by cooling hot wort in the kettle it was boiled in and fermenting in the same vessel without trub or hop separation. This approach is certainly unorthodox, and brewers, including me, get a little nervous when unorthodox techniques are practiced. Today's brewers figure that brewing techniques have developed over the millennia to yield the best beers. If this thought process makes sense, then you should probably conform to the norm and separate your hops.

Q **What are the pros and cons of pellet and cone hops?**

A Hop pellets have very good storage properties and are easy to separate from wort, but they tend to leave a little more trub behind than cone hops, and some brewers consider their aroma qualities to be inferior to cone hops. Cone hops, on the other hand, are more expensive to store, are more susceptible to oxidation during storage, and are more difficult to separate. But they filter out trub during separation, and many brewers think they have superior aroma qualities. (See whirlpooling, page 353.)

Q **What is the fastest time I can brew, ferment, and have *bottle-conditioned* beer ready to drink?**

A So you want to know just how fast you can be sippin' your suds after brewing and you fear that your friends will be afraid of your beer if you tell them that it is 10 days old versus 45! Bottle-conditioned ale can be ready to drink in as little as two weeks, but the beer may be very yeasty and have green flavors that will change over time. Most brewers, including me, feel that a rushed brew is just a source of potential problems.

When I speak to nonbrewers who ask such questions, I tend to leave out the many shortcuts sometimes used in brewing and tell them the story that includes longer fermentation and aging times. An explanation that leaves people with the idea that beer can be brewed and ready to drink in a few days takes away much of the romance and craft appeal to specialty beers.

On the other hand, push can turn to shove and very drinkable beers can be made in short periods if you have the right tools, such as filters for yeast removal if clear beer is desired and kegs to make carbonation quicker than bottle conditioning. A fellow brewer brought a keg of *porter* to a Saturday mud football game to offer to the participants. We all were impressed with the rich, chocolaty flavors and clean yeast character in the beer. Not one of us noticed anything off. When asked when the beer was brewed, our friend replied, "Last Monday!" Three days of fermentation, 1 day to settle the yeast at a very cold temperature, and 1 day carbonating in the keg was all the time available to make the big game. There are some very well-known microbreweries in this country that have pushed their beers to keep up with the fast growth rate in the specialty-beer market. Some have pulled the feat off without a hitch and others have produced products of variable quality under the pressure of time. Homebrewers would be best advised to take this sound advice: "Serve no beer before its time," meaning that fast brewing is possible, but not always advisable.

Q **What are some basic serving temperatures for different beer styles?**

A If this question were part of a beer 101 quiz given to bartenders, I would fail miserably! I simply don't have it in my blood to spell out the conventional rules about serving temperature.

For example, domestic beers with little *body* and flavor are best served at blistering cold temperatures in frosted mugs. Perhaps this practice is either to hide what flavor is present or to trick the consumer into thinking that the cold liquid in his or her mouth is something other than beer with very little flavor. In contrast, beers with more flavor are served warmer, anywhere from 38 to 50°F (4–10°C). The thought behind this practice is that these styles have nice flavors hidden by arctic temperatures and the warmer serving range entices the aromas from the beer. The other historical fact is that commercial refrigeration is a relatively recent invention and the tradition of storing beer in cellars results in warmer beer than refrigerated storage.

This information is a failing answer by any measure. The right answer to this question, in my humble but ferociously opinionated view, is that the serving temperature for any beer style has much to do with the consumer. While studying brewing at UC Davis, I took a class in the Viticulture & Enology Department and interacted with many students in the program. The Davis view on wine and food pairing flies in the face of convention. If you like a big hearty Zinfandel with your poultry, fish, or salad, don't let some food and wine pundit make you feel improper. If you prefer drinking stout that has spent some time in the icebox instead of the 55°F (13°C) cellar, go for it!

The general guidelines ranking beers on a temperature scale from low color and low flavor complexity to darker color and greater complexity can be used as a rough guide to what many beer drinkers and beer writers think about serving temperature. My view is that the person drinking the beer is the VIP in this question, and it's perfectly fine to express one's own preference when it comes to choosing serving temperature. Iced coffee sounds kind of strange to the coffee drinker accustomed to a hot cup of joe, but it tastes really good, and at the end of the day, that's all that matters!

Q What is the best way to pour beer into a glass, and does it matter?

A Pouring method does matter, and the chosen method depends on how you like your beer served. Personally, I like a nice crown of foam towering above the rim of my beer glass, and pour my beer to achieve this effect. I start with a clean glass that has just been rinsed with cool, clean water (not stinky tap water chock full of chlorine, akin to the municipal swimming pool) and allowed to drain so that the surface is wet with no excess water in the glass. Whether pouring from *tap* or bottle, I begin my pour by tilting the glass 45 degrees and positioning the tap or bottle rim about ½ inch from the side of the glass. I hold this glass position until the glass is about three-quarters full and then, while continuing to pour, transition the glass to the upright position. I stop pouring when I see about 1½ inches between the top of the beer and the edge of the glass. The foam should rise and drain so that there is about one inch, or two fingers, of foam on top of the beer. To me, this is a perfect pour.

I like beer foam because it adds *mouthfeel* and texture to beer that headless beers simply lack. The same beer poured with and without foam is perceived differently when consumed. This fact alone is testimony to the importance of pouring technique.

Some beers are trickier to pour and this basic technique may require a few starts and stops to prevent over-foaming. Whatever you do when pouring, do not allow beer to flow over the edge of the glass and down the drain. This sloppy practice is witnessed in almost every bar I have visited in the States and is not a practice to emulate at home! Highly carbonated beer and some finicky draft beers require patience and may require a little longer to achieve the perfect pint.

Some people prefer beer with no foam. I think this preference has something to do with wanting to get every drop of beer crammed into the pint ordered at the local bar. Many beer consumers feel they are getting ripped off if there is any foam sitting atop their beer and occupying precious space that could be beer. I like beer glassware with fill lines clearly indicating to the consumer that the glass is properly filled. I tell our patrons that the foam is a gift from the brewers, because beer without foam is missing something.

However, if you really don't like foam, you should simply stick to wine or cocktails . . . I'm just kidding! Use the same procedure as described above for pouring but keep the glass tilted the entire time you are pouring and only tilt it upright enough to prevent the glass from overfilling. A wet glass and really cold beer helps to minimize foam. I have seen some foam haters in bars borrow a little grease from their face by wiping a finger over their brow or side of nose and using this oil to collapse the foam. If you are guilty of doing this, consider altering your pouring method before resorting to this vile practice.

One other note: If you like frosting your mug, you need to be patient when pouring. Ice crystals on the sides of frosted mugs act as nucleation sites and cause carbon dioxide to escape rapidly from solution. Frosted mugs can be poured like any other glass but just more slowly, using a few starts and stops to prevent over-foaming. Just in case anyone is wondering, I do not frost my mugs and only know the pitfalls with this mug abuse because of friends who like to keep their beer glasses stored in the freezer.

Q **Should I try to leave the yeast at the bottom of my bottles or pour it into the glass?**

A On one hand this is a preference question. Some people like pouring sediment into their glass because they want to drink the yeast for nutritional reasons. Others prefer to pour the beer so that most of the sediment remains in the bottle, which maximizes the clarity of the beer in the glass. Most commercial, bottle-conditioned beers suggest pouring in this manner.

One notable exception to this rule is the pouring of hefe-weizen. These beers tend to have very little yeast sediment, because most are partially or fully clarified and reyeasted before bottling and have little yeast on the bottom of the bottle. All hefe-weizens I have had in Germany are carefully poured to leave the yeast and a small amount of beer in the bottle. After the initial pour, the bottle is placed on its side and gently rolled to suspend the yeast in the beer. This small amount of yeasty beer is poured straight into the glass to give the entire pour a nice, uniform cloud of yeast.

The Aromas of Beer

The seasoned homebrewer develops a good *nose* and might pick up the following scents from the sniff test in his evaluation of a brew: Diacetyl (butter), acetaldehyde (green apple), dimethyl sulfide (DMS) (cooked corn), grain, wort, vegemite, ethyl acetate (solvent), hydrogen sulfide (rotten egg), wet cardboard, or sulfur (burnt match). He might also detect scents that are excessively fruity, phenolic (medicinal), cheesy, grassy, spicy, cooked, meaty, brothy, skunky, or mousy.

Train your nose, and you'll detect these defects by smell alone, with no tasting required.

Q What are the basics of sensory evaluation when it comes to beer?

A For serious brewers with sensory evaluation training, there are really two beer-consuming modes: the detective and the tourist.

The beer detective approaches beer analytically and suspiciously. The beer detective first sizes up the beer based on appearance. Color, clarity, and foam are the things I observe and consider about a beer "under investigation" before I ever get it near my nose or mouth. Is the color appropriate for the style or as envisioned when formulating the recipe? Is the clarity what it ought to be? While unfiltered beers, like wheat beers, should be cloudy, they should not look like yeast slurry! Other beer styles, whether filtered or not, should be clear. The beer detective notes clarity as a fashion critic does color. Then there's foam. Is the foam dense and creamy or light and gassy?

The appearance of beer often has little to do with the taste, but appearance is important because the average beer drinker is usually influenced by what he or she sees. A dark, cloudy beer suggests a flavor profile that is very different from that of a pale, bright beer. Neither appearance is good or bad; they are just different. Some brewers like matching the appearance of a beer with the flavor to come, and others like to surprise their consumers by mismatching appearance and flavor.

After giving the "suspect" a good visual examination, the beer detective is ready to give the sample a good sniff. Most flavors encountered in the world are detected by the nose. The strict definition of aroma is a stimulus perceived by the nose; a taste is a stimulus perceived by the tongue. Flavor is the combination of aroma and taste, and many a flavor experienced when a beverage or food is placed in the mouth is actually an aroma detected when scent molecules travel into the nasal cavity from the mouth. This is called "retro-nasal" by sensory folk. I'll get back to this digression.

The beer detective is different from the tourist because the aromas of interest are defects. (See page 34.) In fact, most flavor defects in beer can be detected by smelling alone, without tasting the beer.

Finally, the detective takes a sip of the sample and evaluates tastes and textures in the mouth. Hop bitterness, malt sweetness, mineral tastes from the water, and body are evaluated. A good beer in the opinion of the beer detective is one that fits within the chosen style, or meets the objectives of the brewer when not brewed to fit a particular style. Any flavors that fall outside of the stylistic guidelines or brewing objectives are flaws, and the beer detective will give demerits for these undesirable traits.

The beer tourist perceives beer in a completely different way from the detective. The beer tourist, or ordinary consumer, experiences beer for what it is. He or she takes in the color, clarity, foam, and flavor and usually responds with some degree of liking, ranging from hate to love. The average beer tourist may use some general terms to describe what he or she perceives, but the terms are typically far fewer and less descriptive than those used by the detective. In other words, an average beer tourist may say, "I really like the brilliant golden color, dense white foam, spicy hop aroma, and bracing bitterness of this *Pilsner*" but will probably not delve into the "elevated DMS levels, subtle yet detectable diacetyl, slight *chill haze*, fish-eyed foam bubbles, slight cheesiness from old hops, atypical malty aroma for the style, and lingering fruitiness more typical of ales" that the beer detective may note.

Sensory evaluation is the single most powerful tool that the homebrewer has to evaluate beer. A good palate requires training; learning from good tasters is one of the best ways to develop this skill. Good tasters use standards for various aromas and tastes and know where to find these standards. They can also tell you if a particular beer has a noticeable level of some flavor and help guide your nose and tongue so that you can recognize and identify the flavor for filing into your flavor library. This takes time and practice and can be very rewarding.

When it comes to enjoying beer, however, I think that it is extremely important for someone with the skills to be a beer detective to also have the ability to turn that part of his or her brain off. When I am drinking a beer as a tourist, I prefer focusing on the positives rather than turning over every stone looking for a flaw, because the truth is that few, if any, beers are perfect. I use my detective skills to improve the beers I formulate and brew. But when I am letting down my hair, I try to forget that I have a trained palate!

Q **What is the difference between alcohol by weight versus alcohol by volume?**

A The difference between alcohol by weight and alcohol by volume is only in the way they are measured. Suppose you have a really big mug containing 100 fluid ounces of beer that is 5 percent alcohol by volume. If you could remove all the alcohol from this sample, you would have 5 percent of 100 ounces or 5 ounces of pure alcohol (ethanol).

If, on the other hand, you knew this sample contained 3.95 percent alcohol by weight, the answer would be a bit different. To begin with, you would need to know how much the 100 fluid ounces of beer weighed. For the sake of this example, assume the sample weighs 6.5 pounds. Since 3.95 percent of 6.5 pounds is 0.257 pounds or 4.1 ounces (weight ounces, not fluid), the sample contains 4.1 ounces of alcohol by weight. These 4.1 ounces (weight) of alcohol occupy 5 ounces of volume because the *specific gravity* of alcohol is 0.79 SG. So, 5 percent alcohol by volume and 3.95 percent alcohol by weight are the same thing.

This example is much easier if the metric system is used. Assume that you have a 1-liter (1,000 mL) mug of beer that contains 5 percent alcohol by volume, or 3.95 percent by weight. Using the alcohol by volume figure, it is clear that 50 mL of pure alcohol is in the beer. One liter of beer weighs the same as its specific gravity because specific gravity can be expressed as kg/liter. If its specific gravity is 1.008 SG, then it weighs 1.008 kg or 1,008 grams. That means there are 39.8 grams of alcohol in the beer. Since the density of alcohol is

790 grams/liter, it can be determined that 39.8 grams of alcohol occupies 50 mL. Again, the same result is obtained as the previous example using pounds and gallons.

To simplify this mess, if you know alcohol by volume, you can convert it to alcohol by weight by simply multiplying alcohol by volume by 0.79. Similarly, if you know alcohol by weight and want to convert to alcohol by volume, just divide the former by 0.79.

The next question is: Why all of this confusion? In the United States, all alcohol except beer is sold by volume. This means if you want to equate the number of beers consumed to the number of mixed drinks, you first must convert alcohol by weight to alcohol by volume. I'm not sure why this practice began, but some argue that it makes the alcohol of beer appear lower than that of other beverages. This supposedly discourages consumers from buying beer based on its high alcohol content, since it appears lower than other alcoholic beverages. This reasoning seems just absurd enough to believe.

In other countries, beer is sold by volume. This is why American tourists frequently insist beer is stronger in other countries. For example, "Man, the Moosehead in Canada is real strong stuff. It's 5 percent alcohol up there! Try some of my stash I brought across the border, but be careful 'cause it's way stronger." I have heard this ridiculous conversation more times than I care to remember.

Recently, many American brewers have begun using alcohol by volume on their labels and, fortunately, this topic is becoming less confusing these days.

Q **Why do beers gassed with nitrogen seem so much creamier than regular draft beers?**

A A nitro beer will do nothing remarkable when poured from a standard beer tap, except for the fact that it usually falls into the glass with absolutely no fanfare — no foam, no cascading, nothing but beer. Taste this beer and it tastes and feels really flat. Pour the same keg of beer through a special faucet (usually called a Guinness tap or a stout faucet) and the whole game changes. You get foam, cascading bubbles, a super-creamy *head* that sticks to the glass like shaving cream, and a wonderfully rich mouthfeel.

The main difference between the two glasses of beer has to do with nitrogen solubility. Beers containing only dissolved carbon dioxide make a huge foamy mess when dispensed through one of these taps because the carbon dioxide suddenly breaks out of solution. Draft systems designed for normal beers are specifically designed to prevent this breakout. To produce its creamy head, a nitrogenated beer is forced at a relatively high dispense pressure — usually around 30 psi — through a plate containing several small holes. Called an orifice plate, its function is to cause gas breakout; normal beer taps do not contain one. When nitrogen breaks out of solution, millions of tiny bubbles form and these bubbles look, act, and feel much different from carbon dioxide bubbles. Any brewer, whether at home or in a brewpub, can serve nitro beers on draft as long as a stout faucet is used. (See nitrogen-carbonated beer, page 275.)

CHAPTER 2

Choosing and Using Brewing Equipment

WHAT BASIC EQUIPMENT DO I NEED TO MAKE BEER?

If you are just getting started, a few basic items are a must. You should be able to find the equipment you need at a homebrewing supply shop or on the Internet.

◆ **Pot.** You will need a 7-gallon (26 L) pot, large enough to boil 5½–6 gallons (21–23 L) of wort plus about 20 percent extra space to prevent boilovers. Most home kitchens are not equipped with a pot this large. Homebrew shops and Internet sites sell a wide array of brew kettles, a good investment for those who want to give homebrewing a serious try. (See brew pot materials, page 46.)

Pot

One thing you need to verify before buying a big pot is that your kitchen stove has enough power to boil that much liquid (a 5-gallon [19-L] pot requires a 10,000 BTU burner). If not, you should use the *high gravity* method or consider buying an outdoor propane burner.

◆ **Wort chiller.** You will also need to make or buy this device to cool the large volume of near-boiling wort to about 75°F (24°C) before pitching *yeast.*

An immersion chiller made from copper tubing is the easiest to build and least expensive type of wort chiller. Many great batches of homebrew are made using immersion chillers, and some brewers stick with them. Other brewers prefer counterflow wort chillers, which are more difficult to build. The main difference is that wort is cooled in the kettle with an immersion chiller and in-line between the kettle and fermenter when using a counterflow chiller.

Copper immersion chiller

◆ **Primary fermenter.** My preference for *primary fermentation* is a glass carboy. Some brewers use plastic buckets for fermenters, but I don't because oxygen goes through plastic very easily. When I was a graduate student at UC Davis, we made a lot of different beers in the pilot brewery; all were fermented in the trusty carboy.

The only disadvantages are that carboys are breakable and they expose beer to light. At Davis, we did fermentations in a walk-in cooler and turned on the light only when someone was in there. I have never had beer skunked during fermentation in glass, but covering the fermenter with something like a towel to protect it from light is a cheap safety policy.

Glass carboy

- **Secondary fermenter.** Racking out of the primary fermenter is not required but is recommended. A second carboy works well.
- **Plastic bucket.** More yeast will settle in the secondary, so the beer must be racked again before bottling; a 5-gallon (19 L) plastic bucket with an easy-to-fit lid and *racking cane* works well as a bottling bucket. I am not so concerned with the plastic at this stage because the beer will only be in it for a short time. One thing to keep in mind is that racking can introduce oxygen into beer by splashing and simply by the fact that the beer is racked into a container filled with air. I have reliably used dry ice to evacuate air from tanks. A little chunk in the bottling bucket could be used to displace the air before filling.
- **Bottle capper.** The last major piece of equipment is a bottle capper. I have used both of the styles available — gooseneck style and hand held — and prefer the gooseneck type.
- **Airlock.** Allows carbon dioxide to escape during fermentation but keeps air from reaching your beer.
- **Racking cane and hose.**
- **Bottle brushes.**
- **Thermometer.**
- **Hydrometer.**
- **Long-handled metal spoon.**

Airlock

- **Food-grade hoses,** such as silicone or Teflon-lined, $3/16$–$3/8$ inches (5–10 mm) in diameter.
- **Bottles.**
- **Supplies to clean and dry bottles.**

You should be able to buy everything you need to get started for a couple hundred dollars, and if you add an outdoor propane burner to that list, your costs will still be quite reasonable. This amount is not a bad investment at all for a hobby that returns on the initial investment!

Thermometer

Q **Do brew pots need to be stainless steel, or can I use aluminum, ceramic, or other materials?**

A A pot needs to satisfy a few simple requirements to become a qualified brew pot. For starters, it should not leak. A good candidate for the job should also be large enough — 7 gallons (26 L) — to hold and boil a whole batch of wort. It is much better to boil the whole volume of wort than do a concentrated wort boil. A concentrated boil affects hop utilization; improves aroma, such as dimethyl sulfide (DMS) removal, during boiling; and develops color much differently. The kettle should also be made from a material that can adequately conduct heat from the source to the wort. The final requirement for the kettle is that it should not harm the wort by leaching compounds into it.

Stainless steel is the most common material for kettle construction nowadays, though its heat conductivity is less than stellar. Stainless steel is inert, is easily formed and welded, and can be heated either by direct flame or with the use of steam jackets and coils. Commercial brewers use steam because it does not result in scorching. Unfortunately, stainless steel kettles are pretty spendy. A 7-gallon (26 L) stainless steel pot can easily cost more than $150.

Ceramic canning vessels and crab or lobster pots meet the basic requirements for a kettle. Canning vessels are usually made of tin with a thin enamel coating. These pots are inert, have high heat conductivity, and are less expensive than stainless pots. One drawback to ceramic is that you cannot weld a valve to them because the coating chips off.

Also, if they get chipped or cracked, the metal under the ceramic is not inert. If you handle these pots carefully and don't mind not having an outlet valve, then they are a viable option. Another drawback is that the handles of canning pots are not very strong; you should not attempt to lift a pot full of near-boiling wort. This is dangerous regardless of the handles and ought to be avoided.

Aluminum pots are readily available in all sizes, are really inexpensive, and have a terrific thermal conductivity. An outlet valve can be welded to an aluminum pot, but you will probably have a difficult time finding anyone who can weld a stainless steel ferrule to an aluminum pot because aluminum welding is a fairly specialized technique. Another issue with aluminum is that it is not inert, making it unsafe to clean aluminum pots with sodium hydroxide (commonly referred to as caustic), and other caustic-based cleaners, which are the workhorse cleaners of the food and beverage industries. Sodium hydroxide is listed on the label of any cleaner containing it, because it is pretty nasty. Drano and Easy Off oven cleaner both contain sodium hydroxide. Some studies have suggested that there may be some cause-and-effect relationship between aluminum and Alzheimer's disease, but I haven't read anything very convincing on that idea. Keep in mind that aluminum is commonly used for making all sorts of cooking utensils. If you don't need an outlet valve and don't use caustics, an aluminum kettle is fine.

The granddaddies of all kettles are made from copper. These dudes look great, have the highest thermal conductivity of all metals, and are traditional. However, copper is expensive, difficult to weld (soldering is typically used on copper and is easy), and not inert. Unfortunately, copper is not commonly used to make big pots, and they are hard to find for an affordable price. I hope you didn't have your heart set on copper!

Many homebrewers convert an old beer keg into a kettle. They make good kettles, but I feel obligated to remind everyone that stainless steel beer kegs are the property of breweries. The paltry deposit is only a small fraction of the true cost of a beer keg. If you use a keg for a kettle, make sure you buy the keg from its true owner. Give breweries a break and don't steal kegs!

Q Is there special equipment needed to make beer from just grain?

A There is special equipment — a mash tun and a hot water storage vessel — required for all-grain brewing, but fortunately it is neither expensive nor difficult to make. My first mash tun was built following Charlie Papazian's *Zapap* design that used two 5-gallon buckets, anger management exercises with a hand drill, and a plastic spigot. I used this for years before building a copper manifold with downward facing slits that fit into the bottom of a cooler. A problem with the Zapap design is that it is not insulated, which allows the mash to cool off some over time. This is not a huge deal, however.

You also need a water cooler that you can use for storing hot water for sparging. Since sparge water is usually held at about 170°F (77°C), you need to make sure the cooler can be used for hot water. If you use batch sparging, you really don't need anything else to get started. If you want to be a little fancier, you can fashion some type of sparge head to go with your mash tun, but that is not required.

■ ══════════ ■

Q What homebrew gadgets would you want in your home brewery?

A This is a terrible question to ask of a guy who designs gadgets for a living! I really dig gadgets and love working with projects where new gadgets are needed.

My dream homebrew setup would feature brewing equipment fitted with stainless steel tri-clamp ferrules like those used on commercial equipment. These fittings make it easy to clamp valves to the equipment and valves make it easier and safer to move hot water and wort in and out of the brewing vessel. The same thing can be done using threaded fittings, but these fittings are not sanitary because they can hide crud that can be a breeding ground for microorganisms. At a minimum, the kettle should have a valve to eliminate the need to siphon hot wort. The downside to adding a bunch of stainless ferrules is that you need to buy valves to attach to them, and you can spend a lot of money in a hurry.

I do not promote the addition of gadgets for the sake of adding bells and whistles. I suggest focusing on the fermentation area of the operation. Most beer tastes best when the fermentation temperature is controlled. Most of the ales I brew at our brewery are fermented at 64°F (18°C), much cooler than the ambient temperature advice offered by most homebrewers making ales. A refrigerator with a thermostat that replaces the original equipment allows a controlled environment for fermentation, so both ales and *lagers* can be fermented at a chosen temperature.

Kegs are great because they allow for all sorts of fun options. Cornelius kegs previously used to store soda syrup are really handy and relatively easy to locate. These can be used as secondary fermenters as well as kegs. One clever technique is to put a couple of gallons of hot water in a Corny keg to heat the keg up and then to empty and seal the keg. As the keg cools, it pulls a vacuum that can be used to start a siphon when racking beer from a carboy. Once the siphon starts, vent the Corny keg through the pressure relief valve and watch it fill!

Once you have kegs, you can build your own tap setup and have draft beer. I think this a great gadget, because it's not just for the brewer, but also friends and family who drink your homebrew. I really like nitrogenated beers, and kegs with a home tap system allow the use of this method.

A submersible pump to pump mash and sparge water from my hot water tank to the mash tun is another item I would put on my gadget wish list. With that, the hot water tank does not have to be elevated.

A malt mill would also be nice, so that you can purchase whole grain and mill it immediately before use. This addition offers some economy, as it allows you to buy malt in larger quantities and store it for months without worrying about it picking up moisture.

I would toss in a counterflow wort cooler equipped with an aeration stone in-line between the kettle and fermenter. And just for the fun of it, add a stainless steel conical fermenter with a racking port on the cone, a bottom connection, a thermometer in the side, and a top lid giving access for cleaning and sneaking peaks of the action inside the fermenter. Oh, and some small wooden barrels to barrel-age some funky *Brettanomyces* brews would be nice! A plastic wine thief is handy to take samples from barrel bungs and carboys for gravity checks.

The last thing I would really want is a dedicated space for brewing. The ultimate space would have a sloped floor with a drain so that equipment could be hosed down and cleaned up without worrying about spilling stuff on the floor. This area would also have some of those nice commercial kitchen

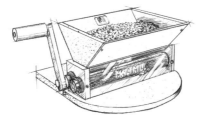

Malt mill

tables for storage and to dress up the space. If you want to boil in your brew space and use a gas flame to boil your wort, make sure the area is ventilated. I have heard of some brewers putting ventilation hoods in their basement, but I would skip that gadget and do my boil outside and gravity flow the wort into my basement through a window.

Q **What are the best ways to chill wort before adding yeast? I let mine sit until it gets down to pitching temperature. This can take a while. I don't know how I can affect the brew by accelerating the cooling process.**

A The best way to cool wort is with a specialized cooling system. The two most common types are the counterflow heat exchanger and the submersion chiller. In the first type, wort passes through a copper tube or some other good conductor of heat while cool water is passing over the outside of the tube. The water flows counter to the wort flow, hence the name.

Submersion chillers are also made of copper or an equivalent conductor. In these devices, however, the cool water runs inside the tube and the whole device is submerged in the hot wort. They both work well and will cool 5 gallons (19 L) of wort within 20 minutes. I like the counterflow chillers because the wort is cooled more rapidly; it enters hot and exits cool about 20 seconds later. The total cooling time for the batch is the same, but since the time for any given wort droplet to cool is quick, you get better cold-break formation.

The bottom line is that hanging around waiting for your wort to cool should make you nervous because of the increased risk of spoilage. The other perk of a specialized cooling system may be a crisper, cleaner barley pop!

Q When measuring specific gravity, is the *original gravity* taken during the mash, during boil, or after the wort has cooled?

A Check the specific gravity of the wort after the boil to determine original gravity. Because original gravity is defined as the specific gravity of the wort before fermentation, this is the only point in the process to determine it.

There are good reasons to check the specific gravity of the wort during sparging and during the kettle boil, namely to hit the target gravity and to make sure that excessive sparging doesn't occur. However, these measurements are very different from the original gravity measurement.

USING A HYDROMETER

Brewers use *hydrometers* to measure density. I like to measure the wort gravity that first flows from the mash tun to know my first wort gravity, a function of mash thickness and how fine the malt was milled. Knowing the first wort gravity allows you to troubleshoot low first wort runnings rather than discover a problem after the boil when it is too late to make a change to the plan. I also measure the wort gravity toward the end of wort collection and avoid collecting wort that is less than 1.008 SG or 2° Plato.

It is important to know the temperature to which your hydrometer is calibrated and to make corrections to your measurements using a correction chart supplied with the hydrometer. I prefer hydrometers with a built-in thermometer and correction scale positioned adjacent to the thermometer; they can be found in laboratory supply catalogs. Hot wort should be cooled before measuring. You can quickly chill samples by plunging a copper sample cylinder into a cold-water bath.

Hydrometers are also great for monitoring the progress of fermentation. I do not believe in the bubble-watching method for knowing when fermentation is complete. The only way to have a good idea of what is happening in the fermenter is to pull a sample and measure the gravity of the beer. This gives you an indication of the apparent extract. (See page 210.)

When measuring the gravity of beer, it is important to make sure that bubbles of carbon dioxide do not buoy the hydrometer and give an artificially low reading. Spinning the spindle of the hydrometer while it is suspended in the sample helps shake bubbles loose. Again, make sure the proper temperature corrections are made.

Finally, you must know whether your hydrometer should be read from the top or bottom of the meniscus. To read the top-reading style, look for the spot where the liquid hits the spindle. To read the bottom-reading design, look across the unit to see the number at the level that lines up with the liquid in the sample container. Many cheaper hydrometers are not labeled: The only way to know if it is top- or bottom-reading is to measure the density of water, which should always be 1.000, provided that it is mineral free.

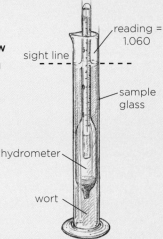

reading = 1.060

sight line

sample glass

hydrometer

wort

Top-reading hydrometer

Q What's the best way to take an accurate original specific gravity reading? I use a sampling thief to collect a wort sample from my carboy before pitching. The readings are different depending on how long the wort settles before measuring and how deep into the carboy I dip to collect the sample. Should the sample come from wort that is relatively free of *sediment*? Should specific gravity be measured before pitching the yeast?

A I usually collect a wort sample from a sample valve placed in-line between the wort cooler and the fermenter. I do this because I want to know my wort density prior to pitching, since liquid yeast will lower the wort gravity slightly by diluting the wort sugars with the liquid in the starter. That said, your method of sampling from the fermenter should work fine, as long as you take your sample before fermentation begins. Just keep in mind that the wort gravity is higher before adding the yeast. This exercise is only of importance if you are strictly tracking your brewhouse efficiency. Otherwise, the difference in gravity is trivial.

There are some oddities about gravity checks that I want to point out. But before I drift too far off, here is one key piece of information for extract brewers — be diligent about mixing your wort and any topping-up water prior to checking your specific gravity. If the wort is not thoroughly mixed, the likelihood of having stratification in the wort gravity is very high. In fact, it's almost a guarantee!

Let's assume, however — for the sake of argument — that you are an all-grain brewer and that the wort is thoroughly mixed. The puzzling part about this scenario is that the wort gravity changes depending on the depth of the sample. If you had pitched, I would suspect that the culprit was your yeast starter not being completely mixed in the wort, especially if you used a large-volume starter. Liquids of varying density are more difficult to mix thoroughly than one would guess. The only other thing that could cause this difference is temperature variation, as temperature affects liquid density and the hydrometer reading. Temperature stratification in liquids is very common. If you are not measuring the temperature of your sample along with the specific gravity, you should.

I usually add some water after wort boiling to adjust gravity and want to know the wort gravity after the water addition to confirm that my calculations and water addition were correct. I have collected multiple samples during the course of wort cooling and have observed that samples do vary slightly from beginning to end. The variation is typically between 0.1 and 0.2° Plato or about 0.0004–0.0008 SG. The only conclusion that makes any sense to me is that the top-up water is not evenly distributed in the wort, even after pumping it to a whirlpool and allowing it to rest before cooling to allow the trub to settle.

Personally, I feel the best place to sample wort is from the kettle, immediately after boiling. At this stage, the wort is well mixed and nothing has been added, such as water for top-up or yeast. The wort gravity combined with wort volume is used to calculate brewhouse efficiency, and this is the place to collect the data. Although suspended solids, such as trub and hop particles, should not affect the hydrometer reading — since hydrometers measure dissolved solids — I collect a sample and first allow the solids to settle, then transfer clear wort to my hydrometer test container.

Q Is it possible my hydrometer might not be calibrated correctly?

A For starters, don't ever assume any measuring instrument is properly calibrated. A hydrometer should indicate that distilled water has a specific gravity of 1.000 SG (a Plato hydrometer should read 0.00°) at the temperature for which the hydrometer is calibrated. Most laboratory-type hydrometers read true at 68°F (20°C), and many homebrew hydrometers read true at 60°F (16°C). In most cases, the sample is at some other temperature and the hydrometer reading must be adjusted up if the sample is warmer than the hydrometer temperature calibration or adjusted down if the sample is cooler than this temperature.

This trivial issue gets nasty when you step back and carefully look at the problem. For example, I have a sample of wort and plunk a hydrometer in it and the reading is 12.5° Plato. Having a good idea that the sample is warmer than room temperature (68°F/20°C) in my chilly, imaginary room, I grab a floating thermometer from the bench, plunk it into my wort sample, and determine that the wort temperature is 78°F (25.5°C). I can go to a table and determine that I need to add about 0.5° Plato to my reading. No problem, right? Wrong. When I put the thermometer in the wort, I changed the wort temperature, since the large floating thermometer was cooler than the wort sample.

One way to get around this problem is to measure the gravity and the temperature at the same time. You can do this with a separate hydrometer and thermometer, or you can buy a hydrometer with a built-in thermometer. These little guys are nice and range in price from about $15 up to $160.

***

Q Is the final gravity taken during the primary or secondary fermentation, and how is this accomplished without infecting the brew?

A Unlike original gravity, final gravity can be determined at many stages in the process. It can be checked once fermentation is complete and sampled from the primary fermenter. The sample can be taken from the secondary fermenter or from a bottle or keg. In all cases, the specific gravity of the beer will be the same because fermentation is complete. There are exceptions to this rule: bottle-conditioned beers or beers with additives such as honey or fruit added after fermentation. These beers have different specific gravities before and after the addition of such materials.

The best method of sampling beer from a fermenter involves a device known as a *thief*. A thief is a large-diameter, turkey-basterlike thingamabob with a small hole in each end. The brewer simply inserts the sanitized thief into the fermenter, covers one end with a thumb, and removes the thief.

Thief

Q How do you convert from degrees Plato to specific gravity?

A A rough conversion between degrees Plato and specific gravity can be made by dividing the specific gravity number behind the decimal (often called points of gravity) by 4. A specific gravity of 1.048 has 48 gravity points and 48 ÷ 4 = 12° Plato. This approximation is pretty good up to about 1.070 SG. After this, the approximation begins to deviate from the actual conversion.

A conversion table between specific gravity and degrees Plato can easily be made in a spreadsheet using the following formula. An example converting 12° Plato to specific gravity is shown (the order of operations is a little confusing at first glance).

$$\text{Specific gravity} = 1 + [\text{Plato} \div \{258.6 - (\text{Plato} \times 227.1/258.2)\}]$$
$$= 1 + [12 \div \{258.6 - (12 \times 227.1/258.2)\}]$$
$$= 1 + [12 \div \{258.6 - 10.555\}]$$
$$= 1 + [0.0484] = 1.048$$

Q How are the Brix, Plato, Balling, and specific gravity scales different?

A This question raises some issues of semantics. In general terms, degrees Brix, degrees Plato, and degrees Balling are interchangeable. All three scales express the weight percentage of sucrose solutions and relate this weight percentage to specific gravity. The Balling scale, established in 1843, is the oldest. Brix later corrected some calculation errors in the Balling tables and introduced the Brix tables. In the early 1900s, Plato and his collaborators made further improvements. Essentially they are the same, but the tables differ in their conversion from weight percent to specific gravity in the fifth and sixth decimal place of the specific gravity number. Specific gravity, by the way, relates the weight of a given volume of liquid to the same volume of water. Liquids heavier than water, like wort, have a specific gravity greater than 1.000, and liquids lighter than water, such as alcohol, have a specific gravity less than 1.000.

Winemakers and the sugar and juice industries typically use degrees Brix, continental brewers typically use degrees Plato, British brewers use specific gravity multiplied by 1,000 (for example, 1.040 becomes 1040), and American brewers use a mixture of degrees Balling, degrees Plato, and specific gravity.

I use Plato and specific gravity because my hydrometers indicate degrees Plato, and specific gravity is always required when doing brewing calculations. For example, if you multiply degrees Plato (expressed in decimal form) by specific gravity, the result is kilograms of extract, a convenient number when doing calculations.

■ ═══════ ■

Q **I have a refractometer and was told that I can check the gravity of my *runoff* when sparging. How would I do this?**

A If you have a refractometer, you certainly can use it to determine density. Most refractometers are scaled in terms of degrees Brix because they are most often used in industries that use the Brix scale. For all practical purposes, you can use the simplified formula (4×°Brix) rule for the conversion. Use caution with your refractometer, because light refraction is temperature dependent, just like specific gravity. Your sample temperature should ideally be around 68°F (20°C). The great thing about a refractometer is that the sample size is small (about 1 mL or 0.03 oz.) and very easy to cool to room temperature before measuring.

I don't like refractometers for two reasons. The first is that they are difficult to read unless they are really high-end. I do like the high-end ones (they resemble a microscope), but they cost thousands of dollars! The second reason I don't like them is that they are not reliable for checking samples from the fermenter because alcohol interferes with the measurement differently than it does with a hydrometer. In other words, a hydrometer measurement on beer may indicate 2° Plato and the refractometer will indicate something different on the same sample. Most brewers express the final gravity as measured by a hydrometer. If you do want to use the refractometer, use it on wort only, and you will be fine.

■ ═══════ ■

Q How do plastic bottles compare to glass bottles, and how good in general are plastic bottles for homebrewing?

A I hate bottles. I mean, taking the soggy cigarette butts out of those bar bottles, getting the labels off, cleaning them, filling them, and then cleaning them again for reuse is a royal pain in the can! The only good thing about the whole process is the drinking stage. Plastic soda bottles obviously cut down on a lot of this effort. You can save them from home use, and it only takes ten 2-liter bottles to bottle off a 5-gallon (19 L) batch.

So what's the downside? Plastic soda bottles allow light to strike your prized beer and eventually allow for the slow transfer of gasses across the bottle wall. This means that, over time, the beer will flatten due to carbon dioxide escape and that the beer will gradually oxidize due to oxygen ingress. If you don't mind skunky, *oxidized* homebrew, plastic bottles will do the trick!

On the upside, however, the gas transfer business is slow, and light can be kept out by putting the bottles in the dark. Research from England shows that beer will hold its carbonation for up to 3 months in polyethylene terephthalate (PET) plastic bottles. These bottles also ward off beer oxidation for the same time period. This means that if you don't drink the beer within 3 months, its quality will start to show noticeable signs of deterioration. No problem — just drink your beer while it is fresh.

Q What is the downside to fermenting in a plastic fermenter?

A Plastic fermenters work fine for fermentation but really should be avoided for prolonged aging. A longer-term aging should occur in stainless steel or glass containers. This opinion stems from the fact that most plastics, including the types used to make most buckets and fermenters, are permeable to gas. This means that oxygen can cross from outside into the beer in a plastic fermenter. The same thing happens with carbonated beverages stored in plastic bottles. Sodas, for example, will lose carbonation over time when packaged in plastic bottles. There are now plastic beer bottles made from special polymers that have better gas barrier properties.

The advantage to stainless steel and glass vessels is that they allow no gas transfer. Also, stainless steel and glass are more difficult to scratch if treated with a modicum of care. Plastic, on the other hand, is easier to scratch. Scratches are the sort of crevices that bacteria love and make sanitizing that much more difficult. Even without scratching the plastic surface, it is often the case that heavy-wall plastics are rougher on a microscopic level than steel or glass.

■ ══════════ ■

Q Does a conical fermenter help create better tasting beers?

A I would not say that conical fermenters alone make beer that tastes better, but I would agree that they are the ideal shape for a multipurpose vessel. The real advantage of conicals is that yeast will settle in the cone and can be removed from the fermenter with minimal beer loss. Most commercial brewers will reuse some of the yeast harvested from the cone of a fermenter and will discard yeast that is either not suitable for reuse (the first and last layers off the cone, for example) or yeast that is in excess of what is needed. This use of the cone comes early in the process, typically within a few days of the fermentation's end.

Another use of the cone comes later in the process, during aging. To use the cone during aging, you need to age the beer in the fermenter. If you buy into my gas barrier argument, you are probably aging in stainless steel. During aging, more yeast will continue to settle from the beer. Over time, this yeast will begin to die and autolyze or decay.

Yeast autolysis is bad for two reasons: It imparts *off-flavors* to beer and it increases amino acid concentration in the area surrounding the dead yeast. Most beer spoilage bacteria do better in high amino acid environments; the bottom of a fermenter full of autolyzing yeast is a perfect environment for bacteria growth. When beer is aged in a conical fermenter, this layer of dead and decaying yeast is very easily removed from the bottom and the problems with yeast autolysis can be greatly reduced or even eliminated.

The last real advantage to fermenting and aging in one vessel is that it allows a single beer transfer. This means you have only one fermenter to clean per brew and the chances of contamination and air pickup encountered during racking are reduced. All-in-all, the conical fermenting (and aging) vessel, often referred to as a *uni-tank,* is a great tool.

■ ━━━━━━ ■

Q I am thinking of stepping up to a stainless steel conical fermenter. I notice that most are listed as seamless with no welds, but some brag about being welded. What is the difference, and which is better?

A Weld quality is a very big deal; it affects stainless steel corrosion and its ability to be cleaned. I want to give a little background on welding, because both welded and seamless kettles can be excellent pieces of gear.

As a general rule, welds are only used when required, as they are for big vessels, because stainless steel coils come in a standard width of 48 inches (122 cm). The standard method used to build tanks is to form a tube and attach bottom and top heads to the tube to complete the tank. Fermenters typically have a cylindroconical bottom and dished top head. The heads and tube all have weld seams, and the welds are ground flush on the interior of the vessel. A good weld must have full penetration to provide strength and to eliminate crevices where microorganisms grow.

Excessive heat applied to a weld leaves a large heat-affected zone around a weld, and the alloy composition around this area is different from stainless steel that is not exposed to the heat of welding. Corrosion is more likely to occur in the heat-affected zone, especially when the welds are made using too much heat. Various testing methods, such as radiography, are used to evaluate welds. Tube or pipe welds can be really problematic if the tube or pipe is not properly purged before welding. Improper purging causes *sugaring* inside the tube; this black, granular oxide is a veritable breeding ground for bacteria.

Most long pipe runs are fit up with very small tack welds and the joints taped. The line is then purged with an inert gas, usually argon or a blend of argon and nitrogen, before the welds are made. A good pipe weld, like that used to attach a valve or ferrule into a line, is fully penetrated, has only one start and stop, is smooth (often having the appearance of a stack of dimes slid off into an even and overlapping row), and has very little discoloration. Pipe and tube welds often cannot be ground on the interior, and boroscopes are used to visually inspect the weld for penetration, starts and stops, and color.

If welding can be avoided, it is, because of all the associated concerns. One way to build a pot without welding is through metal forming. Stainless steel has very good mechanical properties and can be stretched and formed without tearing the material. Although stainless does not look elastic, it is really like a sheet of dough and can be formed into a variety of smooth shapes with the proper tools. Spinning dies can be used to stretch and form the steel into the shape of a bowl or pot, for example, and most stainless steel cookware is made using such methods. Knuckles can be added to a dish-shaped head using special dies to add strength to the head. These methods do not require welding and avoid the potential problems associated with welds.

Here is the take-home message: Excellent equipment can be purchased with or without weld seams. The key is to know how to properly inspect equipment before purchasing. All beer contact surfaces should be smooth. Polished surfaces should not be scratched or pitted. Welds should be uniform and free of crevices and discoloration. Once you pick out your gear, you then want to maintain it in this condition. Do not use abrasive scrubbing pads to clean stainless steel and be very careful of the metal tips many scrub brushes have; they can quickly scar a perfectly smooth stainless surface. (See cleaning stainless steel, page 103.)

Q How many times can you reasonably use flexible silicone hose for siphoning before it needs to be thrown out?

A I have no trouble recommending that you use a section of hose for as many times as you can, as long as the hose is kept clean and the inside surface is not cracked. Hose cleaning is one of those things that are sometimes overlooked. If you cleaned your blowoff tube with a hot bleach solution after using it, I bet it would look like new! Make a good cleaning solution by mixing ½ cup unscented bleach per gallon (118.3 mL/3.8 L) of hot tap water.

Hoses should be cleaned by either recirculating cleaning solution through the hose (this requires a pump) or by soaking the hose in a cleaning solution. This cleaning is best done soon after the hose is used, so that the soil has little time to harden inside the hose. Many hoses have some type of barbed fitting connected to the end. It is a good idea to routinely remove the fitting and clean the area around the connection or, better yet, cut a small portion off the hose and reattach the fitting to a smooth hose section. This helps to keep the intersection between the fitting and hose clean and the crevices in this region to a minimum. When I have a long piece of hose and am unsure if it is in good condition, I cut a piece off the hose, split the sample in half, and inspect the inside of the hose. If there are small cracks, or if the hose has a buildup of *beer stone* (calcium oxalate deposits that look like brown-tinted glass), I will toss it. Otherwise, there is no reason to waste good hose.

One thing to be careful about at home is pressure. Hoses that are not reinforced with braids should not be pressurized, especially with hot liquids. When silicone hose is heated, it gets soft and is easy to rupture when pressurized, for example, by a pump. If you pump wort or beer, or move wort or beer using compressed gas, you need to buy braided hose. As long as the braided hose has an interior made of silicone, you can treat it as you do your nonbraided hose. I use the same sections of commercial-grade hose continuously for several years without any problem.

Q What would you recommend for optimal distance between grain mill rollers? Does it depend on the particular grain being milled?

A The gap between rollers in a malt mill does depend on the type of grain being milled as well as the roller size and surface texture. Most commercial mills with large-diameter rolls (6–8 inches/15–20 cm) have a gap setting of 1 to 1.2 millimeters. This setting is typically used for pale malt and may be set tighter for smaller grains, such as wheat and rye malts, and special malts for which husk integrity is not an issue. In fact, some brewers prefer very finely milled *roasted barley* and roasted malt because less grain is needed to provide a given color. This may also have a flavor benefit because less roasted/burnt husk material is added to the mash. The best way to determine the best gap setting is to start with coarsely milled malt and gradually tighten the gap over time while monitoring the ease of wort collection. The best gap setting is one that gives good extract yield while also allowing for easy wort recovery during lautering.

Thermometer Accuracy

Some thermometers, especially dial thermometers, can be significantly out of calibration. I have encountered many such thermometers that were the source of error, especially wort-fermentability problems, from seemingly normal mashes.

The best way to check a thermometer is to measure the temperature of melting ice and boiling water. These temperatures should be 32°F (0°C) and 212°F (100°C), respectively.

To calibrate a thermometer, fill a glass with ice cubes and then fill the glass with water. In a few minutes, the water temperature will drop to 32°F (0°C). If the thermometer is a dial type, it most likely has an adjustment screw or the face can be rotated. Simply adjust the thermometer so that it reads 32°F (0°C).

Alcohol-filled thermometers cannot be adjusted and are typically more reliable than dial thermometers because they are calibrated when made and don't change over time.

Q I recently saw a filtration kit with three cartridges: 5 micron, 1 micron, and ½ micron. What would be filtered out by each of these cartridges?

A This is a difficult question because filters can remove particles based on two properties: size exclusion and adsorption (sticking). Size exclusion is the mode of filtration that most filters are designed to use. This method essentially removes particles that get trapped in the filter or on the filter, depending on the filter type.

Cotton filters, paper pulp filters (sheet filters, for example), and diatomaceous earth (DE) filters (swimming pool filters and commercial beverage filters, for example) remove particles based on size and are known as depth filters, the first type of size-exclusion filters. The flow of liquid through a depth filter follows a tortuous path that is responsible for the removal of solids. The key feature of depth filters is that they are rated in nominal sizes. Your 5-micron filter and perhaps the 1-micron filter are depth filters rated on a nominal rating system. This means that they effectively remove particles of 5 and 1 microns respectively, but the size of the openings in the filter are much larger than the filter ratings. This means these filters can remove relatively high solids loads, but will also let through some particles the same size as and smaller than the filter rating. Depth filters are extensively used for beverage *clarification*.

The second category of size-exclusion filters is the membrane filter. A ½-micron is probably a membrane filter, referred to as an absolute filter. This means that the pore sizes in the membrane absolutely will not allow particles larger than ½ micron, the size of the membrane pore, through the filter. These filters are terrible at handling high solids loads, like cloudy beer, because the surface of the filter quickly becomes blinded. Membrane filters are used only after beer clarification, and the absolute filter is useful primarily to remove spoilage organisms. Most yeast cells are between 5 and 10 microns in diameter. A 5-micron filter is a good size to remove yeast and will remove most chill haze caused by protein/polyphenol interaction.

The key to filtration is to filter as cold as possible without freezing the beer. If you want a really clear beer, then you may want to filter twice. Yes, twice, starting with 5 microns and then again with 1 micron, which removes more of the nonyeast beer haze. Double filtration is not necessary, but it will make your 1-micron filter last longer. Finally, if you want to remove bacteria and extend your beer's shelf life, then pull out the ½-micron filter. Make sure the beer is brilliantly clear before using this size; if it is not, the membrane will quickly blind.

Q I want to add a spigot to my kettle. Should I weld it on or could I use another method?

A You can go with a welded outlet or a bulkhead fitting. A bulkhead fitting is inserted in a hole and sealed with a gasket and nut. The advantage of this kind of fitting is that it requires no welding and is easy to replace. The disadvantage is that the gasket and nut present a crevice on the inside of the kettle and are not as easy to clean as a smooth, welded connection. I prefer welded fittings for this reason.

If you have the outlet welded to the kettle, you can either weld a valve directly to the kettle or have a fitting welded to the kettle. I prefer using a fitting and then attaching my valve to the fitting. This allows the valve to be removed for maintenance or replacement if it becomes damaged.

If you want to use a ball valve with a threaded connection, you can have an NPT coupling welded so that it will mate to a ball valve. I have a personal thing against threaded connections and prefer sanitary fittings. I would have a ferrule welded in the kettle and attach my valve with a clamp and gasket. This method requires a more expensive outlet valve which is also more difficult to find than the ubiquitous ball valve available at every hardware store.

Q **I've heard that brass contains lead and shouldn't be used in brewing. Is this true?**

A Brass is an alloy consisting of the elements copper and zinc; brass contains no lead. Brass, like copper, can be soldered, and if lead-containing solders were used, then a brass fitting would contain lead. Brass by itself, however, does not pose a health risk.

I have a personal beef with brass, though, and want to add some meat to this answer. Most brewhouses found in commercial breweries contain metals other than stainless steel. Even an "all-stainless" brewhouse will incorporate a bit of copper somewhere to contribute a small amount of copper and usually trace amounts of zinc to wort. These elements play an important role in fermentation. Copper helps bind volatile sulfur, and zinc is a yeast micronutrient. Other metals found in older brewhouses include carbon steel (the type of steel that rusts), brass, and bronze. Excellent beers can be made when these metals are part of the "hot side" of brewing — although carbon steel can cause some real problems and is best avoided because it easily releases *iron* into liquids.

After yeast is pitched, the rules change in my book. Yeast rapidly decreases the pH of wort from about 5.2 to around 4.5 and begins to produce flavor compounds that are very susceptible to oxidation. Oxygen is not the only element capable of filling the oxidant role; metal ions from equipment can and do act as oxidants. In beer, the ones to look out for are copper and iron, because the equipment we use often contains these two elements. Filter sheets and filter powder such as diatomaceous earth (DE) can carry iron that will contaminate beer being filtered with this very potent oxidizer. Most brewers are very picky about specifying low-iron filter materials. Iron can also come from carbon steel used in the construction of brewhouse equipment, and the use of carbon steel in brewhouses is virtually nonexistent today.

In my opinion, brass, copper, and carbon steel should never touch the actual beer . . . never. In wort, these metallic flavors are absorbed by yeast or react with products of fermentation when wort is fermented. Once fermentation is complete, however, metal ions will make the beer taste metallic. After a while, the beer will begin to taste oxidized if enough metal is present, just as it would if it were in contact with air or oxygen.

This blanket statement really flies in the face of much written about beer. After all, brass is the most common metal used to make beer faucets, and many fittings used in kegging equipment are also brass. The fitting used to tap into a keg is commonly made of chrome-plated brass (the chrome plating really does not last long where it touches beer, and what lies below is plain old brass). The little barbed pieces with nuts used for connecting the keg tap to a beer hose are also made from chrome-plated brass. Chrome is an alloy of chromium and other metals, usually molybdenum. Chrome is not bad, but when it is plated on top of brass and begins to wear, the plating comes off and brass is exposed. Some people even use copper tubing to cool beer in a *jockey box* on its way from keg to faucet.

The point to all of this is that when you start thinking about how beer flavor is affected by the materials you use in the brewery, you realize that improvements in flavor can often be made by focusing on your equipment rather than your brewing technique. You don't have to worry about lead from a brass nut, but you may find that a flavor improvement can be realized by using a different material.

Q **I am looking to expand my home brewery and was wondering if there are any issues with using CPVC pipes instead of copper to move my wort around?**

A The most important thing to consider when evaluating construction materials is product compatibility. CPVC, or chlorinated polyvinyl chloride, is a heat-resistant type of PVC rated for continual exposure to water at 190°F (88°C). The main use for CPVC is in hot water lines in new homes. This type of pipe has advantages: It is heat resistant; it is easy to cut and "weld" together with liquid PVC bonding agents; and as a food-grade polymer, it stands up to a wide range of brewery cleaning solutions, including strong bases like sodium hydroxide (caustic) and acids like phosphoric acid.

I prefer rigid piping or tubing, such as copper or stainless steel, for permanently installed wort lines, because these lines just feel tougher. With this personal opinion aside, I can't think of any red flag issues concerning CPVC in the home brewery other than the obvious — you don't want to use this plastic with boiling wort as it's not rated for temperatures that high. Another thing to be mindful of is keeping this material away from the flame under your wort kettle or hot water tank.

Q I was told that all the equipment that comes in contact with a *lambic* beer I want to make will have to become my exclusive lambic equipment, and if I use it to brew anything but lambics, the other beers will get off-flavors. Is that true?

A The really big problem with lambic cultures is not the yeast: It is the bacteria. The bacteria in lambics include *Lactobacillus* and *Pediococcus* species. These two genera of bacteria just happen to be the most potent beer spoilage organisms of regular beers. They produce sourness and diacetyl (*buttery* aroma). The other feature of these bacteria is that just a few cells of the buggers can cause beer to spoil. When lambics are made, there are more than just a few cells, since the growth of these bacteria is actually encouraged — unthinkable for any other type of beer! Some of the yeasts used in lambic fermentations are considered "wild," meaning they are not brewing strains. One such example is the genus *Brettanomyces*. This yeast imparts the wet-horse-blanket aroma to lambics.

The bottom line is that all these microbes are bad news for brewing regular beer. It's the brewing equivalent of introducing a population of toxic, food spoilage bacteria into your kitchen. As with cooking, these bacteria can be carried from a batch of lambic to a batch of regular beer. One way to avoid this *cross-contamination* is to use only certain pieces of equipment for certain tasks, the way a cook might have separate cutting boards for raw and cooked meats. This preventive measure keeps kitchenware that has not been cleaned properly from carrying bacteria from raw to cooked meat. The same rule is not usually applied to utensils like cutting knives, because they are easier to clean. This philosophy can also be applied to brewing equipment.

In general, glass and metal (usually stainless steel) utensils are smooth and hard and should not have crevices that make cleaning difficult. These tools can be used for lambics and for regular beers if they are designed for thorough cleaning. For example, a stainless steel fermenter with a threaded fitting is a poor design with respect to cleaning. Racking canes, hoses, tubes, plastic fermenters, and other soft materials also fall into the cutting board category. I would recommend having separate soft tools for lambic brewing to help prevent cross-contamination.

SABCO's Brew-Magic RIMS

Q **How exactly does a RIMS (recirculated infusion mash system) work differently than a regular three-vessel system?**

A The recirculating *infusion mash* system is a cleverly designed assembly that allows the homebrewer to use the temperature profile or step–infusion mash method without having a heated mash tun. Most RIM systems have a mash tun, a brew kettle, and a hot-water pot used to heat the mash and sparge water. The only vessel that is unique is the mash tun. At first glance, it looks like a normal mash tun made from a stainless steel pot or old keg, but closer examination will reveal a pump and a heater. These two elements are the heart of the RIM system.

Mashing begins normally in the RIM system, but usually at a lower temperature because the mash is later heated. When the first temperature rest is complete, the recirculating and heating begins. Basically, wort is pumped from beneath the mash tun false bottom, through an in-line heating element, and on top of the mash bed. This process is continued until the wort entering the pump equals the temperature of the next step of the mash profile.

Some fancy RIM systems have little programmable logic controllers (PLCs) that will automatically run the mash profile, whereas the simpler (and more affordable) systems are manually operated. The in-line heater uses the principle of external heat transfer. Many large breweries use external heaters for wort boiling because these heaters can be cheaper to install than internal wort boilers. They also operate with more energy efficiency, and are more easily cleaned (the cleaning solution is pumped through the heater) than their internal heater cousins. RIM systems are essentially small-scale adaptations of large, industrial, external vessel heaters.

* ———————— *

Q I have been looking for information on how to calculate the volume of exhaust and makeup air required for a 200,000 BTU natural gas ring burner. How can I figure this out?

A Safety and brewing is a topic near and dear to my heart. No matter how much fun the hobby of homebrewing is, one cannot forget that some of the brewing procedures done at home can be dangerous. And firing up a 200,000 BTU/hr burner in the comfort of one's living quarters qualifies as a legitimate safety concern. My local building codes require 1 standard cubic foot per minute (scfm) of airflow per 2,400 BTU/hr of burner capacity. Based on this guideline, your whopper of a burner requires 80 scfm of makeup air. Fortunately, most high-end kitchen exhaust fans I checked into supply this sort of air volume.

The key fact to keep in mind is that fresh air must be supplied to the room where your burner is located. In the brewery where I work, we have a large louver panel that opens when our 2,000,000 BTU/hr boiler flame is on. This means that when the flame is burning, we have makeup air flowing into the boiler room, and the combustion gases from the boiler exit the space through a chimney. Makeup requirement is something that the burner manufacturers provide; I suggest that you call the supplier of your burner to determine the recommended scfm required for your unit.

Speaking of your unit . . . it's a monster! Your 200,000 BTU/hr flame-thrower is one tenth the size of the boiler that simultaneously heats our 1,000-gallon hot-water tank and powers our 500-gallon kettle's peak demand. Either you have a huge brew kettle or plenty of horsepower under the hood. Good luck and stay safe!

■ ══════════ ■

CHAPTER 3

Cleaning and Sanitizing

Q Are cleaning and sanitizing the same thing?

A When it comes to this topic, there are two classes of chemicals: cleaners and sanitizers. Cleaners are formulated to remove soils. Some cleaners, like sodium hydroxide, are also lethal to microorganisms, especially when the cleaner contains sodium hypochlorite (bleach). However, these cleaners typically do not guarantee a sanitized surface. Sanitizers are designed to kill microorganisms, and some sanitizers are more effective at killing yeast than bacteria. Most sanitizers do not work well if the surface is dirty; they are best used after a thorough cleaning step. The best sanitizer is hot water or pressurized steam coupled with time. Many people assume that very low temperatures accomplish the same thing, but this is not true. Bacteria and yeast easily survive freezing, even for long periods of time.

Q What cleaning supplies do I need?

A The cleaning supplies used for homebrewing fall into two categories: household cleaners and specialty cleaners. I suggest selecting one all-purpose cleaner for all equipment. A dish detergent can be used to clean brewing equipment, but many of the soils found in the brew kettle and fermenter are not so easily removed. If you use a gentle cleaner, you will need to use brushes and elbow grease to clean your equipment. It is very important not to use implements that may scratch your equipment. Scratches make equipment more difficult to clean over time.

Personally, I like stronger alkaline cleaners, such as sodium hydroxide and sodium metasilicate, with good dissolving power, as my go-to cleaners. I periodically use acid cleaners to remove mineral deposits and beer stone. After the equipment is cleaned, I sanitize it with hot water or one of the many food-grade sanitizers on the market.

The only other special thing you need to clean homebrew equipment is an appropriately large container to soak and rinse equipment. Unless you have a really big kitchen sink, you may find that the bathtub or laundry sink is a better place to do some of your scrubbing. Plastic 55-gallon (208 L) chemical drums cut in half are pretty handy makeshift cleaning tubs and can also be used to ice kegs.

Q **What are the different types of cleansers available, and how should they be used?**

A Sanitization is one of the most important things a brewer can do to ensure good beer. I believe in and practice rigorous sanitization methods when I brew. Many brewers fail to recognize the cleaning component of a sanitization program. To properly sanitize any equipment used for food or beverage handling, the item must be cleaned first.

Cleaning means that organic debris is loosened and removed from the surface prior to using a sanitizer. Cleaning increases the effectiveness of your sanitizer, because organic debris consumes the sanitizing power of most chemical sanitizers. Just as a shield can fend off the blows of a sword, organic debris can prevent microorganisms from coming into contact with sanitizing chemicals. In fact, many microorganisms secrete extracellular slime that helps them attach to surfaces and protects them from chemical sanitizers.

Cleaning also drastically reduces the microbial load. In other words, cleaning washes microorganisms away. Most dishwashing detergents used in the home do not contain sanitizing agents and effectively remove microorganisms from smooth surfaces simply by acting as a detergent (known in cleaning lingo as a surfactant).

In practice, sanitizing should serve as an insurance policy to good cleaning. The fact is that a properly cleaned, unsanitized piece of equipment could most likely be used with minimal risk of contaminating the brewery. Many common cleaners used in the brewery, such as hot sodium hydroxide, or caustic soda, will also kill microorganisms. Do an excellent job cleaning your equipment and use a sanitizer as a second line of defense to your cleaning. For the record, I recommend sanitizing everything that touches beer or wort after boiling.

There are many good cleaners. The safest is a good dishwashing detergent coupled with elbow grease. Other cleaners, such as trisodium phosphate (TSP) and sodium hydroxide, have the added advantage of dissolving soils, but they are also less safe to handle. Certain mineral soils, such as beer stone, are not soluble in alkaline cleaners like TSP and sodium hydroxide. Acids such as white vinegar effectively remove mineral deposits. I keep a gallon under my sink and use it to clean everything from hard water spots in the bathroom to my coffee maker. You can use just about any chemical cleaner on your brewing equipment as long as you thoroughly rinse it from the equipment before the sanitizing step.

One last piece of advice: Don't rinse "no-rinse" sanitizers. Rinsing water can contain spoilage organisms and undo all your work. As long as the sanitizer is diluted as directed on the product bottle, you should have no reason to rinse your equipment after cleaning and sanitizing.

Q What makes a good sanitizer for my equipment?

A Sanitizers that brewers use have some common traits. The best sanitizers do not affect beer flavor or foam stability, are cost effective, and are not toxic when used at the proper concentration. Food-grade sanitizers that meet the requirements include sodium hypochlorite (bleach), iodophor solutions, peroxyacetic acid (my favorite), *quaternary ammonium compounds* (quats), and hot water or steam. Bleach can cause off-aromas and damage stainless steel if used incorrectly, but it is a great sanitizer and is safe. Iodophor can also lead to off-flavors, and quats are notorious for ruining foam.

- ◆ **Stronger alkaline cleaners.** Sodium hydroxide and sodium metasilicate, with good dissolving power, are my go-to cleaners.
- ◆ **Acid cleaners.** I periodically use acid cleaners to remove mineral deposits and beer stone. My favorite acid cleaner to use at home is white vinegar. I keep a gallon under my sink and use it to clean everything from hard water spots in the bathroom to my coffee maker.
- ◆ **Sanitizers.** My advice on sanitizers is to keep more than one type on hand. Quaternary sanitizers are great for certain tasks, while peroxyacetic acid (PAA), iodophors, bleach, and hot water work great for others.

Q Everybody talks about bleach, iodine, and commercial products as a sanitizer. What about alcohol?

A Alcohol is a great sanitizer; its most effective concentration for use is 70 percent. Many brewers use rubbing alcohol (isopropyl alcohol) in a spray bottle to spray valves, small fittings, and the like before use. Rubbing alcohol is a very effective sanitizer but is not intended for consumption. You don't want any appreciable amount of isopropyl alcohol in beer. Rubbing alcohol is much more toxic than ethanol, the kind of alcohol we homebrewers make, but it's not highly toxic in small doses, like methanol (wood alcohol).

I use isopropyl alcohol to sanitize sample devices, keg valves, and certain pieces of bottling equipment prior to use. I let the alcohol evaporate before using these implements, and I always flush beer through surfaces sanitized with alcohol before running the beer into a bottle or keg. The bottom line is that rubbing alcohol is not a food-grade sanitizer and should not be used for sanitizing fermenters, transfer lines, and other pieces of brewing equipment.

Ethanol is also a very effective sanitizer at the 70 percent (140 proof) concentration. However, it is expensive because it is taxed. Industrial-grade ethanol is cheaper than beverage ethanol, because methanol is added to the industrial version to make it toxic if consumed, thereby eliminating the taxes placed on beverage ethanol. Do not use industrial-grade ethanol for anything to do with brewing or cooking!

You can use alcohol for a sanitizer, but if it is likely to end up in your beer, you need to use ethanol and not isopropyl alcohol. As a closing comment, homebrewers typically follow the trends used by commercial brewers. Commercial brewers would probably not use ethanol even if it were cheap as a sanitizer, since it is flammable and electrical equipment (pump motors, light switches, and in-line instrumentation, for example) gets much more expensive when designed as "explosion proof" or "intrinsically safe," as is required for use around flammable liquids and gases. If you want to use alcohol at home for sanitizing, go for it!

Q When is it appropriate to use bleach and when is it not?

A Household bleach, or sodium hypochlorite, has a bad reputation primarily because of what it can do to beer flavor. When phenols — which are present in malt, wort, and beer — react with bleach, a potently aromatic compound called *chlorophenol* is formed. Chlorophenols are described as medicinal and remind me of the aroma of the throat spray Chloraseptic. The strong medicinal aroma of chlorophenol is a defect in all beer. Avoid this particular problem by keeping bleach out of your wort and beer; this means that you must thoroughly rinse equipment sanitized or cleaned in bleach until the rinse water has no bleachy aroma or taste. Of course, if your local water is heavily chlorinated you might have chlorophenol problems without using a bleach sanitizer — but this is another issue. I prefer using compounds other than bleach for sanitizing. My favorite is peroxyacetic acid (PAA).

Bleach is a strong oxidizing chemical and works extremely well as a sanitizer and as a cleaner. In fact, adding bleach enhances many industrial caustic cleaners (usually sodium hydroxide). These so-called chlorinated caustics are much more effective in the removal of protein films than regular caustic, and many brewers use them in the brew kettle, where cleaning is most difficult.

The major downside to chlorinated cleaners is that chlorine can corrode stainless steel when the pH of the chlorinated solution is low (or acidic). Caustic cleaners are alkaline and have a high pH, so stainless steel can be safely cleaned with chlorinated caustics.

Household bleach is also alkaline and has a pH around 12. This means that bleach can be used on stainless steel. However, when multiple cleaners are used for cleaning, it is possible for a chlorinated liquid residue to become acidic and thus corrosive. This can happen, for example, when a vessel is cleaned with a chlorinated cleaner followed by an acid-based cleaner or sanitizer.

This whole topic is pretty controversial among cleaning experts and stainless steel experts. Some argue that as long as the pH of chlorinated cleaners is kept alkaline, then chlorinated cleaners are OK on stainless steel. Others argue that chlorinated cleaners should be avoided at all costs because of this multiple cleaner scenario. My advice is to avoid using chlorinated cleaners unless you clearly understand how and when they can cause corrosion.

If you do use bleach, I recommend cheap bleaches that contain only sodium hypochlorite. Avoid bleaches such as lemon-scented Clorox. Bleach works great for soaking hoses, cleaning glass, and for special cleaning projects on stainless steel. For instance, I periodically — perhaps every one in ten cleanings — add plain bleach to caustic to remove a protein film that builds over time in our whirlpool. This film accumulates despite the fact that we clean our whirlpool with caustic after every use. Do not use bleach as an everyday stainless cleaner, because of its potential corrosiveness. Finally, bleach is a great sanitizer if you don't mind running the risk of the dreaded chlorophenol nose!

The concentration required for good sanitizing action is really pretty low. The state of Kansas, for example, requires restaurants to use 100 ppm for dishwashers with a cool-water sanitize step (that's roughly 2 teaspoons of bleach per gallon [10 mL/3.8 L]). The Montana State University Extension Service Web site recommends 50 ppm for household sanitation of dishes and 100 ppm for sanitizing countertops and appliances. Cleaning is another issue — concentrations from 6 to 12 ounces per gallon (47–94 mL/L) of water are more common. When I add bleach to caustic, I add about 12 ounces of bleach to 2 gallons (355 mL/7.6 L) of a 2 percent caustic solution. That's one potent cleaner!

Sterilize Versus Sanitize

After most equipment in a brewery is cleaned, it is then sanitized with some sort of chemical or heat treatment. Sanitize is based on the Latin root *sanitas*, and in food safety circles, "sanitary" means that bacteria, viruses and other things that are health concerns have been removed or destroyed by cleaning and sanitizing the equipment to a point where human safety is not compromised. "Sanitize" and "sterilize" are not interchangeable words. Sterilize in its simplest form means to completely destroy all living matter. The standard dunk in bleach or another sanitizer does not sterilize equipment.

Is sanitation important during mashing and sparging?

Sanitation is very important in every part of the brewing process. During wort production, it is important that your homebrewing equipment start off clean, like plates stored in your cupboard. The only time microorganisms really cause problems in the brewhouse is when wort sits around long enough that it starts to grow bacteria. This is uncommon at home, but it happens in commercial breweries where cleaning is more challenging. I read many recipes stressing the importance of sanitizing all brew pots, mash tuns, and tools, but it is not necessary. What is needed is for these brewing implements to be clean.

As soon as the kettle boil is over and wort cooling begins, the rules change. This is because wort is a nutrient-rich liquid that can support the growth of just about anything that falls in. Sanitizers (such as hot water, iodophor, and bleach) actively kill anything on your equipment to ensure it doesn't make it into your wort and spoil your beer.

What is the best way to clean and sanitize a plastic fermenter?

Be careful cleaning your plastic. Extremely stiff bristles safe for glass carboys can scratch plastic if applied with force. Some brushes use a twisted wire design to hold the bristles together and act as a handle; this can scratch surfaces. Scratches provide future safe havens for all kinds of microscopic contamination. If you simply want to swab the sanitizer across the surface of your equipment, use one of the sponges with a plastic handle used to clean glasses. Then you will not have to worry about scratches. Another problem with plastics is their ability to hold aromas. As a result, be careful using chlorine bleach products.

Q A homebrewer told me that as long as bottles were clean and free of residue, they could be sterilized in the oven. His method was to stack the bottles in a cold oven, bring it to near 500°F (260°C) and then let it cool gradually, removing the bottles when completely cool. Have you ever heard of this method, and does it produce good results?

A Dry heat, like that of an oven, is not as effective as moist heat when it comes to killing microorganisms. Sterilizing devices, like autoclaves and pressure cookers, use steam for heating and are vented during the heat-up phase to eliminate air. Air acts as an insulator in steam sterilizers and slows down heat transfer from the steam to the item being sterilized. Items — such as surgical instruments or lab waste — usually become sterile after 20 minutes in a pressure cooker or autoclave held at 15 psi. The method you describe can be used, but the sterilization time required is longer than if you used steam. Unfortunately, I cannot find any solid numbers for exactly how much time is required, since all of my references related to heat sterilization are based on moist heat. I would guess that 30 to 45 minutes of dry heat exposure would be pretty effective at killing beer spoilage bacteria and yeast.

There is a practical problem to heating beer bottles: glass fatigue. At one time in my brewing career, I sterilized bottles in a steam cabinet (basically an unpressurized steaming device similar to a big seafood steamer). After several cycles, the bottles became weak, and one day, several exploded during counterpressure filling. Luckily, I was wearing a face shield. After that experience, I quit using heat to sterilize bottles.

My advice about bottle cleaning and sterilization is to begin with clean bottles. If you reuse your bottles, thoroughly rinse them immediately after use. This makes cleaning much easier when you need a batch. Some dishwashers accommodate bottles and do a good job of cleaning them. Or you can soak bottles in a hot, diluted solution of a heavy-duty cleaner such as sodium hydroxide or sodium metasilicate. If the bottles are already pretty clean, hot dish soap will work fine. The idea with cleaning is to remove organic soils that interfere with the activity of most sanitizers.

After cleaning and rinsing, I prefer to use a liquid sanitizer instead of heat. One way to do this is to soak the bottles in your sanitizer of choice; chlorine bleach and iodine solutions are two popular choices for homebrewers that, if allowed to dry, should not impart aromas. (See chapter 7 for more information.)

Q
What sanitizing solution is friendly enough for a septic system?

A
There are many different sanitizers available to home-brewers. In your particular case, you want a sanitizer to effectively kill bacteria and *wild yeast* that may spoil your beer. But you don't want to kill the bacteria — at least not too many of them — that make your septic system function.

I don't know the size of your septic system, but in all likelihood, you could use just about any sanitizer available on the market to sanitize your homebrewing tools without harming the septic system. Since most sanitizers work by chemical oxidation, they lose their sanitizing ability after they have done their oxidation dirty work. This is why using a sanitizer such as bleach on a dirty surface doesn't guarantee success; the dirty surface uses the oxidizing potency of the sanitizer before the sanitizer kills the bugs. The amount of oxidizable matter in the drain line between your home and your septic tank will probably take care of most sanitizers that you might use.

Chemical cleaners are a different matter, especially those cleaners containing phosphates. Most states have laws regulating the types of soaps and detergents that are permissible for sale; many soaps are especially designed for septic systems. Detergents are designed to wet surfaces and carry crud away from the surface. They include chelating agents that make them foam, even in the hardest of waters. In the scheme of things, soap selection is much more important to your septic system than sanitizer selection.

Although I probably sound like a card-carrying sanitizer abuser, I don't like chemical sanitizers for a set of different reasons. The only way to really sanitize anything effectively is to apply the sanitizer as the last step of the cleaning process. Last means last and leaves no room for a water rinse — especially well water! Many people have the notion that water is somehow bacteria-free purity flowing freely from the taps of their homes. As nice as the concept sounds, tap water carries no guarantee of being free of bacteria. In most cases, it probably doesn't carry the bacteria that spoil beer, but when it comes to cleaning procedures, "probably doesn't contain" translates to "may contain."

I don't like many of the sanitizers (such as bleach) commonly used by brewers because they affect the beer flavor and appearance when left on the surface of the item being sanitized. Some make the beer taste medicinal, and many ruin its foam. We use sanitizers to keep the beer free of bacteria, but if it ends up with a different problem, what's the point? Funky beer is funky beer.

The two nonrinse sanitizers I really like for sanitizing the big items, such as fermenters and hoses, are peroxyacetic acid (PAA) and hot water.

Peroxyacetic acid leaves no foreign by-products and has gained popularity with commercial brewers. It is a combination of hydrogen peroxide and acetic acid. The sanitizer is stable in the absence of oxidizable matter but breaks down into peroxide and acetic acid when exposed to organic debris. Assuming the item being sanitized is clean, the organic debris is probably some microbial bug rapidly killed by the very aggressive peroxide component. The ultimate by-products of PAA are water and acetic acid (vinegar). Spoiled beers often have high levels of acetic acid, but all beers contain a very small amount.

Hot water is also a wonderful sanitizer for brewing equipment. Nothing destroys microorganisms like wet heat. The rule of thumb for killing beer spoilage organisms with hot water is 20 minutes at 180°F (82°C) or hotter.

Q After I empty my bottle into a glass, I fill the bottle about three-quarters of the way with warm water, turn it upside down, and shake it vigorously while it drains. Then I repeat this procedure. I park the bottle upside down to dry and then store in the case, again upside down. At bottling time, I just use my bottle tree to let the bottles dry after dousing the inside with iodophor solution. Is what I am doing adequate, or is there a big potential for a problem?

A Remember, there are two stages to cleaning when it is applied to food or beverage implements: cleaning and sanitizing. Cleaning is simply the removal of debris, usually organic in nature, from the surface of the object being cleaned. Sanitizing is used to kill yeast or bacteria that may spoil beer or food. Cleaning usually begins with a rinse to remove loose debris. Your warm water rinse falls into this category of "prerinsing."

The next step is to use some sort of energy input to remove soil that remains on the item being cleaned. There are three modes: mechanical, thermal, and chemical. For example, when you wash dishes with hot, soapy water you are using 1) elbow grease or mechanical energy, 2) hot water for the thermal factor, and 3) soap as a chemical cleaner. This step is critical because organic (schmoo) and inorganic (beer stone) components in beer adhere to surfaces and are largely unaffected by rinsing, even in cases where the object looks clean!

This is not to imply that prerinsing is not important. If loose soils are not removed before cleaning, they will reduce the cleaning power of your cleaner. Those dishwashing liquid commercials that show greasy plates being dunked into the dishwater are the perfect example of how not to clean. This does nothing more than make the cleaner less effective for the next greasy plate until the cleaner becomes so dirty that it begins to make the surface dirtier than it was before cleaning. Believe it or not, this actually happens; cleaning gurus call it redeposition.

After cleaning, it is then time to use a sanitizer. This segregation of duties is important because most sanitizers work by oxidizing things. If the sanitizee is clean, then the stuff being *oxidized* is most likely very tightly adhered to the sanitizee surface. The only things routinely left after cleaning are bacteria that form tight bio-films on surfaces. This is what the sanitizer is intended to oxidize. If the surface still has other organic debris, then the sanitizer will be used up on the remaining crud.

I think your prerinsing of bottles is an excellent start, because it prevents beer schmoo from drying on the surface. I would not consider this surface clean enough to be sanitized. I would strongly recommend cleaning with detergent between your water rinse and iodophor application. If I were doing the work, I would accumulate prerinsed bottles over time, clean them all at once, and then sanitize immediately after cleaning to make the work more efficient.

Q **I use iodophor to sterilize and mix it according to the directions on the bottle. Do you have to rinse after you sterilize with it?**

A Iodophor is a very effective sanitizer and, unlike bleach, can safely be used as a no-rinse sanitizer without adversely affecting the flavor of your beer. Iodophors require no more than 30 minutes to effectively sanitize a surface at the recommended concentration of 25 ppm. Most iodophors are diluted so that the typical use rate is somewhere around 1 ounce per gallon (7.8 mL/L). They are always labeled with instructions giving suggested usage rates. If you use it at this concentration and allow your equipment to drain properly, you will be in good shape. Iodophor does have a flavor, and when used at higher-than-recommended strengths, it can impart an iodine flavor to beer — especially if it is not drained from the equipment surface.

Q I have heard that some brewers soak their bottles in iodophor and place the bottles on a tree to drip dry and use them up to a week later. Would you recommend a bottle tree?

A Your primary concern with the use of bottle trees is the issue of recontamination. Any sanitized surface can be contaminated after the sanitizing step, and contact with contaminated surfaces should be eliminated. Using a bottle tree does not necessarily pose a risk if the tree is kept clean and sanitized. If you soak your bottles in the iodophor along with the tree and place them to drain on the tree, you should be fine. But I would not wait a week until using them. After the bottles drain on the tree, they should be used immediately because iodophor sanitizers work on contact and have very little residual activity.

■ ━━━━━━ ■

Q I would like to know if I can use a quaternary sanitizer to sanitize homebrewing equipment. This stuff is used in the food industry as a no-rinse, air-dry sanitizer. I don't want to ruin a batch of beer if it is inappropriate to use in homebrewing.

A Quaternary ammonium compounds, frequently called quats or *QACs*, are effective no-rinse sanitizers used in the food industry for a wide range of purposes. Quats are natural wetting agents and are very similar to soap. This means that they are good at penetrating surfaces.

Quats kill a wide range of bacteria and also leave a bacteriostatic film on surfaces. This film prevents microorganisms from recontaminating a previously cleaned and sanitized surface. Quats are frequently used to prevent the growth of microbes, especially molds and mildews, in food-processing areas. Restaurants also use quats in sinks as the final dip for dishwashing. This practice is used to wash glasses in bars.

Quats are gentle on the skin, stable when stored, and maintain their effectiveness when exposed to organic soils (dirty equipment). They also leave no odor or flavor on equipment or glassware. So far, quats are sounding pretty good, but there's a catch.

In general, brewers don't use quats on beer contact surfaces because quats can ruin beer foam. It's unfortunate that many bars and brewpubs use quats in their glass-washing sinks. That said, I do use quats in a fittings soak tank for small items and also use them to sanitize hoses and pipes. When used for hoses or pipes, I also rinse the quats out with clean water before passing beer through the line so the foam won't be destroyed.

Quats can be used to sanitize fermenters and other beer vessels, but I don't recommend them for these applications. Personally, I use a sanitizer called peroxyacetic acid (PAA) for beer vessels because it's effective and leaves nothing but water and vinegar (acetic acid) on the surface. (See sanitizing with PAA, page 90.)

My advice on sanitizers is to keep more than one type on hand. Quaternary sanitizers are great for certain tasks, while PPA, iodophors, bleach, and hot water work great for others. Just like household cleaners, one sanitizer is never going to be the best choice for all circumstances.

■ ══════════ ■

Q Are there any cleaners I need to avoid using on my new stainless steel pot?

A The one commonly used household chemical that can really damage stainless steel is bleach. Bleach (sodium hypochlorite) is corrosive to stainless steel when the pH is less than about 12 and causes the steel surface to develop small pits. Eventually, the pits can turn into holes, transforming a pot into a strainer. Pits are also hard to clean and can be a place for bacterial contaminants to hide.

■ ══════════ ■

Q How do I clean my stainless steel brew kettles?

A For those of you with expensive stainless steel cookware or brew kettles, here is some money-saving advice. DO NOT use any metallic abrasive pads when you clean. That includes 3M green scouring pads, copper balls of metal, stainless balls of metal, and all metal tools. (By the way, 3M makes many of the polishing abrasives used by stainless companies, but they are much finer than the pads used to remove cheese from a casserole dish.)

I recommend using Teflon scouring pads that are far too soft to scratch the surface of stainless steel vessels. We use a product made by 3M called a Doodlebug mop to clean the outside of our fermenters. It's a snazzy tool that has a big pad (which looks like one of those buff puff facial pads) stuck on its end. Again, the key is using something that does not scratch!

When there is a big cleaning problem, I am a proponent of chemical cleaners. What you want to do is select a cleaner that will dissolve the soil and not damage the steel. Although chlorinated cleaners can be used safely on stainless steel, I usually discourage their use because they can cause damage if used inappropriately. Cleaners like powder brewery wash (PBW) and sodium hydroxide, or caustic (my favorite), are good at dissolving soils. The key is to allow the chemicals to do the work for you. It is very important to wear eye and hand protection when working with industrial cleaners — even if you use a brush (metal free, of course) to do the scrubbing, since brushes have a way of spitting stuff toward one's face. Information abounds about cleaning chemicals, so I will be brief here. My point is that chemicals should be used on dirty equipment — not drills with abrasive scrubbing attachments.

And finally some words on passivation: This term describes a very particular type of cleaning performed on stainless steel. The main goal of passivation is to remove all contaminants (oils, soils, and especially, iron) from the surface of stainless steel in order to allow the "passive" film of chromium oxide (that makes stainless steel "stainless") to form spontaneously. The only chemicals widely used for this task are nitric acid and hot citric acid. Nitric acid is extremely dangerous, and the citric acid method is pretty intricate. In any case, you really don't need to worry about passivating stainless steel unless you contaminate the surface with iron. A rust-producing abrasive or tool is actually one of the best ways to go about contaminating the surface with iron, so this is another good reason not to use metal for cleaning.

Q I've read that the best way to sterilize my copper immersion wort chiller is to put it into the boiling wort for the last 15 minutes of the boil. When I do this, my boil stops and it takes 10 minutes to start up again on my electric stove. Is this normal, and are there other ways to sterilize the chiller?

A Using the wort boil to sanitize your wort cooler is really the easiest and most effective method. To ensure you get your proper boil time, knowing your chiller will stall the boil, you could simply extend your boil by 10 minutes before adding the coil. Try preheating the copper coil in a pot of boiling water. Copper has excellent heat-transfer properties, which means it doesn't take very long to preheat. The stalled boil is common when adding a copper chiller, because the copper absorbs energy from the wort faster than your stove burner can transfer energy to your brew pot. If you want to use a

Using a sanitized immersion wort chiller

chemical sanitizer instead, make sure it is a sanitizer with a low pH, such as iodophors and quaternary ammonium compounds (quats); they are copper friendly and won't cause corrosion. (Read more about quats for sanitizing on page 101.)

■ ──────────── ■

Q **I discovered that my copper counterflow chiller fits inside my pressure cooker. To sanitize, or actually sterilize it, I will run it through at 10–15 psi for about 15 minutes. Can this be harmful to my brew or me?**

A Pressure cookers are wonderful discoveries, especially if you name them something else. I call my pressure cooker an autoclave. Autoclave sounds less like some pot that granny used to make pot roast or can green beans from the garden. I use my autoclave to sterilize wort, contained in little Erlenmeyer flasks, and media bottles to grow yeast. The autoclave is also great for sterilizing media to make Petri dishes containing various microbiological media. And of course, when one considers that surgeons sterilize scalpels, forceps, hemostats, sutures, and all sorts of other surgical implements in autoclaves, they become an obvious tool for use in a brewery.

Autoclaves can sterilize if the steam pressure (temperature) and duration of the process are sufficient. Usually when equipment is sterilized, the process is targeted to destroy a specific group of bugs, and the term "commercially sterile" is used since absolute sterility is not practical. Some heat-resistant spores, such as *Clostridium botulinum,* are very difficult to destroy. Those spores can kill people if canned foods are not properly processed. Beer does not support the growth of pathogens, but heat-resistant bacteria certainly can make for some awful tasting beer. Heat exchangers are a good place for these little buggers to hide.

Cleaning beer and wort lines is also very important. At our brewery, the wort line is cleaned after every brew and heat-sanitized by recirculating 203°F (95°C) water through the line for at least 20 minutes. We do the same thing with our beer filter. We measure the water temperature at the outlet of the filter and maintain a minimum temperature of 176°F (80°C) for 20 minutes before we cool the filter with cold water that was previously boiled. Heat is a wonderful method of killing bacteria because bacteria cannot hide from heat, provided that the heat is uniformly distributed through the equipment being sanitized or sterilized.

When equipment is exposed to very hot water or steam, as in an autoclave, it is important to verify that all parts can tolerate high temperatures. Heat-treating materials not rated for extremely high temperatures can result in failure. If the piece of equipment being treated is to contain something potentially dangerous, like hot wort, a failure can cause serious injury.

Make sure your chiller or any other equipment you choose to put into the pressure cooker has no plastic parts that might not be as heat tolerant as they need to be and end up harming the chiller or causing flavor problems in your beer. You should note that hoses are rated for specific pressures and temperatures. These two numbers mean that a hose can hold, for example, 100 psi of pressure at 120°F (49°C). The rating does not mean that the hose melts above 120°F (49°C), but that it may burst if pressurized above 100 psi at the same temperature. When heat sterilizing in an autoclave, you really don't care about the pressure rating, because you are not using the hose to hold liquid pressure. You do want to ensure that the hose is not damaged. Simply remove the hose and autoclave the chiller if you cannot determine the hose's temperature rating. When I autoclave things, I use 15 psi for 20 minutes, and most home pressure cookers have a weight designed to provide 15 psi of steam pressure. The time and temperature used in an autoclave depends on what bugs you are targeting. You can get data on the kill rate of various bacteria at different temperatures if you so desire.

CHAPTER 4

Hops, Grain, and Ingredients

Q I've heard you can evaluate malt grains by chewing them. How does this work, and what do I look for?

A The practice of chewing malt grain is used to evaluate textural components that have meaning in the brewery. Poorly modified malts have cell wall material that has not been enzymatically broken down during malting. Since the enzymes released from the germinating grain originate from the embryo located at the end of the barley kernel, the progress of *modification* is uneven. In poorly modified malt, the tip of the grain is often hard. These "steely tips" are something that can be detected by chewing. The term steely refers to the appearance of the barley-like endosperm of the grain. As cell walls break down during malting, the steely, gray appearance of the endosperm transitions into a mealy white color.

Chewing also gives the brewer an idea of how friable (easy to crush) the grain is. Roasted malts, crystal malts, and well-modified pale malts typically are very friable. Raw wheat, barley, rice, and corn are less friable and are harder to crush. So, by chewing, you can get an idea of modification and a feel for ease of milling.

The other nice thing about chewing grain is that you get an idea of some of the flavors that will ultimately end up in your beer. While beer does not taste much like the malt from which it is made, there are some flavors from malt that do survive into the finished beer. Burnt, roasty, smoky, peaty, caramel-like, and nutty flavors from special malts and malty flavors from higher kilned pale malts do end up in beer. I often chew malt samples when I am searching for a certain flavor I want in the finished beer.

Q **Are *caramel malts* the same as crystal malts?**

A Caramel, cara, or crystal are synonymous terms describing a large family of malts made by changing the kilning process. All malts are kiln-dried to arrest germination. To make caramel malts, the maltster adds a key step, known as *stewing* or *saccharification,* before drying. The stewing step heats moist, unkilned malt (or rehydrated kilned malt) to about 158°F (70°C). The malt is held at this temperature for 1 to 2 hours with minimal ventilation to minimize drying.

Most caramel malts are made in roasting drums where ventilation and temperature are easily controlled. Stewing allows the starch inside the malt kernel to convert to sugar, just like mashing. After the stewing step, the malt is then dried and roasted at various temperatures and times.

Caramel malts contain high concentrations of Maillard reaction products (MRPs). The Maillard reaction is a complex series of chemical reactions initiated when "reducing sugars" react with free amino nitrogen. This occurs in hot, moist environments. Reducing sugars include sugars like *glucose* and maltose that are formed when starch is broken down by *amylase* enzymes. The stewing step drastically increases the concentration of reducing sugars inside of malt kernel. Free amino nitrogen refers to the nitrogen end of a protein or polypeptide not chemically tied up in a peptide bond (the bond between two amino acids in a protein or polypeptide chain).

The concentration of free amino nitrogen increases when barley is converted to malt. Well-modified malts have a higher concentration of free amino nitrogen than poorly modified malts. When sugars participate in the Maillard reaction, they become unfermentable; that's why using a high proportion of crystal malt increases the final gravity of beer.

The Maillard reaction is responsible for the formation of a wide array of aromas, including toffee, caramel, toast, nuts, raisins, and sherry. The reaction is also responsible for an increase in color. Toasted bread is a classic example of the Maillard reaction and can be used to illustrate how the reaction can progress from subtle to very pronounced colors and flavors. Some crystal malts are very light in color and flavor and are made using kilning regimens (after stewing) similar to pale malts. Darker crystal malts are kilned at higher temperatures for longer periods after stewing. Maillard reaction products are also widely believed to improve mouthfeel as well as beer foam stability.

Q

What's the difference between LME and DME?

A

Liquid malt extracts *(LME)* and *dry malt* extracts (DME) both begin as wort from a mash just like that used in all-grain brewing. LME is highly concentrated wort, usually 70 to 80 percent solids, and is made using some sort of evaporator. Most evaporators used to concentrate food products, such as tomato paste and orange juice, are multieffect vacuum evaporators.

In these devices, liquid is heated as it runs through a tall evaporation column; the hot liquid flows into a separator where water vapor flows out the top and the liquid is pumped to a second column. The condensed water vapor is used to heat the next column in the series. Because of the removal and condensation of water, each column in a multieffect evaporator has a deeper vacuum than the previous column, thus lowering the boiling point of water. Concentrated liquid flows from the end of the system. In the case of homebrewing ingredients, the product is LME.

Dry malt extract is made using a spray drier like those used to make powdered milk. In a spray drier, liquid is sprayed through very small nozzles into a tall vacuum column with hot air flowing up through the bottom. Liquid is evaporated and carried out of the column. The dry solids fall through to the bottom of the column, are collected in a cyclone separator, and conveyed out.

Food products made in multieffect evaporators or in spray driers pick up some color and flavor during the process. That's one reason that very light-colored beers can be difficult to make using LME or DME. Other than the differences in method of production, LME and DME are fairly similar.

Liquid malt extract does not store as well as DME and will darken over extended storage periods. Another difference between LME and DME is that LME is sometimes made from hopped wort, whereas DME is not. Personally, I prefer DME to LME because I think the DME is lighter in color and is easier to use.

Q What is the difference between *two-row* and *six-row* barley?

A In North America, both two- and six-row barley are grown. In Europe, only two-row varieties are grown. Six-row varieties have three fertile florets (kernels) at each node on the plant's rachis (the part the kernels are on). When the head is viewed from above the rachis, there appear to be six rows of kernels because each triad of florets is offset down the rachis.

In two-row varieties there is only one fertile floret per node. As with the six-row varieties, this position is offset, giving the appearance of two rows. Big deal! Well, it kind of is, because the two-row floret has more space to expand on the ear. This means two-row barley tends to be plumper than six-row, and plumper means more extract and less protein.

Six-row varieties also have higher enzymatic power.

In general, all-malt beers are made with two-row varieties because many brewers feel these varieties are best for flavor and because plenty of enzyme already exists for all-malt brews. More enzymes usually mean more protein. More protein means less carbohydrate, which is really why we mash to begin with!

Two- and six-row barley

Q I have heard that it is sometimes better to buy malt in 50-pound increments to save money on grain. However, I do not plan to brew with more than 10 pounds at a time. How should I store the extra crushed grains? Can crushed grains be stored in the freezer, or should I just leave the grain in its paper sack at room temperature?

A The key to storing grain is keeping it dry. Whenever crushed grain is left to sit around, it begins to take up moisture from the air. Most malts have a moisture content between 4 percent and 6 percent, and there are very few climates in the world that do not cause malt to absorb water over time. My rule with crushed malt is to use it as soon as possible, which means don't mill your malt until brew day. This, of course, requires a mill.

If you buy precrushed grain and want to store it for some time, you have a few options. One option is to measure the grain into convenient quantities, such as 5- or 10-pound lots, and bag it in sealable plastic bags. You can use a fancy vacuum packer, but large freezer bags will do the trick, too. You also can store malt in a sealable container, such as one used for flour.

Some malts are even sold in woven nylon bags that have plastic liners. These bags work pretty well for extended storage if you roll up the open part of the bag and secure it to reseal the bag. Malt can be stored at room temperature for extended periods without harm. As long as it stays dry and free of bugs, malt will keep for about a year — although like anything else it will lose its fresh flavor over time. Because malt does contain a small amount of oil, it can go rancid if left unused for too long. This is more likely to occur if the malt is stored in a very hot environment.

I would not recommend storing malt in the freezer, mainly because it is not necessary. The other problem with freezers is their amazing ability to make things taste like they were stored in a freezer! I can't imagine a beer that ended up tasting like a freezer, but I would guess that it wouldn't be all that great.

Q Whenever I try to crack grains rated 300°L–500°L (Lovibond), they turn to powder. Since the chocolate and black grains are just used for flavor and color, can I leave them whole and achieve the same results?

A I think of brewing ingredients such as chocolate malt and black patent malt as similar to coffee beans. If you steep them without crushing them, you will not get the same release of color and flavor. On the other hand, if you turn them into powder they can create problems when it comes to wort collection. Finely milled coffee can cause the same problem when it is packed too tightly into the thingamabob on the espresso maker.

Most really big brewers (domestic and abroad) who make dark beers use some sort of malt extract for coloring, because of the problems that dark-roasted grains cause during *run-off*. I have often considered treating roasted grains like coffee and making my own dark malt extract at the same time I am mashing. The malt "coffee" could be made using a wide array of kitchen gadgets, such as a strainer and several large coffee filters used to make a liner. I would then add it to the kettle, along with the wort from the mash. This strainer would give me the color and flavor I want from dark grains and alleviate the problems with very fine particles from milling.

Unfortunately, I cannot recommend using unmilled dark grains. If the small bits are causing problems, give my malt coffee idea a whirl or simply try adding the dark grains to the very top of the mash after the other grains have been mashed-in.

Q What are the main differences between adjunct brewing and all-malt brewing?

A Go down to the local mini-mart and pick up a few six-packs of adjunct beers to get an idea of what different adjuncts do to flavor. Michelob contains a small portion of rice in addition to malted barley. Budweiser contains more rice; Busch uses corn instead of rice. I think beers brewed with rice have a crisper, drier flavor profile than those made with corn, which have a sweeter, fuller flavor.

Both rice and corn are composed almost entirely of starch, and lack enzymes. When used in brewing, they contribute fermentable sugars but add little flavor and no color. They increase the physical stability (for example, chill haze) by diluting wort protein and polyphenol levels. They are also cheaper than malt, a fact that affects the commercial producer much more than the homebrewer.

When using rice or corn, I prefer to begin with whole rice or corn grits (white or yellow) as opposed to flaked rice or corn. Any kind of rice will work. You can purchase rice or corn syrup, and de-germed flakes at homebrew stores. The raw form is more challenging to use and adds to the fun of brewing an adjunct beer. The typical mash profile used for adjunct brewing is called the "American double mash" and is a hybrid form of *decoction mashing*. The first of the double mashes is the cereal mash. It contains all of the adjunct, which needs to be milled into a very fine *grist* (like grits), and about 10 to 20 percent of the total malted barley. (For milling rice, a coffee mill will work better than a homebrew grain mill.) High-enzyme malts, such as domestic six-row and domestic two-row, are preferred because the adjunct dilutes the enzyme concentration of the mash. European malts, especially British ale malts, are usually lower in enzymes than North American malts and are not recommended for use with mash adjuncts.

The cereal mash begins at about 158°F (70°C) for roughly 15 minutes and then is quickly raised to boiling. Boiling helps to gelatinize the adjunct starches, which have a higher *gelatinization* temperature than malted barley and wheat. Boiling typically lasts for 20 to 30 minutes.

In the meantime, the second mash is begun and held at around 120°F (49°C). This main mash accounts for between 65 and 75 percent of the total mash volume. When the cereal mash boil is complete, it is added to the main mash and the mash temperature increases. The exact volumes and temperatures vary with the type of beer being made, but in the traditional double mash, the cereal mash heats the main mash from its initial temperature to between 154 and 158°F (68–70°C). As with any other multitemperature mash, some brewers use different intermediate *rests,* but all double mashes follow this general sequence.

I've had success in using one vessel for adjunct brews. I first perform the cereal mash-in in a full-sized mash vessel. Then I cool the boiling cereal mash with cold water. Once the mash temperature is near my first temperature step, I add the remaining malt and enough hot water to get the proper mash consistency and temperature. The remainder of the mash profile is like any other step mash.

You can also brew adjunct beers using flaked rice or corn. The flaking process gelatinizes the starch, which means the flakes can be added to any type of mash without boiling them. If you typically use a single-temperature infusion, you can add the flaked adjunct directly to the mash. Remember that the adjunct dilutes the enzyme concentration and that the amount of adjunct should not exceed more than about 40 percent of the total grist.

Q Why is oatmeal used as an ingredient for stout, and can it be steeped for partial-grain batches?

A For starters, oatmeal must be mashed to convert the starch into fermentable sugars. If the oatmeal is simply steeped, you will extract starch and viscous gums (beta-glucans) from the oatmeal. Oatmeal is added to beers, especially stouts, because it is believed to enhance the foam stability and body of the brew. Some brewers believe that the beta-glucans increase beer *viscosity* enough to increase foam stability. This benefit is arguable. Furthermore, oats are rich in lipids (oil), and lipids are not good for foam. Oatmeal is also well known for making wort separation difficult because of the viscous beta-glucans. Brewers using oatmeal often use it sparingly so that wort separation is not an absolute nightmare. I think oatmeal does little for foam stability, but it does add a certain mouthfeel to beer that some brewers describe as slick or oily.

Q **What roasting times and temperatures should I use to make my own chocolate malt and black patent malt at home?**

A Roasted malts can be made using pale, previously kilned malt as the raw material. The methods are not very different from coffee roasting. Commercially produced, roasted grains are made in drum roasters. Roasted malts include amber, brown, chocolate, and black. The principal difference among these grains is the roasting temperature and roasting duration. Roasting pale malt at 200°F (93°C) for 15 to 20 minutes, and then gradually heating to 280–300°F (138–149°C) and holding for some time (determined by visual inspection by the roaster) is one way to make amber malt. Chocolate malt is made by roasting pale malt at 420–450°F (215–233°C) for 2 to 2½ hours; if this time is extended, black malt results. It is critical that the roasting temperature not exceed 480°F (250°C) because grain converts to charcoal (literally!) above this temperature.

Quenching, or spraying water on the hot malt, quickly stops the roasting process and causes the grain to swell. In a commercial roaster, the water is sprayed inside the roasting drum before the drum is opened. This is crucial, since opening the hot roasting drum is a sure way to ignite the combustible fumes contained inside the drum. At home, you could roast your malt on a cookie sheet and use a spray bottle to apply the quenching water; the idea is to cool the grain and flash the water off as steam, so you don't want to go crazy with the application.

Q Can I make my own brown malt for brewing porters?

A Yes, you can make your own brown malt by roasting pale malt in the oven. Roasting temperatures for brown malt are 400 to 450°F (204–233°C). The malt should be taken out of the oven when the right color is achieved and quickly spread on a cooling *rack*. Brown malt is lighter in color than chocolate malt and has a distinctive nutty, roasted flavor. The original brown malts were made by drying the green, or unkilned malt, over a wood fire, giving them a smoky flavor. This method is no longer used to make brown malts, so they lack smokiness. Used in porters and other dark ales, brown malts impart flavors that would not be found if you simply replaced the brown malt with chocolate malt.

Q From a practical standpoint, does a 5–10 gallon homebrewer who is just looking to make good beer need to worry about anything that is reported on malt specification sheets?

A Malt specifications, also called specs, have some very useful information to give brewers a feel for what they are using in their brews. Commercial brewers take these specs very seriously, because they are in the business of creating the same beer day after day. Standard malt specs include color, degree of modification, protein content, extract, enzyme content, beta-glucan content, and moisture. All are pieces of data required to evaluate malt. Most malt-sters make malt to suit the needs of their customers, so most malt is made in accordance with the biggest customers in mind. That's because out-of-spec malt delivered to a medium- to large-sized brewery is likely to be rejected and sent back to the maltster. Maltsters on the whole do a good job converting barley, also purchased based on stringent specifications, into malt that brewers want to purchase. In some years the barley crop is bad because of weather, and malt quality is affected, but for the most part, brewers enjoy a ready supply of good malt.

When I buy malt, I know the general specs for what I am buying. This means I know the color, the protein range, the degree of modification, and the approximate enzymatic activity. The extract content of the malt, expressed as hot water extract or the laboratory yield, is actually a number I personally do not fuss with much because most malts of a similar type almost always fall into a very narrow range. It has been my experience that some of the challenges I have had with malt, be it flavor or wort separation issues, do not show up on malt specs, and that a problem lot can seem totally normal when appraised using a spec sheet.

Pale malt is typically purchased in railcar quantities or by the truckload, and the malt specs normally go directly from the malthouse lab to the brewery needing the information. Homebrew ingredients are handled by distributors who often repackage malt in smaller bags than the standard

50-pound and 25-kg bags used in North America and Europe, respectively. It's easy to lose track of lot numbers during that process, but not impossible to trace. Then the malt goes out and is sold by retailers (homebrew shops, usually). Sometimes the malt is blended into ingredient kits or sold in bulk, where lots are mixed. Even if the lot number and specs left the malthouse with the malt, chances are they were separated from each other long before you bought your malt. Even if you did have a bag of malt from a maltster with a printed lot number and decided to call the maltster to ask for specs, you'd be up against the wall. The person on the other end of the phone is tasked with supporting a plant producing literally thousands of tons of malt daily, and a call from a homebrewer about 50 pounds of malt purchased from a retailer separated two or three degrees from the malthouse is probably not going to be placed on the must-do list for the day.

Again, the good news is that if you know the product you are buying, who produced it, and what the product specs are, you will be fine because companies who produce two-row, 50° Lovibond crystal malt, for example, are going to do their best to produce a consistent product to satisfy their customers' needs. Malt specs do indeed exist, and they contain valuable information. Commercial brewers are required to know this information in some detail, but at the homebrew level, malt analysis is less available and less important.

SMOKING YOUR BEER

There are three common methods to make smoked beer. One is to use peated malt as one of the grains. Peated malt is used to make Scotch whiskey and has a powerful medicinal-phenolic aroma. I don't like peated malt in beer, but if you do use it, be careful! More than 1 percent peated malt is usually too much.

Another method is to use liquid smoke. This product is intended for cooking. I can't stand its nasty flavor in food, but I have heard that it can be used successfully in beer.

The most famous smoked beer is the German *rauch-bier* (*rauch* means smoked). It is principally brewed in Bamberg and is made using a very lightly smoked Munich-style malt. Rauch malt is smoked over beech-wood and has a wonderful smoked meat flavor. Because the smoking process is relatively cool, enzymes are not destroyed and rauch malt is used as a high proportion of the malt in the mash. Most rauchbiers contain well above 75 percent rauch malt. Aside from the ingredients, rauch-bier is brewed like other *lagers.*

The key to rauchbier is obtaining the malt. One German maltster, Weyermann, exports rauch malt to the United States. If you want to try this style of beer, buy some Weyermann rauch malt and go for it! You may want to taste a rauchbier before brewing it; Schlenkerla Rauchbier is available in the States.

Q **What purpose do hops serve in beer?**

A Historically, hops served an important role in stabilizing beer and slowing the growth of some spoilage organisms. Many of the more bitter beer styles were brewed for export across the seas. India Pale Ales (IPAs), export lagers, and foreign stouts are all designations used today that have their origins as beers with higher hopping rates brewed specifically to have longer shelf lives than less bitter beers.

These days, the association between hopping rate and shelf life has been lost because of improvements in sanitation and the widely used practice of pasteurization by larger breweries. The role of the hops today is mainly that of a spice. The bitterness balances malt sweetness. In the view of many brewers and beer drinkers, their aroma is just plain wonderful!

■ ══════ ■

Q **What is the difference between hop pellets, plugs, and whole hops?**

A Hops have a low density after harvesting and kilning and must be converted into a form that increases their density and makes storage and shipping more practical. Compressed cones, also know as whole hops or cone hops, are the most basic form for compressing and storing hops. Whole hops are packed into large hemp-fiber bales resembling giant bales of hay; they weigh about 200 pounds (91 kg). Brewers using whole hops cut the bales open, transfer the hops to a container for weighing, then add them to the brew kettle. After use in the boil, the cones must be separated from the wort using some sort of screening device.

Pelletized hops have only been in use since the middle part of the twentieth century. Compressed whole hops are milled, then compressed into little pellets using special dies. The advantage of the pellet is that the hops are denser than compressed hops. Pellets are easy to handle, have better storage properties than whole hops, and are easily separated using the whirlpool method. On the downside, many brewers believe that whole hops have better aroma than pelletized hops because the lupulin glands containing hop oils are broken during milling and some aroma loss is believed to occur. Pelletized hops have become very common these days and are used by more brewers than cone hops.

Hop plugs are really just a special form of whole hops, but instead of being compressed into giant bales, hop plugs are small. Hop plugs are intended for dry hopped cask ales

Hop plug

Whole hops

Hop pellets

and fit through the bung of casks. Because of their small size and weight, they are convenient for use at home where smaller quantities are needed.

Q How different are hop varieties?

A I'll put it this way . . . all hops are not created equal. Many breweries have jumped onto the explosive growth of wine consumption and are using hop varieties in their marketing much as grape varieties and growing regions are used to market wine. I think the trendy word *terroir* has even popped up in more than one beer ad.

Hop breeding has been going on for centuries, and many related varieties have similarities in aroma. For example, Cascade, Chinook, and Centennial are all American varieties with assertive citrus and pine aromas. There are many varieties, such as Liberty and Mt. Hood, related to the Hallertau hop. To me, these varieties have a floral, herbal note in their aroma profiles. Then there is the spicy Saaz hop most famous for its use in Pilsner beers.

This short list of aroma varieties barely scratches the surface of hops available for use in brewing. The bottom line is that beer flavor can be dramatically altered by using a different hop variety. In fact, it can be a lot of fun to brew the same recipe with different varieties to see how pronouncedly different two beers can be from changing the hop variety.

Q I just planted some hops in my backyard and was wondering when I should expect to harvest them?

A If you planted these hops in the spring, you may not have a very good yield the year of planting. Assuming the hops began sending out shoots (bines) the same spring as planting, you should have started training two or three of the bines up a wire trellis. During the growing season, hops need to be fertilized with a good nitrogen fertilizer. In the old days, manure was used. Be careful; if you overfertilize, you will get excessive bine growth and the cone yield will suffer. If everything goes right, you should start seeing hop cones in the fall. Incidentally, hop cones are the fruit of the female plant. Male plants flower but do not produce anything of value for the brewer (sorry, guys).

It is important to pick the hops when they are ripe but not overripe. When hops are ripe, the cone will be tight and compact, will easily come off the hop plant, and will have just changed from bright green to greenish-yellow. If the cones get too ripe, they will begin to loosen up and become easily damaged by the weather.

Q **Can I use freshly picked hops, or do I have to dry them out first?**

A Fresh, unkilned hops can certainly be used in beer, and there is no right or wrong way to use them. I think fresh, or green, hops are best for late hopping, because of the great aroma they impart. They also contain a lot of moisture (about 80 percent), and you would have to use a huge amount for bittering.

Sierra Nevada brewed the first green-hop beer I ever tasted. Called *Harvest Ale,* it has an intoxicating hop aroma that smells completely different from a hoppy brew made using kilned hops. The beer itself is pretty intoxicating, too. Its original gravity is around 1.068 SG, but it is so smooth and tasty I thought it was a normal-gravity beer. Oh, well! The key to using fresh hops is to use them immediately after harvesting. Sierra brewed Harvest Ale by coordinating the shipment of hops from the hop field directly to the brewery using an overnight express freight service. Grant's in Yakima also brewed a beer with fresh hops, but its hop delivery was easy to coordinate because Yakima is in the heart of Washington hop territory.

The first year I brewed a fresh hop ale, I added about 1 pound (.45 kg) of fresh hops per barrel of wort (31 gallons/117 L) right at the end of the boil and got a nice, fresh, hop character. The aroma has a pungent grassy note, kind of like fresh-cut hay. The next year, the hop yield was not so great, so I decided to dry hop with the green hops. This time, I added 2 pounds (.90 kg) of green hops to one barrel of pale ale, and it went from fairly hoppy in the nose to super hoppy! A year later, the nose was still intense and the flavor was delicious.

Don't substitute fresh hops for kilned hops in a recipe. I would use the fresh hops for aroma at a fairly heavy-handed rate, keeping in mind that they have a lot of extra weight because they are moist. I have used 3 ounces (85 g) per 5 gallons (19 L) with nice results. If you use fresh hops of good quality, you won't be disappointed!

Q How can I dry homegrown hops if I want to use them later?

A The best way to do this is to spread the cones a few layers deep on a cookie sheet and place the sheet in a 130°F (54°C) oven. Move those on the bottom to the top a few times and allow about 10 hours for drying. In commercial drying operations (oasthouses), the hops are layered up to 2 feet (.61 m) deep, and hot air is forced up through the bed. If you have a food dehydrator, you can reproduce this practice. Then brew with the hops, using an educated guess at their alpha acid content derived from the variety. I would estimate a percent or two less than the published values, since homegrown hops tend to have a lower alpha content than commercially grown hops.

Q **How is alpha acid measured for hops?**

A Undoubtedly, some homebrewers want to measure the alpha acid content of their hops. This goal is unrealistic for homegrown hops. The most common method used by hop growers is a method called the lead conductance valve (LCV). In this method, a methanol extract of hops is titrated with lead acetate and the conductivity of the solution is monitored during the titration.

The conductivity initially decreases until it hits a minimum value and then begins to increase as more lead acetate is titrated into the solution. The volume of lead acetate required to bring the conductivity of the solution to its minimum point is the LCV; this value correlates with alpha acid content. This method is not practical to perform at home.

The other method involves using high performance liquid chromatography (HPLC). An HPLC is a very expensive piece of laboratory equipment that separates compounds based on affinity between various compounds contained in a mixture and the column material.

After this separation occurs, a detector is used to quantify the amount of the various fractions contained in the mixture. This method is even less practical for the homebrewer. The bottom line: If you grow hops at home, you are probably going to be doing a little bit of guesswork when it comes to alpha acid numbers!

Q What is a good way to see if my hops are fresh?

A Although visual inspection gives some information if you know what you are looking for, the best and easiest thing is to give the hops a good rub. This method of aggressively rubbing small samples of hops between the palms of your hands warms the hops and releases their aromas for sniffing. Aromas associated with aged hops are usually described as cheese or wet sock and are due to the release of short-chain fatty acids when hops deteriorate. The other thing you can observe when rubbing are the lupulin glands in cone hops — in both pellet and cone hops you can get a feel for the type of aromas associated with the oils. I like the piney, citrus, and resinlike aromas to come through in a big and assertive beer.

———

Q I have been thinking about buying ingredients in greater quantity and storing them. I know that hop pellets don't age as fast as whole hops, but can and should you freeze hop pellets to extend their life?

A This is a good question with a very straightforward answer — storing hops at freezer temperatures does extend their life and will not damage the hops. If the hop variety has good storage properties, and if it is packaged properly, hops will remain fresh for 2 to 3 years. Most pellets are vacuum packed to minimize oxygen in the package. This process is key, since oxygen is the primary concern during hop storage. The other two concerns are time and temperature. Storage time can be maximized whenever exposure to oxygen and temperature are minimized.

I want to make a few points about this question. For starters, hops are not frozen during cold storage because hop pellets and compressed cones have very little moisture. The small quantity of water in processed hops is called bound water and does not freeze or crystallize like free water, which can also cause freezer burn.

The other point is that commercial freezers are much different from the type most of us have at home. The main difference is that they don't have a refrigerator full of smelly food sharing the same air. If hops are not stored in an airtight container — something like glass, or a foil bag that does not allow gas migration — the hops can pick up flavors from other items stored in your refrigerator or freezer. If you happen to have one of those vacuum sealers lying around, you could split up your hops into small bags of some convenient weight — 1-ounce (28 g) packs, for example — vacuum seal the bags, and then place them in a big glass jar with a metal lid. The jar will prevent any stink from touching the hop bags, and the vacuum-packed hops would have little oxygen to damage them.

If you don't have a vacuum sealer, you can get handy foil bags from coffee shops that are fitted with a zipper lock and check valve. Just fill it up with your hops, zip the bag closed, and squeeze the air out through the check valve.

Find a coffee shop with this type of bag, and ask if they will sell the bags to you for a reasonable price.

I would err on the safe side and put this bag into a jar, just in case some particularly persistent molecules are emanating from the freshly sliced onion stored in the neighboring refrigerator. If the hops remain sealed in their original foil package, they can just be stored in the fridge or freezer. The bag should keep oxygen and odors out.

■ ══════ ■

Q **Many articles on brewing say that hops lose their flavor and aroma after an hour of boiling and retain only their bittering characteristics. However, many recipes still call for large quantities of low-acid, -flavor, and -aroma hops for bittering. Why not just use good quality bittering hops?**

A This question is difficult to answer definitively, because it depends on one's flavor preference. In short, many brewers feel that certain hop varieties, particularly some of the lower-alpha hops, have a more pleasing bitter taste than others. These hops have a "soft" or "subtle" bitterness that isn't "harsh" and doesn't linger on the palate. These descriptions convey the bitter quality delivered by these hops, but the use of such fluffy terms (those in quotes) makes the more analytical brewer want to puke! I feel that certain hops produce beers with a more pleasing bitterness than others; I can't really describe the difference in bitterness, but I simply prefer certain types of bitter tastes more than others.

Over the centuries of using hops in beer, a group called *noble hops* has risen to the top. Most brewers simply view these varieties as those with the best aroma qualities and dismiss any role they may play in bitterness. The noble hops include Hallertauer, *Tettnang*, Saaz, Spalt, and Goldings, to name a few. While all of these varieties have excellent aroma qualities, they also tend to have low levels of cohumulone (between 20 percent and 30 percent of all alpha acids). Cohumulone, humulone, and adhumulone are the three principal sub-types of alpha acids. Because adhumulone is roughly 10 to 15 percent of the total alpha-acid content in all hop varieties, the variation in cohumulone and humulone is viewed as a varietal indicator.

Many brewers not only seek low cohumulone hop varieties for aroma, but also believe that the bitterness associated with humulone is more pleasing than the bitterness associated with cohumulone. Hence, some brewers use low-alpha, nice-smelling hops for bittering even though the fine aroma will be lost in the boil.

Not all brewers share this view. Many use high-alpha hops, regardless of the aroma, for bittering, and fine aroma hops for late hopping. Their logic is like yours: Why pay the extra price for fine aroma when the only person who will smell it is the brewer? There are dozens of high-alpha hop varieties to fill this need in the market. Chinook, Galena, Nugget, Columbus, Symphony, Super Styrian, and Eroica are some examples of hop varieties ranging between 12 and

20 percent alpha; these guys are loaded with the sticky, yellow lupulin sacs that contain the bitter acids. There are probably more brewers in the world who prefer these varieties for bittering than who prefer low-alpha varieties for the same application.

The only way to develop a good feel for your position on the debate is to experiment. I have said many times that homebrewers are in a better position to try things and develop opinions based on experience than are many commercial brewers; the commercial brewer simply doesn't have the time to play! Do a series of brews and let your palate answer the question.

■ ══════════ ■

Q **I'm a bit confused about how to handle hops. Some folks recommend cheesecloth *hop socks*. What do you think?**

A Handling hops is one of those topics lightly dealt with in homebrewing literature, because almost any hop type — pellets, cones, or extracts — can be used on a small scale without too much hassle. Some homebrewers who have crossed the ranks to professional brewing have been surprised to discover that very few small brewing setups are designed to use whole hops. Small breweries use hop pellets because cone hops require special equipment for separation.

The hop sock is a simple device that enables the homebrewer to get the hops out of the wort before cooling. If you are using multiple additions of hops, you might have two or three hop socks floating about in the kettle. The advantage of this technique is that it's really easy to remove the hops at the end of the boil. The disadvantage is that hop utilization (the conversion of alpha acids to iso-alpha acids) can drop significantly because the hops are bundled up too tightly.

An alternate method is to place a perforated stainless-steel screen in the bottom of your brew kettle. Simply toss whole hops into the wort and the screen will strain them out at the end (assuming you're draining the wort from a point below the screen). The hops also act as a natural filter bed and will remove much of the trub.

For brewers using pellet hops, socks and screens are not required because pellet hops settle to the bottom of the wort along with trub. Commercial brewers use whirlpool vessels for this task, and no extra equipment is required. Homebrewers can whirlpool wort containing pellet hops. (See whirlpooling, page 353.) Hop-free wort can then be transferred to the cooler, as long as the wort is drained from the side of the kettle, away from the trub pile.

Leaving hops in the wort during fermentation will not lend much more bitterness to the beer because heat is required to transform the insoluble alpha acids into the soluble iso-alpha acids. This is why *dry hopping* adds aroma but not bitterness.

Q What do you recommend using as an accurate way to estimate my hops utilization?

A This is a rather weighty question about a topic that continues to spark interest and debate among the numerical brewers of the world. The key to calculating the contribution of bitterness from hops added during brewing is the elusive utilization. This efficiency term relates the amount of alpha acid added to the wort to the iso-alpha acid in the finished beer. Hop utilization ranges from nil to about 40 percent and depends on a whole multitude of factors. A short laundry list of contributing factors includes: wort gravity, boil duration, hop form (cone or pellet), wort pH, type of kettle (influences losses in foam among other things), wort protein and trub content, yeast type, krausen formation during fermentation, and method of beer clarification. That's quite the list of variables!

Simple charts like those in Charlie Papazian's books are a good start, and some brewers don't venture beyond these rules of thumb. Other more sophisticated methods to estimate utilization based on curves are also found in home-brewing literature. The curves first postulated by Jackie Rager in 1990 and later by Glenn Tinseth and Mark Garetz are the ones that I have seen cited most often. These curves focus on wort gravity and boil duration, the most obvious factors affecting utilization. Garetz's approach added multiple factors to the equation including hopping rate, temperature (elevation), yeast, filtration, hop type (pellet or cone), and whether the hops are in a bag. These methods do not give the same answer, and I honestly do not know which curve is the most accurate. Rager's numbers are the highest utilization estimates, Garetz's are the lowest, and Tinseth's are between the two.

"Why?" you may ask. Well, to my knowledge, these tables were developed without actually measuring the resulting bitterness. This resulted in much debate, lasting now for more than 15 years, about whose method is best. The real discussion ender would be to take beers brewed using these estimates and analyze them in a lab. Instead, there are countless postings to bulletin boards and bantering in book reviews about who has the best utilization estimates.

The bottom line is that hop utilization is empirically determined, and a method to determine the hop bitterness is an absolute must. I strongly believe that sensory evaluation is a great way to do this. You can simply compare homebrewed beers to similar commercial beers with known bitterness. The utilization table that Rager published has values in line with those I have used as utilization estimates and range from 2 to 5 percent on the low end for hops added toward the end of the boil up to about 30 percent for hops boiled for an hour or more, with a deflation factor added in when wort gravity goes above 1.050 SG. My experience is based mainly on using pellet hops in normal gravity beers (12–14° Plato or 1.048–1.056 SG). I work in a small brewery and we do not have analytical equipment to measure our bitterness, but I have had our beer analyzed by outside labs and the analytical bitterness is pretty darned close to our targets.

I cannot hide my bias on this subject. While I calculate bitterness and have my quirky ways of tweaking numbers and abstracting what the beer recipe on my spreadsheet will taste like, I personally don't put much stake in numerical bitterness. The beer consumer perceives bitterness in a more complex way than an analytical instrument. The instrument measures bitterness without influence from the surrounding world. The perception of bitterness by the beer drinker is influenced by other variables, such as malt character, sweetness, mineral composition, carbonation level, and alcohol content.

I use hop calculations to maintain consistency of bitterness for a given recipe and use sensory evaluation to critique and fine-tune the result of the brewer's art. That's what it's all about in my view. I can't speak for how other brewers fill out paperwork for competitions and can only speculate that most use calculations to estimate color, alcohol, and bitterness. The only thing most homebrewers know for certain is the original gravity (OG) and the final gravity (FG).

My suggestion to you is to put as much focus on developing your sensory skills as you do on your calculation skills. A brewer who is balanced can lean on technical knowledge when required and strong sensory skills to evaluate and improve brews. You will soon discover what target bitterness numbers and utilization rates you can choose in order to make brews that fall within the flavor profile that suits your taste.

Calculating Hop Additions

Calculating hop additions to hit target bitterness is simple. To calculate a hop charge, use this equation with metric units:

$$\text{Hop Charge (grams)} =$$
$$((\text{L of wort}) \times (\text{Target Bitterness})) \div$$
$$((\text{Hop Utilization}) \times (\text{Alpha acid Content}) \times (1000))$$

By the way, 1 *International Bitterness Unit (IBU)* equals 1 milligram of iso-alpha acid per liter of beer (0.0001 oz./gal.). If you are into units, you can see how the units cancel in the above equation. When I formulate recipes, I consider the percentage of the total bitterness from each hop addition and apply a different utilization to each addition. Almost every brewer who calculates recipes uses something akin to this method . . . it's simply the way it's done. One thing to note is that the alpha acid content of hops is highest when harvested, so they lose alpha acid content with storage. Also, some hops store better than others. These factors may result in a beer that is less bitter than anticipated.

Q What is the goal of dry hopping?

A The aim of dry hopping is simply to get hop aromas and flavors directly into beer without boiling the hops in the wort. Dry hopping imparts a distinctive aroma to beer that is lost when hops are boiled. As in most aspects of brewing, keeping things simple is the best approach.

Breweries that reuse their yeast tend to add the dry hops after harvesting yeast because the yeast can actually remove some of the dry hop character. The harvested yeast may be used in a different beer that is not dry hopped, and the hop character can be carried with the yeast. Although yeast can dilute the dry-hopped character, it wouldn't hurt to add the hops right to your primary fermenter. In fact, many breweries add dry hops to the primary. The best time to do this is at the end of the primary fermentation to prevent the hops from clogging up your fermentation blowoff. After the hops are added, let the beer stand for at least 1 week and then carry on as usual.

If you are looking for a more advanced approach to dry hopping, you should use a secondary fermenter. After the primary fermentation is complete, rack the beer into the secondary, add the dry hops, and attach an airlock. If possible, transfer the keg or carboy to a cool area of your house (50–60°F/10–15°C) and let it stand for at least 1 week. Then bottle the beer as usual. This method may give better aroma retention because of the lower yeast density in the secondary and will give a clearer finished product.

Q **Can I please get a rundown on dry hopping versus a hopback when brewing?**

A Most brewing techniques are touted by a long list of advantages. Dry hopping, which means adding compressed hop cones or hop pellets to beer or fermenting beer, can be sold by its ability to contribute a nice, fresh hop aroma. Why put hops in the kettle or use a hopback when you can add them straight to the fermenter?

Hopback advocates almost always mention the bonus of having the hops and the hopback sanitized in the process. This casts a cloud over the method of dry hopping, because it implies that hops are covered in bacteria and require sanitization (an argument that is not well supported). Dry hoppers feel pretty confident about the method — after all, dry hopping would not be popular if it routinely produced contaminated beer. Plus, dry hoppers avoid the scrubbing action of primary fermentation.

When reading the hype surrounding these methods, it is hard to get a feel for the salient features of each method. When I want a really hoppy beer with a fresh hop oil aroma, I prefer dry hopping. The aroma of dry-hopped beer is often described as grassy and frequently has the distinct aroma of myrcene (a particularly aromatic hop oil). Hopping rates vary depending on the hop variety and oil content, but ¼ to ½ ounce of hops per gallon (7–15 g/3.8 L) of beer is a pretty normal range for dry hopping. When I dry hop, I do it after primary fermentation is complete and before moving the beer to a cool location for aging.

But I personally prefer adding hops to hot wort, usually in the kettle at the end of the boil for most beer styles, because the grassy and oily aromas are less pronounced. Sierra Nevada, for example, uses a generous late-hop addition in all of its standard beers and only dry hops the Celebration and Bigfoot. Hops added late in the boil or to a hopback can certainly produce a very hoppy beer, but the hop aroma is less raw in comparison to dry-hopped beers. Hopping rates for late-hop additions and hop-back additions vary, but ¼ to ½ ounce per gallon (7–15 g/3.8 L) will produce beers with pronounced hop aroma.

Q **I want to brew a big hop monster of an ale. What is the best technique to get an aggressively bitter beer?**

A One of the most important considerations about hopping is the hop. When brewing ales high in bitterness units, it helps to use high alpha hop varieties for the first hop addition. You can use low alpha varieties, but then you have to use more hops — and the separation of wort from hops can become challenging (I'll get to that later). I personally subscribe to the low-cohumulone school of hopping, and I avoid high cohumulone varieties. My favorite all-around high alpha variety is Nugget.

Hop age has a profound effect on beer bitterness, since hops lose alpha acids with age. With this chemical change comes a decline in the bitterness contributed by hops. To complicate aging, not all varieties deteriorate at that same rate, and packaging method and storage temperature have a huge impact on stability. I prefer using hops that are less than 1 year old; I use older hops only if forced to do so by availability of certain varieties.

Good hops in hand, it is now time to touch on brewing tips. My advice is to add hops directly to the kettle and not use a bag if at all possible. If you use pellets, the best way to separate hops from wort is to use the whirlpool method (see page 353).

If you use whole hop cones (either from compressed bales or in the plug form), you really need to make sure the hops are loosened up before adding them to the boil. I am not suggesting tossing them into a blender, but sorting through the hops and gently breaking up compressed bits will help. I have seen bags used for dry hopping with dry spots after weeks in the fermenter and have heard the same from other brewers. At home, it's easy enough to avoid this problem . . . if the hops ain't wet, you haven't gotten all of 'em.

At home, you can easily use whole hops either by putting a screen in the bottom of your kettle or by building a simple hop strainer large enough to hold all the swollen hop cones used in the boil. I prefer using a screen in the bottom of the kettle, because it is simple and effective. This requires installing a valve in your kettle, which makes things easy and safe for all types of brews and, in my opinion, is more of a requirement and less of a luxury if you brew frequently. Whole hops should not clog the screen, but they can plug an outlet valve if the screen does not fit into the bottom of the kettle properly. Most commercial brewers using whole hops use a whirlpool following hop removal to separate trub.

Now that you have selected the hop variety of choice, given the hops the thumbs up after a cursory evaluation, and tweaked your brewing setup so that hops can be used and removed without confining them to a bag (which can reduce yield if the bag is too small), it's time to formulate a hop monster.

Hopping techniques are a matter of art, and empirical evidence will help shape your brewing method. My standard way of approaching hopping is to get about 80 percent of the bitterness from the first hop addition and boil these hops for 1 hour. The second addition comes midway through the boil and amounts to about 15 percent of the total bitterness. Finally, the late hops are added right at the end of the boil and account for just 5 percent of the bitterness but most of the hop aroma. This is where homebrewing and commercial brewing differ considerably.

Wort transfer from the kettle to the whirlpool typically takes 20 minutes in a commercial operation, the whirlpool rest takes about 20 minutes, and transfer through the cooler and into the fermenter requires another 30 to 45 minutes. Total exposure time between those late hops and hot wort is at least 20 minutes for breweries using hop cones and a hop separator (after the kettle) and well over 1 hour for pellet users. During this time, some isomerization occurs, albeit very little, and (more importantly) the hop oils have plenty of time to be extracted in the wort. Some of the oils are lost during this time, but the surface-to-volume ratio is in the favor of brewers with bigger pots — as kettle size increases, this ratio decreases and the retention of volatile oils increases.

In my quest for big aroma, my go-to method is dry hopping. I have tried all sorts of strategies in the brewhouse to get the big fragrant nose desired in certain styles and have personally determined, like so many before me, that dry hopping delivers the one-two punch and definitely delivers the hop bang! I have used both pellet and whole cones and prefer the aroma of the whole cones as well as the ease of use. I wait until fermentation is complete and rack the beer into a clean fermenter containing the bag of hops. It is important to add a stainless steel weight to the bag or somehow tie the bag to the bottom of the fermenter (if you have a racking port you can tie off to it). A floating bag does not deliver the whole enchilada. Two weeks of dry hopping is long enough to get the good stuff out, yet not too long to give you that grassy, freshly baled hay aroma found in some dry-hopped beers.

I have detected an ever-so-slight oxidized aroma in dry-hopped beers and recently borrowed a technique used by some winemakers to purge tanks of air. Whole hop cones are like little sponges; they contain air. That's why they float. I figure that this could be a bad thing when added to beer. We toss dry ice into the bottom of the fermenter before adding the hop bag and allow the dry ice to completely sublime before racking the beer onto the hops. This method slowly pushes the air out of the fermenter and probably displaces much of the air from the hop cones. One mole (44 g or about 1.5 oz.) of carbon dioxide expands into about 23 quarts (about 22 L) at atmospheric pressure, and a little goes a long way. This method has become a standard at our brewery when we dry hop. If you try this, do not seal off the fermenter, as it will build pressure! Fit it with an airlock and wait until the bubbling ceases before racking your brew.

Doubling Up

You can double the amount of ingredients to double a recipe, provided that you are using similar brewing techniques and equipment. Different techniques and equipment setups do affect ingredient yields. If you double the batch size and use a different type of equipment, adjustments in your calculations will need to be made to account for extract yield differences and/or hop utilization differences.

I have successfully scaled up 5-gallon (19 L) batches to 500-gallon (1,892 L) batches with very minor adjustments in my calculations to account for the better yields of larger equipment. At home, there will not be much difference if you are scaling a 5-gallon (19 L) recipe up to 10 gallons (38 L).

Q Can I use a linear scale-down to convert a larger volume brewpub recipe to 5 gallons (19 L), or are there other factors that need to be considered?

A When small brewers think about scaling down a recipe, the assumption is that there will be a reduced yield on a small system. This may or not be the case, as many small brewers don't have much better malt yields than homebrewers. As a general rule, yield becomes higher and more important as brewery size increases. Most brewers will tell you their yield if you ask.

The hard thing about scaling up and down is the hopping. The list of reasons includes lower surface to volume ratio in large kettles, more vigorous boils in large kettles, lower surface to volume ratio in the fermenter with big batches, and so on. The key here is the surface-to-volume ratio, and the idea is that hop acids and oils stick to surfaces. The more surface area per volume of wort or beer, the more loss you get with hops. This same thing occurs in fermentation when the foam from fermentation is yet another surface that scrubs hop goodies from beer.

Clearly the homebrewer must use more hops per gallon when scaling down a recipe due to decreased hop utilization at home. The other thing about hops is their oil content; these are also lost more in a small kettle, for a similar reason. This is the interfacial area between the liquid and air. This means that as batch size decreases, hop oils are harder to keep in the wort where they are needed if the finished beer is going to have a nice hoppy aroma.

The take-home message with hops is practical. If a commercial batch is scaled down, more hops will be required for bitterness. That's easy; just add more hops. The additional amount will probably range between 25 and 33 percent above what is used in a commercial brewery for a given wort volume, assuming your recipe is coming from a small brewery. The hop oil loss is not so easy to balance, because when you add more hops to make up for the oil loss, you add bittering acids and plant matter that can begin to add vegetal flavors to beer when heavy hopping rates are used.

My advice to you is that when you want to scale down a commercial recipe, you first must carefully study the beer you want to brew. Smell it, taste it, and really focus on the hops in the beer. Are the aromas similar to any homebrews you have previously made, or is the aroma something more intense? You may indeed find that the easiest way to duplicate the hop aroma is to use an entirely different hopping method. Cloning a commercial brew has much more to do with using all of your skills as a brewer to attempt to match the flavor of your homebrew with your chosen model. Simply copying the technique used by another brewer may get you close, but the devil is always in the details. Copying technique will probably fail when it comes to the subtleties of hop aroma.

Q **What is the best way to eliminate chloramines in my brewing water?**

A Dechlorination is important to brewers for flavor reasons. Compounds called chlorophenols are formed when beer interacts with chlorine. These compounds have a fairly unpleasant aroma.

Although many reducing agents can be used to dechlorinate water, the ones that are most accessible to homebrewers are sodium metabisulfite or its cousin, potassium metabisulfite (commonly found in the Campden tablets used by winemakers). These compounds will remove chlorine from water treated with sodium hypochlorite (bleach) or chloramine. The reaction converts chlorine into chloride and sulfite into sulfate. Chloride has no affect on aroma, is found in most water, and many brewers add it in the form of calcium chloride. Likewise, sulfate is a normal constituent of water, and brewers add it in the form of calcium sulfate. When this reaction occurs with chloramines, ammonium ions are released into the water. Again, this is no big deal, because ammonium ions are found in a brewer's mash and come from the malt. Keep in mind, we are talking about very low concentrations of all of these reaction products.

In easy-to-use terms, a ½-ounce (15 g) Campden tablet can dechlorinate 20 gallons (76 L) of water. This reaction occurs very rapidly. All you really need to do is dissolve the metabisulfite in your water and let it sit for a minute or two. You are finished with the dechlorination process. Many brewers boil water prior to use to drive chlorine out of the water. The boiling method works very well with water chlorinated with hypochlorite but is less effective at removing chloramine. The metabisulfite method is fast acting, easy to perform, and very effective.

Q Would you please enlighten me on brewing with softened water?

A Water softeners replace calcium and magnesium ions in water with sodium. Two atoms of sodium are added for every atom of calcium or magnesium removed from the water. If your well water has 100 ppm of calcium and 20 ppm of magnesium, the softened water will contain a whopping 240 ppm of sodium. Sodium adds palate fullness and sweetness to brewing water up to about 100 ppm. At higher concentrations, sodium makes beer too salty.

The real problem with using softened water for brewing is that most homes equipped with water softeners have harder than average water. Thus, the water produced by the softener is in turn very high in sodium. For this reason, softened water is often only used for utility water — water for showers, toilets, washing machines, and the like. Water piped to sink faucets bypasses the softener. The above example of 100 ppm calcium and 20 ppm magnesium would most likely not warrant a water softener.

Let's assume that you do not have abnormally hard water, but simply have a softener. As long as the sodium does not lend a salty flavor to your water or beer, you can use it for brewing. The "salts" listed in most recipes are calcium sulfate and/or calcium chloride. You certainly would want to add these, since calcium is required for pH adjustment in the mash, is a cofactor for alpha-amylase, aids in trub formation, and also helps yeast cells flocculate at the end of fermentation.

If you actually did use softened water for brewing as described above, this is what happens: 1) You remove calcium and magnesium and replace it with sodium; 2) You add calcium back to the water because calcium is important for brewing. In my opinion, this seems like a roundabout way to add sodium! Most breweries were historically located near good wells and it might be your signature touch to simply use your well water as is and not to worry much about water softeners.

The more likely case is that you have a water softener because you have hard water. I would not recommend using softened water from well water that is indeed hard. Homes with hard water are easy to spot, because of the white mineral deposits near water taps. Unfortunately, most hard waters in North America come from limestone aquifers, and limestone is calcium carbonate. The only beers well suited to these waters are dark ales and lagers, for example, porter, stout, and dunkel. The preferred hard water type for brewing lighter-colored beers, like *pale ale,* is hard water from a gypseous aquifer. *Gypsum* is calcium sulfate.

I am a strong advocate of the KISS (Keep It Simple, Stupid) approach when it comes to water. I prefer using the local water supply as is, with chlorine removed by charcoal filtration or reacting with metabisulfite when applicable. Alternately, you can use deionized water or distilled water from the supermarket and add various salts to turn the water into the type needed for the particular task. If it is possible, get an analysis of your well water and determine what type of water you have. Based on this information, you can take a more calculated approach to water treatment.

■ ═══════════ ■

Q What is the difference between temporary and permanent hardness in brewing water?

A The most basic difference between hard and soft water is that hard water reacts with soap to form solid soap scum and soft water does not form soap scum. The formation of soap scum on your skin is the reason that soap seems easier to rinse from your body when you shower with hard water.

Hardness in water is caused by the presence of calcium ions, magnesium ions, or both. As their concentrations increase, water becomes harder. The combined concentration of calcium and magnesium is frequently referred to as total hardness. When hard water is boiled in the presence of carbonate (CO_3^{-2}) or bicarbonate (HCO_3^-), the calcium and/or magnesium ions react with the carbonate and bicarbonate ions to form solid calcium carbonate, magnesium carbonate, or both.

Much of the groundwater in the United States is trickled through underground labyrinths of limestone (calcium carbonate) and has high concentrations of both calcium and carbonate. This type of water wreaks havoc on plumbing, especially water heaters. Much of the total hardness in this sort of water is composed of temporary hardness.

Temporary hardness is complex, because its concentration is a function of the concentration of carbonates in relation to their reaction with calcium in magnesium. Suppose your water has 100 ppm of total hardness before boiling and 60 ppm of total hardness after boiling. This means it has 40 ppm of temporary hardness. The good thing about temporary hardness is that it is easy to remove by boiling or through precipitation with lime (calcium hydroxide).

Permanent hardness is simply the hardness that is not removed by boiling. If your water is gypseous — that is, it has passed through gypsum in the ground — it will contain calcium and sulfate. When gypseous water is boiled, very little hardness is lost because calcium is not precipitated by sulfate.

Many brewers add calcium chloride to their brewing water. This addition is another source of permanent hardness. The good thing about permanent hardness is that it is stable. This fact applies more to commercial brewers than to homebrewers, but if water is stored hot in large hot water tanks and contains temporary hardness, the concentration of calcium will change over time. This problem doesn't happen with water in which most of the total hardness is composed of permanent hardness.

One trivial point worth noting is that distilled water adjusted with calcium sulfate still contains some temporary hardness, because carbon dioxide from the atmosphere contributes a small amount of carbonate to water. This means that no teapot or bathtub is completely immune to calcium and magnesium deposits.

With modern water-treatment systems able to do just about anything to any sort of water, the difference between the two types of water is less significant than in the past. However, for homebrewers using local water without any major treatment, the difference between temporary and permanent hardness is important. A quick survey of traditional brewing centers reveals that the dark-beer cities have water dominant in temporary hardness and the cities known for light/pale beers are more skewed to the permanent-hardness side.

Q How are oak chips used in brewing?

A Whether using oak for flavor or beechwood to help with aging, the weight of the wood chip is not the most important consideration. Rather, the surface area is the key factor. The flavor from the chip is released into the beer only where the beer and the chip are in contact. You could have a bag of thin oak chips and a bag of thick oak chips that both weigh the same, but the thin chips would have a greater surface-area-to-weight ratio. So the thin chips would add more flavor than the same weight of thick chips.

If the chips are 2 inches wide, 4 inches long and 0.25 inches thick, each will provide 19 square inches of surface area (two sides at 8 square inches, two edges at 1 square inch, and two edges at 0.5 square inch). Eight of these chips per gallon (3.8 L) of beer will give about the same surface-to-volume ratio (149) as an oak barrel. Set aside 43 of these chips for a 5.5-gallon (21 L) batch.

Chips will float, and it is important to keep the entire surface of the chip in contact with the beer during aging. A hop bag weighted with some stainless steel bolts (or some other inert weight) will do the trick. Sterilize the bag, chips, and weight with either steam or hot water. I choose to fill my barrels with 195°F (91°C) water and let the barrels sit for several hours prior to use. Either method will work for sterilization. Some sanitizing solutions will damage the wood and perhaps flavor the beer. Burning sulfur is one method of sanitizing barrels used by winemakers, while using a dilute solution of Campden tablets is another. I like hot water because there is nothing added to the barrel except water.

The next step is to place the chip bag into a vessel for the aging process. This poses a dilemma, since the chip bag won't fit into a carboy and a plastic secondary allows oxygen into the beer. The ideal container is a 5-gallon (19 L) Cornelius keg. Place the chips in the keg and rack the beer from the primary into the keg for aging. Try to minimize the amount of yeast carried into the secondary as excessive yeast will impart autolyzed flavors from yeast death over the aging period. The beer can be primed at this time, or you can wait until later. Priming at this stage will be easy, since the yeast viability is still excellent. If primed later, more yeast will most likely need to be added.

Now it's time to wait. This step is most important to oak aging. It is tempting to place the keg in a cool corner and to forget about it for several months. Vigilance and restraint are required during aging. Sample the beer on a regular basis — say once every 3 weeks — to keep tabs on its progression. The purpose is to prevent the beer from becoming excessively oaky. The oak should add complexity to the beer but not dominate its flavor. Once the flavor reaches the intensity you desire, you can rack the beer into a second keg or bottle it.

Q I understand that some microbreweries like to age their beers in old sherry or bourbon barrels. How can I imitate sherry casks with oak chips?

A The popularity of beers aged in a variety of used oak barrels has really blossomed. My take on these beers is that the used oak barrel acts as a vector to flavor beer with what was previously in the barrel. Stouts aged in old bourbon barrels taste like stout flavored with bourbon, and beers aged in old sherry casks taste like sherry-flavored beer. This observation is pretty obvious, but it has a practical implication for homebrewers who do not have access to used oak barrels — or do not brew enough beer to fill a barrel.

Homebrewing is very different from commercial brewing in that homebrew is not taxed and the regulations governing commercial brewing do not apply. At home or in a pilot brewery, a brewer can make an oaky bourbon stout by adding oak chips to a stout during aging to get the desired effect from the oak and then blend this beer with bourbon, whiskey, or scotch to add whatever flavor and intensity is desired from the liquor.

"Sherry cask" flavor can be further broken down into oak character and sherry character. If I were brewing this sort of beer, I would address the flavors individually. Add oak chips or age beer in a barrel to add oak character. I would lean toward buying a new small oak barrel, because oxygen slowly diffuses into a barrel during aging and this probably has an influence on barrel-aged beer. To my palate, many of the strong beers aged in oak have flavors associated with oxidation. This term is almost always a negative connotation in the world of beer, but not all oxidation is necessarily bad when very strong beers are aged. In high-alcohol beers, oxidized flavors may remind one of raisins, dates, and sherry. In my experience with aging beer in new oak barrels, a couple of months are required before the beer really starts to take on appreciable oak flavor. Tasting throughout the aging process is important, and there is no magic time frame.

The same is true if one chooses to add oak chips to the secondary fermentation. After I got the brew where I wanted it with respect to beer flavor, oak flavor, and aged flavors, I would begin to play with adding the wine or spirit component. This type of blending is always best done by preparing several samples of beer with varying levels of blended mixtures, so that the flavor impact can be tasted over a range of concentrations. You may find that even a small amount of the planned flavor additive makes for a vile brew, and avert a disaster.

This method is probably not for every brewer; it is actually quite unorthodox. For that matter, aging beer in an old bourbon, sherry, or whiskey barrel is pretty strange in the minds of many brewers. However, if the purpose of homebrewing is to create beer with a certain flavor profile, it seems that the finished product is more important than the method used to make it. If you really want to add flavored chips, soak the chips in the wine or spirit of your choice and then add the infused chips to your beer. I think the flavor would be less difficult to control, and the method is no more "pure" than adding the two ingredients independently.

Q I'm trying to find a conversion formula for how many cups of honey are needed to replace 1 cup (237 mL) of corn sugar. Can you help me?

A Honey contains about 25 percent water and 75 percent solids. Corn sugar has about 98 percent corn sugar and 2 percent water. I like to convert ingredient figures into the easiest-to-use number for ease of calculation. In this case, 1 cup (237 mL) of honey contains about 0.75 cup (176 mL) of dry solids, mainly sugars, and 1 cup (237 mL) of corn sugar contains 0.98 cup (232 mL) of dry solids. This means you need to use 1.31 cups (310 mL) of honey to equal 1 cup (237 mL) of corn sugar.

The dry solids basis is handy for evaluating raw brewing materials, because dry solids increase the specific gravity of water when they are dissolved. Suppose you had some unusual sugary liquid and wanted to use it as an ingredient and had the same question. You would read the nutritional label and find out how many grams of carbohydrate are contained in the serving size. Suppose there are 17 grams of carbohydrate per 28-gram serving. This equates to 61 percent carbohydrate. Assuming there is not much protein, this number represents the amount of solids in the ingredient. This mystery ingredient would require 1.61 cups (381 mL) to equal 1 cup (237 mL) of corn sugar.

The Time is Ripe to Add Fruit

I like adding fruit to beer after primary fermentation because of the good retention of fresh fruit aromas and colors. If fruit is added to the primary, special care must be used to prevent potential carboy bombs. The fermentation lock can get plugged and pressure can build up inside the fermenter. The safest method is to ferment the beer in a plastic bucket with a large lid and an airlock. A blowoff tube on a carboy can also be used, but it, too, can clog, creating a dangerous situation.

Q **I've heard you are supposed to use pectic enzyme when you use fruit in a recipe. How much do I use? Do I use it with all fruits?**

A Pectin is a type of carbohydrate found in fruits that acts as a structural member of the fruit, kind of like beta glucan in cereal grains. In cooking, pectin is useful for its ability to form a gel when heated in a sugar solution with a low pH. This is why jams and jellies are thick and stay on your toast or bagel instead of running off. Although all fruits contain some pectin, many do not contain enough for making jams and jellies. Many fruit spreads use pectin from other sources than the fruit being used. Certain varieties of apples, such as Granny Smith, are well known for their especially high pectin contents.

When it comes to brewing and winemaking, pectin levels are usually kept low for two main reasons. The first is that pectin may cause haze; pectin hazes are due to the very large size of the pectin molecule and the tendency for the molecule to form gels and are analogous to starch hazes. This is a cosmetic issue that some of us don't worry too much about, depending on the style of beer being made. The other thing about pectin is that filtration becomes very, very difficult. The reason for this is again the large size of the molecule and its gelling properties.

Pectinase enzymes reduce the size of the pectin molecule and also prevent the fragments from gelling. To check for the presence of pectin, simply add one part of the wort, beer, or wine to one part 70 percent alcohol. Ethanol and iso-propanol (rubbing alcohol) both work. I use iso-propanol because it's cheap. This test will cause pectin to gel. When this occurs, the sample becomes cloudy and the pectin begins to precipitate and will eventually settle on the bottom of the sample glass.

Although this method is not quantitative, you can get a feel for the pectin concentration. If the haze is detectable, but very slight, you may decide not to worry. If after adding the alcohol, the sample looks like orange juice, you probably will choose to deal with the pectin. Fortunately, it's simple to address this problem. The easiest thing to do is to add some pectinase to the fruit mush before adding the fruit to your beer. You can use dry or liquid pectinase; follow the recommendations with the enzyme regarding usage rate. The other approach to take, especially if you don't like adding stuff unnecessarily to your beer, is to do a test after fermentation is complete and the fruit has been added. If the sample indicates a pectin problem, then add your enzyme at this stage.

As I stated earlier, all fruits contain some pectin. Tart apples, citrus fruits, cranberries, currants, gooseberries, and sour plums all have high pectin levels. Interestingly, all of these fruits also rank high in natural acid levels and make great jams and jellies without requiring an exogenous (outside) source of pectin. Strawberries, peaches, pear, pineapple, apricots, and rhubarb have a low pectin content. Cherries, blueberries, blackberries, and raspberries have a medium level of pectin. Most brewers typically make fruit beers with fruits that have a low or medium pectin level.

■ ═══════════ ■

Q **I'm getting ready to brew a batch of all-grain porter, and I plan to put a little cherry extract in the brew. When should I put it in so I don't lose the essence and flavor? How much should I add?**

A When flavoring beers with essences, it is best to add them after fermentation and prior to bottling. Most essences add no significant amount of fermentable sugars and don't do much for the beer other than adding flavor. Adding these flavors early in the process only reduces their impact in the finished beer.

Some fruit flavors do add a significant amount of fermentable sugar and should be added to the wort prior to or during fermentation. If you planned to add whole cherries to the porter, these would definitely need to be added to the wort during boiling or added to the fermenter while the yeast is still active.

Fruit beers such as lambics are aged with the fruit in the beer for several months before racking the beer off the fruit sludge. This practice allows the yeast to ferment the fruit sugars and, in the case of cherry beer, also gives sufficient time for some of the pit flavors to be leached into the beer. Fruit purees are frequently used for fruit beers, and these also should be added to allow the sugars to ferment. If you use a fruit flavor with fermentable sugars at home, be careful! These flavors will create several dozen bottle bombs if you add them at bottling time.

As far as the usage rate, most of these products have a suggested range. If you stick to this range, you'll be okay. If you have an unfermentable fruit essence, you can make up a few test concentrations using a commercial porter and get a good idea of how the flavor will taste in your finished beer. When it's time for bottling, add your essence and bottle condition as usual.

CHAPTER 5

Choosing and Using the Right Yeast

BREWER'S CHOICE
Pure Liquid Yeast

Top Fermenting
Saccharomyces cerevisiae
for
Ales-Porters-Stouts-Alts

The first innovation in Brewing Yeast.

No starter bottles are needed.
Follow the instructions on the reverse side.

LABORATORY TESTED
MAKES 5 GALLONS

GERMAN ALTBIER YEAST

Ale
Beer Yeast

active
dry
lager
yeast

REDSTAR

Q What is the difference between liquid and dry yeast strains?

A The main difference between dry and liquid yeast is that dry yeast can be stored over very long time periods without much loss in viability. Dry yeast is made using a process similar to that used to make dry malt extract (DME) and can be a very reliable form of yeast. Liquid yeast autolyzes quickly, even when stored cold, and should not be stored more than 3 to 4 weeks before use. Commercial brewers harvest liquid yeast and want to use it within a few days after harvesting.

The real downside to dry yeast is the limited availability of strains. Since liquid yeast does not have to be dried, labs can quickly grow yeast from cultures and supply a vast array of yeast strains to brewers. I like using liquid yeast because of the great selection of strains I can readily purchase.

Liquid yeast is also less likely to carry contaminants. The process used to dry yeast is set up for relatively long run times, and any bacteria that may be in the drier can grow and contaminate the dried yeast. In the late '80s and early '90s, many brewpubs were using dry yeast. Occasional problems with contaminated dried yeast gave dry yeast a bad name, and many brewers quit using it. I know some really good dry yeast suppliers who are using improved methods, and I would not hesitate to use dry yeast because of some problems more than 15 years ago.

With that said, I believe liquid yeast is probably cleaner than dry yeast because of the drying step. I buy liquid yeast from a yeast lab and use it for 10–15 *generations* before discarding the yeast and buying fresh yeast. I would not feel comfortable doing the same with dry yeast, because any contaminants increase when yeast is used over several generations.

ATTRIBUTE	LIQUID	DRY
Storage	3–4 weeks	More than 1 year
Variety of strains	Vast array	Limited
Purity	Less likely to carry contaminants	Bacteria from the drying process can contaminate
Life cycle	10–15 generations	2–3 generations

LIQUID VERSUS DRY YEAST

Q What do you look for when choosing which yeast strain to use in your beer?

A I consider flavor, *attenuation,* and flocculation when selecting yeast. I tend to prefer beers made from clean yeast: I like my ales to be low in *esters* and diacetyl, and my lagers low in acetaldehyde and diacetyl with just a little sulfur. Yeast strain descriptions will give you an idea of how the yeast will come through in the finished beer.

I also have a preference for beers that finish fairly dry and look for yeasts that have an apparent attenuation somewhere in the 75 to 80 percent range. Again, yeast suppliers list the typical apparent attenuation of their strains. Since most of the beers I brew are filtered, I like yeast that has good floc-culation properties, but not so flocculent that it may have problems with diacetyl and acetaldehyde reduction.

In our brewery, I go yeast shopping when we brew spe-cials that cannot be brewed using our house ale or lager strain. We brew a hefe-weizen as our summer seasonal, and I like *weizen* yeast strains that give a nice balance between banana fruitiness and clove spiciness. Some weizen strains produce too much banana for me; I tend to steer clear of those. When brewing Belgian-style beers, I look for strains that produce some phenolic aromas, but not too much.

What I am saying is that I choose yeast that will produce a beer flavor that suits my palate. Some brewers like fuller, maltier ales with a hint of diacetyl and would choose totally different yeast strains from those I would choose. The great thing about homebrewing is that the homebrewer is brew-ing beer to suit his or her preferences!

Q **How are lager yeasts different from ale yeasts?**

A The traditional answer to this question is the top (ale) and bottom (lager) fermentation story. To me this is more of a description of the appearance of yeast dur-ing fermentation than anything else. In conical fermenters, both ale and lager strains are cropped from the bottom of the fermenter, and since this method of fermentation is the most common method used in newer breweries, the top and bottom distinction is somewhat outdated.

Ale yeast, in general, can be used at warmer temperatures to produce good beer. Ale fermentations are usually conducted somewhere between 60 and 75°F (16–24°C); some cases go as high as 85°F (30°C) and usually last no longer than 5 days. Most ales have a detectable ester profile in the aroma and are often referred to as fruity yeast. That is a generalization, as there are many ale strains that produce a very low ester profile and are easily mistaken for lagers.

Lager yeast produces better beer when the fermentation temperature is below about 60°F (16°C); most lager fermentations are held between 50 and 57°F (10–14°C). Lagers that are fermented too warm often become too fruity and usually produce too much sulfur. To my palate, it's the subtle sulfur aroma and very low ester profile that separates ales from lagers. Most lager fermentations take anywhere from 5 to 10 days to finish primary, and the cool aging or lagering period usually lasts from 2 to 4 weeks.

I think the most notable difference between ale and lager strains is that there is much more diversity in the ale family of yeast. Wit, weizen, stout, pale ale, Kölsch, *Trappist* and Abbey ales, alt, and *saison* are all ales that have distinctly different yeast-related aroma profiles. The differences among lager styles are related to the malt, hops, and water used in brewing and have less to do with different lager strains.

Q What is the best way to cut down on yeast off-flavors?

A I will answer this question assuming that you have selected an appropriate yeast strain for the style and that no contaminating organisms exist in the yeast slurry. The best advice I can offer on reducing yeast off-flavors is to begin with well-aerated wort, add enough yeast so that you are not underpitching, control fermentation temperature, and rack the beer off the yeast after primary fermentation to avoid autolysis.

Aeration is very important because growing yeast cells require oxygen to synthesize cell wall components. Yeast health can be compromised if wort oxygen is too low, and beer flavor can be affected by changes in how metabolic intermediates flow through biochemical pathways. The most notable thing about beers made from under-aerated worts is that they tend to be very estery. Wort oxygen level also influences fermentation speed. Starting off with well-aerated wort is just good practice; the ideal level is about 8 mg/L, which is the maximum amount of oxygen wort can hold if aerated with air (as opposed to pure oxygen).

One mistake that many brewers make is not pitching enough yeast. Underpitching causes some of the same problems as under-aerating because the growing yeast cells run short of oxygen, resulting in many of the same off-flavors and fermentation behavior. Lagging and stuck fermentations are common problems when insufficient yeast is added, causing problems other than yeast related off-flavors.

When using liquid yeast, I always like to make a starter so that I am pitching 1 to 2 quarts (about 1 L) of active yeast slurry into a 5-gallon (19 L) batch. If you harvest yeast for subsequent reuse, you will need about a quart (250 mL) to get a good pitching rate. Rules for dry yeast vary, because not all yeast sachets contain the same weight.

Controlling fermentation temperature is another key to cutting down on yeast off-flavors. I am not suggesting buying elaborate and expensive temperature-control systems, unless you are at that stage of the hobby where you really want that type of control. Most homebrewers can do a pretty good job controlling temperature simply by selecting a cool part of the house to conduct ale fermentations. I suggest keeping most ales below 72°F (22°C) to get the best results. When it comes to lagers, most homes are not cool enough; a garage corner in the fall or winter or a refrigerator is required to ferment and age lagers.

Finally, racking beer off yeast after fermentation reduces the chances that your beer will pick up autolyzed flavors. I suggest racking no later than 2 weeks after primary fermentation is complete and most of the yeast has settled to the bottom of the fermenter. If you are using a conical fermenter, you can simply remove the yeast from the bottom of the cone without transferring the beer to another fermenter.

Q Can you explain what yeast generations are?

A Each time you use yeast is called a generation. The first use from the lab is referred to as *first generation yeast*. When you crop the yeast from the first brew and reuse it in a second batch, it becomes second generation yeast (the semantics here are important to clarify, since yeast typically increases by about fourfold during one batch, and the generation count would be very different if defined by a different rule). Most lager breweries discard their yeast after no more than 10 generations and replace this with fresh yeast propagated from the lab. Ale breweries are much more varied in their yeast management. Some have yeast management programs akin to lager breweries; others repitch their yeast with very infrequent replacement.

Q What is the best way to get yeast samples from commercial beers?

A My marauding kit consists of one cigarette lighter, one sterile mason jar, one plate of wort agar, and one metal microbiology loop (all micro stuff available from homebrew supply stores). To collect a sample, order a pint of unfiltered beer and inconspicuously break out your mobile yeast lab. First flame the loop, dip it into the beer and then streak it out on the wort agar plate. The plate is then sealed with Parafilm (a wax tape) for transport. Just in case the plating on site goes awry, pour a sample of the beer into the mason jar is a backup.

An easier way to get yeast from a brewery is to culture it from a bottle-conditioned brew. If you do this, be careful. If the brew has any bacteria in the bottle, your yeast propagation process will also increase the bacterial population — not exactly the idea. Some breweries, like Sierra Nevada, are known for clean yeast in the bottle. Ask around to get a feel for the quality of yeast in the bottles of whatever brew you are looking to get yeast from. Be careful with some of the more exotic bottle-conditioned beers — many are filtered and dosed with a yeast strain that is different from the fermenting yeast. Some Belgian ales and hefe-weizens use this practice. Although these yeast may produce good beer, they are not what fermented the host beer.

Q **Is there any way I can improve my yeast-starter technique with respect to culturing yeast from bottles?**

A The best way to use yeast from a bottle-conditioned beer is to do some true microbiological selection before propagation. Essentially, this involves streaking a small sample of the yeast sediment onto a petri dish

Petri dish

containing some type of microbiological medium. When yeast growth is visible, you can select a single colony to propagate into a volume large enough to pitch into a fermentation. This method is preferred, because there may be some bacterial contaminants or nonbrewing yeast in the yeast sediment that could ruin the beer being brewed. This technique will usually give better control over the yeast concentration in the propagator because the colony that you start with is known to be alive and of high concentration. Yeast concentration, viability, and purity are not known if you simply add a volume of yeast sediment to a quart of wort for propagation.

Q What is the best way to go about reusing yeast?

A Yeast storage and reuse is one of those topics that strike fear in many homebrewers, because of the importance yeast plays in beer quality and the real possibility of ruining a batch of beer with bad yeast. With that said, you only need to keep a few key things in mind when harvesting and storing yeast for use in subsequent brews.

Commercial brewers routinely harvest, store, and reuse yeast, because beginning every batch of beer with a new culture is not feasible without considerable investment in both time and equipment for large-scale yeast propagation. Furthermore, the quality of yeast available for harvest following fermentation is excellent in most breweries. The optimal time for harvesting yeast is after primary fermentation has completed, when yeast viability is high and the yeast is easy to crop either from the top of an ale fermentation or the bottom of the fermenter. This technique is most easily accomplished with the use of conical fermenters, which have become the norm.

Sanitation is of the utmost importance when harvesting yeast: All tools must be clean and sanitized prior to use. Since yeast slurries are rich in nutrients, especially as yeast ages, dies, and autolyzes, bacteria can grow during storage and the slurry can turn into a source of bacterial contamination. With this being said, good techniques can easily be used to successfully harvest and store yeast.

Once harvested, the yeast slurry should be stored cold to minimize metabolic activity and loss of viability. The general practice in commercial breweries is to maintain the yeast slurry between 32 and 38°F (0–4°C) for a minimal time period before repitching. Most large breweries harvest yeast from the fermenter and store it in an agitated, cooled vessel to minimize hot spots in large volumes of yeast. At home, where much smaller volumes are used, a slurry can easily be maintained at a uniform temperature in the refrigerator. Many small brewers leave their yeast in the bottom of their conical fermenters and remove the yeast for reuse immediately before pitching. This method works well as long as the yeast does not sit in the bottom of the tank for too long. Anything beyond 2 weeks is getting a bit long, based on my experience.

A method I have successfully used in 5-gallon (19 L) batches fermented in carboys is to harvest the yeast after primary has completed and the yeast has settled to the bottom of the fermenter. Moving the carboy into a refrigerator greatly helps with yeast flocculation. The beer can be racked off the yeast into a secondary fermenter, keg, or bottling bucket after about a week, and the yeast can easily be recovered by swirling the sediment in the bottom of the carboy with a little beer left behind after racking. This slurry can then be poured out of the fermenter into a clean and sanitized storage container and refrigerated. I suggest using a glass container fitted with a sterile cotton plug or a plastic container with a screw top, because yeast slurries can build up pressure even when stored cold.

The other thing to consider when harvesting yeast for reuse is its history. I do not suggest harvesting yeast from high-alcohol beers, beers that had a sluggish or unusual fermentation, or batches of beer brewed from "high generation" yeast. Every time yeast is used in fermentation, the generation number increases. First generation yeasts come from a lab propagation. When the fermentation is complete and yeasts are harvested, the next batch or batches contain second generation yeast (it is common to harvest enough yeast from one batch to brew two or three batches).

As the generation number increases, so does the likelihood of using yeast that has mutated and lost some of its desirable brewing qualities (such as flocculation characteristics). The potential for contamination also increases with each generation. Most commercial lager breweries do not use yeast older than 10 generations, while some ale brewers reportedly never go back to a lab culture and are always repitching yeast from a fermentation.

Now for some unsolicited advice.

Bad yeast will wreck a brew, wasting both time and money in addition to creating a shortage in beer! There are several sources of very good homebrewing yeast out there, and the price of yeast is relatively low in the grand scheme of things, especially if one values his free time. There are several reasons to reuse yeast, but if one is in doubt about technique and does not brew relatively often (every couple weeks), I would seriously consider the pitfalls before using this method on a routine basis.

What are the keys to a healthy yeast starter?

Propagating yeast is like growing any other life form: You need to provide a good environment and a supply of nutrients. Growing yeast is relatively simple on a small scale and becomes more difficult as the size of the propagator increases.

A pure strain of yeast is essential. This means there should be only one strain of yeast present in the starter and no bacterial cells. If unwanted yeast strains or bacteria are present, they will be propagated along with the yeast you really want to grow. The only way to really know if you are starting with a pure culture is to have a laboratory. Since most homebrewers don't have labs in their basements, it is common to rely on the skills of a reputable yeast supply lab and hope everything goes well. Fortunately for American homebrewers, there are several excellent yeast suppliers around the country.

After acquiring a yeast strain to propagate, you need an appropriate nutrient media. Luckily for us brewers, wort is the perfect media for growing yeast. Wort contains amino acids for protein synthesis, nucleic acids needed to synthesize DNA and RNA, essential vitamins and minerals, essential fatty acids for membrane growth, and an abundant supply of fermentable sugars. The three most important points to note regarding propagation wort are specific gravity, hops, and sterility.

The healthiest yeast is produced from moderate wort strengths, usually in the 1.040 to 1.050 SG range. If the wort gravity is too high, then the ethanol concentration can reach levels that begin to damage the yeast. If the gravity is too low, the growing yeast soon run out of food. Hops should always be added to propagation worts to suppress the growth of certain beer spoilage organisms. Although hops do not suppress the growth of all bugs, they do prevent the growth of many that will grow in wort and beer. The third point to remember is sterility. Always boil the propagation wort for at least 30 minutes and store it in a clean and sanitized container. The best method is to sterilize the wort in the propagation container — canning jars and a pressure cooker work well for this method.

Once you have yeast strain and a sterile, hopped propagation wort in hand, it is time to start the propagation. If you're starting with a concentrated liquid starter, use approximately 1 part starter to 100 parts of wort. After inoculating the wort with your starter, set the environmental conditions. Yeast grow fastest and produce higher cell counts at higher temperatures. If you are after high cell counts, conduct the propagation at 75 to 85°F (24–29°C) for ale strains and 65 to 75°F (18–24°C) for lager strains. Although these temperatures will stimulate rapid growth, they may lead to the production of funky flavors, so it is important to pick a temperature that produces a good flavor with your particular yeast strain.

The next important growth factor is oxygen. Although yeasts grown in full-strength wort (1.040–1.050 SG) always produce energy through fermentation (as opposed to respiration), they still require oxygen for the synthesis of sterols and fatty acids. These compounds are the foundation of new cell walls. When yeasts are growing, they must produce a lot of new cell walls.

Oxygen can be infused into the growing yeast with an aeration stone or can be absorbed from the atmosphere. On a large scale, the only way to provide the yeast with adequate oxygen for maximum growth is through some sort of direct injection. However, small-scale propagations can absorb enough oxygen from the atmosphere for good growth. For this to occur, the propagator must not be equipped with an airlock.

Sterilized cotton wads have been used for more than 100 years in brewing labs for yeast growth. The cotton wadding allows oxygen to enter the propagation container but traps airborne contaminants. Continuously shaking or stirring the propagator dramatically increases the absorption of oxygen into the wort and increases the yeast cell density. Magnetic stir plates and shaker tables are the two most common ways of incorporating atmospheric oxygen into growing cell cultures in labs. Shaken or stirred propogation really does make a big difference in the cell count of the slurry.

Q Because the object of making starters is to grow more yeast, how big an increase in starter volume is required to grow more yeast? I usually use a factor of 10. Is this the best way?

A The approach you use is the conventional method used to grow yeast in commercial breweries of all sizes. In growing yeast, the oxygen content, specific gravity, and nutritional quality of the wort along with the propagation temperature will affect the maximum cell density of the culture. To keep the population growing, the volume must increase. As a rule of thumb, increase your propagation volume by a factor of 5 to 10. Make larger increases early and progressively drop them as the total volume approaches that required for pitching.

One problem with propagating yeast that bothers many homebrewers is the dilution of the recipe's wort with the propagation wort. The best way to minimize this problem is to allow the last step of your propagation to complete its fermentation and the cells to flocculate (clump and sink). Then you pitch the bottom of the starter. This method not only concentrates the yeast cells to a much smaller volume, typically about 5 to 10 percent of the propagation volume, but it also selects flocculent cells from a potential mixture of flocculent and nonflocculent cells. Many brewers want to know the secret of great beer. In my opinion, great beer can only be made time after time if the basics of yeast are understood. The key to yeast is to have it clean, alive, and in sufficient quantity to take off quickly. Your approach to handling is a great start to guaranteeing success with yeast.

Q **My last batch had a huge fermentation with foam spilling out of the airlock. Did I do something wrong?**

A Although you had a giant mess on your hands with your excited fermentation, you may have added a normal amount of yeast. One to 1½ cups (237–355 mL) of yeast solids per 5 gallons (19 L) of wort is a good pitching rate. Now the bad news: The *krausen* spewing out of your carboy is directly related to your pitching rate. A wimpy rate usually results in a thin krausen that will rarely leave the fermenter. Airlocks can vent the gas from such a fermentation. Increasing your pitching rate increases fermentation rate, decreases certain aroma compounds, decreases the chance of contamination . . . and increases the odds of making a mess! The minimum precaution when fermenting in a carboy is to attach a blowoff hose. Still, I don't think you contaminated your beer by neglecting to use a hose. Any microscopic invaders were most likely pushed onto your floor along with the krausen. Usually the headspace provided by a 6.5-gallon (25 L) carboy is plenty for a 5-gallon (19 L) fermentation, but sometimes foam happens!

Q Is it important for a lager yeast starter to be fermented at the same fermentation temperature as the main batch of beer?

A Two schools of thought butt heads on lager yeast propagation and fermentation. The traditional approach is to propagate the yeast and begin fermentation at lager fermentation temperatures. This method results in a slower propagation rate and tends to start the fermentation off a bit slower, compared with warmer propagation and initial fermentation temperatures. Proponents of this method argue that the finished beer tastes better.

The other school of thought basically argues that warmer propagation gives better cell counts at pitching time and that a warm start to fermentation gets things off to a vigorous start. This method reduces the chances of a bacterial problem. Although both arguments are strong, opponents cite studies showing an increase in fruity aromas in lager beers produced using these higher temperatures.

Some brewers use a blend of the two philosophies. They propagate at warm temperatures, usually around 68°F (20°C), and carry out the entire fermentation at cool temperatures, typically between 46 and 54°F (8–12°C). My personal preference is to propagate lager yeast at 68°F (20°C) and conduct the entire fermentation at 50°F (10°C).

■ ══════════ ■

Q **Should I use wheat dry malt extract (DME) in my yeast starter when making a wheat-based beer, or can I use extra-light plain malt DME as a neutral base?**

A Strictly speaking, any wort with a gravity ranging from 1.040–1.052 SG works well in starters with respect to growing yeast. But flavor questions arise if the starter and the wort the yeast is going into are very different. I typically use my palest standard wort (a wheat-beer wort) as the starter for my yeast. My experience tells me that the flavor of this wort is light enough not to dominate the flavors of the other beers I brew.

In general, some things I would avoid in a starter wort are dark colors, malty flavors, high bitterness, late hop aroma, and gravities higher than about 1.052 SG. I personally would not get too worried about trying to make a special starter for every beer. This is my opinion, and I know some brewers don't agree with this advice, but there is no absolute answer to this question.

I like making things easy for myself when possible. I typically steal a bit of wort from a batch and put it into media bottles instead of making a special batch just for starters. After the wort is in the bottle, I pressure cook it with the lids of the media bottles loose for 20 minutes at 15 psi pressure. After 20 minutes, I remove the pressure cooker from the heat and allow the pressure to slowly fall. Once the pressure is down to 0 psi, I remove the bottles or jars, tighten the lids, and store at room temperature. This wort will remain preserved until needed.

Q **Every time I've seen reference to a yeast starter being prepared, it calls for plain, light, dry malt extract (DME) as the growing medium. Is there some reason not to use corn sugar?**

A There is a very good reason not to rely solely on simple sugars, like corn sugar, for yeast starters: nutrient content. Yeast cells require many of the same basic "building blocks" of life that we require, and corn sugar is not a good source of anything other than sugar. Wort, on the other hand, is an excellent source of amino acids, nucleic acids, phosphates, and carbohydrates, among many other organic compounds. These substances are used to synthesize proteins, DNA, RNA, cell membranes, and energy.

Wort lacks or is deficient in some things, however. Cell growth requires vitamins and minerals, such as B-vitamins and zinc; many brewers boost the content of these compounds in their starters. In fact, some brewers add these compounds to wort as part of their normal brewing practice. Oxygen is also important because of its use by growing yeast to produce unsaturated fatty acids and sterols, which yeasts require for healthy cell membranes.

Dead yeast cells are one of the best sources of yeast nutrients. Brewers have used dead, autolyzed (enzymatically self-destructed) yeast as a nutrient supplement for years. With a good source of yeast nutrients, you get healthier yeast cells, shorter lag times, faster fermentations, and healthier yeast for reuse. Improvement in yeast health improves beer flavor. I have used various yeast nutrients as part of my standard brewing practice for several years, with great results.

In short, yeast starters should, at minimum, be made from wort. The use of yeast nutrients, in combination with periodic aeration or oxygenation, will allow for the growth of even healthier and denser starter cultures.

Q **I recently decided to give dry yeast a try and pitched one rehydrated, 11.5-gram (0.4 oz.) package of dry yeast into my carboy. The carboy began showing signs of fermentation within 4 hours. By the**

next morning, the fermentation was violent and I was losing a substantial amount of brew out of the blow-off tubes. I don't understand why I had such a violent reaction. I did not rehydrate the yeast, but I don't think that is the problem. Do you have any ideas on how I should proceed for my next attempt with dry yeast?

A I also don't think rehydration was the problem. Hydrating dried yeast in water before pitching is recommended, because it allows the cell wall and internals to establish their normal size and transport functions before the yeast is tossed into wort. I have used dried yeast many times without rehydrating and made good beer, but the microbiology folk who understand the cellular reactions do suggest rehydrating for the benefit of the yeast.

The "problem" is that you are accustomed to yeast strains that don't form such a large krausen volume. Not all yeasts behave the same; some strains require a considerable amount of headspace in the top of the fermenter to avoid mega blow-off. A standard beer fermenter, if such a thing exists, has about 25 percent headspace in the top of the tank. When sizing cylindroconical tanks, I calculate the beer level for a given tank geometrically, typically a 2.5:1 height to diameter ratio, and then I make sure there is 25 percent additional length in the straight side of the tank. There are other ways of calculating headspace, but this is how I do it.

Most yeast strains perform fine in a tank with 25 percent headspace, but others can cause messy beer loss when mega blowoff occurs. Hop components are lost, too, when the krausen is skimmed. This loss of hop bitterness can be a bummer if you did not expect it. Your finished beer may be different from what you planned. However, some of your loss may not be such a bad thing.

If you have ever tasted the foam on the top of fermenting beer, you will know that it is very bitter and that hop compounds become concentrated in beer foam. Cold break trub that forms upon wort chilling is also carried up into the yeast and *head*. German brewers call this stuff *braun hefe,* or brown yeast. Braun hefe does not taste very good, so traditional brewers using open fermenters skim it off the top. More than one large American brewer uses fermenters specifically designed to remove braun hefe during fermentation to make a cleaner tasting brew.

Next time around, use much more headspace than you think is required, something like 40 percent. Once you get an idea of how a particular strain behaves, you can adjust the fill height in your fermenter accordingly. You may decide that a little blowoff is a good thing and end up filling in order to achieve a controlled amount of self-skimming.

Q What is the best way to pitch lager yeast?

A Some yeast manufacturers suggest pitching lager yeasts at ale temperatures and then moving the fermentation to a cooler environment within 12 hours of seeing active fermentation. The idea here is that yeast do not begin producing flavor compounds until they are actively fermenting. Even then, there is a delay between yeast activity and the concentration of flavor compounds, such as esters (fruity aromas), higher alcohols (spicy, winelike aromas), and sulfur compounds (burnt match and rotten egg aromas).

Fermenting lager yeast at warm temperatures is not a major cause of yeast mutation, but it will result in a beer with a very different aroma. Anchor Steam is a lager beer fermented at warmer temperatures, around 65°F (18°C), and it is much more fruity and alelike than lagers fermented at cooler temperatures.

I do not know of any medium to large lager brewers that start their fermentations warm and then cool them down. In fact, many lager brewers begin their fermentations cool and let them slowly warm to a defined maximum temperature. Many German brewing references indicate that it is common to cool wort to 46°F (8°C), pitch the yeast at this very cool temperature, and allow fermentation temperature to rise to a maximum of 50°F (10°C). Why pitch yeast in cool wort? It is believed the resulting beer has better flavor. Why pitch into warm wort? It is well known that bacterial problems become likely as the lag time preceding fermentation increases.

I have used both techniques and prefer beers made by pitching at or slightly below fermentation temperature to beers made by pitching warm and then cooling. To be honest, one of the problems with starting warm and waiting until seeing active fermentation is that this might happen at night or on a day when you are not at home checking your fermenter. I use a German Pilsner yeast, pitch at 50°F (10°C) and allow the fermentation to rise to 54°F (12°C), where it is maintained with cooling control on the fermenter until fermentation is complete. I typically see signs of fermentation within 24 hours. I have tried starting at 46°F (8°C) and fermenting at 50°F (10°C), but the fermentations were sluggish and took too long to finish for my particular demands. Yeast strains vary, and the best temperature for fermentation is a function of yeast strain, brewing practices, and the types of beers being brewed. In other words, suggestions about temperatures should be taken as suggestions and not as rules set in stone.

Q If I want to harvest yeast, should I start removing it as it falls or wait until after fermentation?

A One method — not necessarily the most common one — goes a bit like this: Add yeast and wort to the fermenter, and fermentation begins. When this happens, yeast begin zooming around in the fermenter; some trub solids remain on the fermenter bottom, and some trub solids are suspended by the fermentation. (Trub is the proteinaceous precipitate that forms in the wort. Hot trub precipitates during wort boiling. Cold trub precipitates when the wort is cooled.) If your fermenter has a valve on the bottom, some brewers would briefly open the valve to remove trub solids on the bottom of the fermenter at this time. They may repeat this step a few times during fermentation.

The next phase of the operation happens when fermentation slows and the yeasts begin to flocculate and fall to the bottom of the fermenter. Brewers hold off on purging trub during this phase, because a lot of the stuff in the cone is good yeast. If they cool the fermenter for *secondary fermentation,* they do so before harvesting the yeast, because more yeast will settle out when the beer is cooled.

When I harvest yeast, I usually have multiple cleaned and sanitized containers handy. The first container holds the trub-laden bit intended for the sink. This portion looks like hummus with tiny chunks of chocolate. The second container is for the good yeast I plan on using. I use the third, if needed, for the last bit of yeast, after about 500 mL (about 2 cups) of good yeast is collected. Good yeast looks like plain hummus (without the chunks). Usually my second container has plenty of yeast for another batch. Typically, I end up pouring the contents of container one and three over my hands. I observe the color of the yeast and the amount of trub mixed in with the yeast. I also smell and taste the yeast. (Obviously, this yeast is not used for brewing after I've touched it.) Fresh yeast smells very breadlike and does not have off-aromas. I want fresh-smelling yeast that is trub-free and has a creamy white or tan appearance. Autolyzed yeast is usually darker and more liquidlike than fresh and healthy yeast.

What I am most keyed into are the signs of yeast autolysis, which can be detected from aromas of soy sauce or vegemite. If I pick up autolyzed aromas — especially if the aroma is present in both containers — I become concerned about the quality of the yeast in the second container. If the yeast in the first sample is slightly autolyzed and the third sample has no detectable autolysis, I usually don't worry. The very bottom of a cone bottom fermenter does not circulate and has the greatest likelihood of harboring a small amount of decaying yeast. The yeast intended for pitching should be used as soon as possible at a rate of about 8 ounces of yeast to 5 gallons (237 mL/19 L) of wort. If you have to store the yeast, refrigerate it for no longer than a few days prior to use.

I also like to know the history of the yeast. I really don't like using yeast that doesn't meet the following profiles. Lager yeast should be less than seven generations old, only used in normal-gravity fermentations for paler worts, harvested from a fast to normal-length primary fermentation (usually 7 to 10 days), and without detectable off-flavors. The time span between the brew day and the harvest day should also be less than 3 weeks. The ale yeast profile is similar, except that I will use ale yeast up to 10 generations. The normal time span for primary fermentation should be 3 to 4 days and the span between brew day and harvesting should be less than 2 weeks. These numbers work for me in my brewpub. Homebrewers are less likely to use yeast for this many generations, simply because the frequency of brewing is usually less at home, except for you guys who brew twice a month no matter what!

CULTURING YEAST AT HOME: STEP BY STEP

1. Select the type of medium you want to use. A good all-purpose growth medium, such as a universal beer agar (UBA), works well for growing yeast and anything else that may be in the inoculum. However, if you suspect the yeast culture that you will be plating may not be pure or may be contaminated, then medium selection is the way to sort through your unknown culture.

2. Buy or round up the other basic tools you will need. This includes media, Petri dishes, inoculating loop, alcohol flame, media bottles, a decent scale, a small pot robbed from the kitchen, a funnel from the same place, and a pressure cooker. Petri dishes, media, and media bottles must be purchased from a lab supply company or homebrew supply house that carries more advanced equipment.

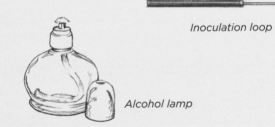

Inoculation loop

Alcohol lamp

3. Mix your dry medium powder with water and slowly bring it to a simmer in the small pot. Don't worry: All-purpose media don't contain toxic compounds. However, differential media contain things you do not want floating around the kitchen. A common medium used in brewing labs to suppress the growth of brewing yeast contains cyclohexamide; this compound is a teratogen, meaning that it may cause birth defects. Don't use this stuff at home! Once the liquid medium is mixed up, it is time to transfer to the media bottles using the funnel and sterilize them in the pressure cooker.

4. After pressure cooking (I suggest 20 minutes at 15 psi), the pressure cooker should be slowly cooled and *unloaded* after the pressure has fallen. The medium must be poured when it is hot and then allowed to cool and solidify in the dish. This takes some skill: If you pour the plates too hot, the lids fill with condensate; if you wait too long and pour the plates when the medium is beginning to solidify, you get lumpy plates. The other important thing here is to pour the plates

Pressure cooker

in a clean environment where you can cool the plates with the lids halfway on to prevent lid fogging. If the environment is not clean, you get moldy plates. This whole headache can be skipped if you purchase pre-poured plates. But then your selection of medium is somewhat limited. Not a big deal if you just want to grow yeast.

5. Streak the plate . . . and no, I don't mean crossing home plate nude! Streaking begins with flaming the inoculum loop with an alcohol or natural gas flame until it is red hot, dipping it in the yeast slurry or beer sample, and then transferring this sample to the plate. A more complicated procedure used in labs is called "streaking for isolation" and will result in isolated colonies of yeast or bacteria.

6. Incubate the sample. Seal the plates with a wax or plastic film to prevent contamination during the incubation step. It typically takes 1 to 2 weeks to develop plates, depending on what you are growing. Yeast grows faster than bacteria. Yeast plates usually show good growth within 1 week.

This process gets you to the point where you can now store your plate in a refrigerator for several months. You can routinely grab a single yeast colony and transfer it to a small flask of wort using a flamed loop; 20–25 mL (0.7–0.8 oz.) is a good starting volume. Then propagate this colony up to about 2 quarts (about 2 L) if you are pitching into a 5-gallon (19 L) batch of wort.

It is critical during this entire process that you use good lab techniques to prevent contamination of the culture. Proper lab methods are required, and nothing beats lab classes in which an experienced instructor demonstrates the methods. Reading the intricacies of lab technique in a book is not a very good substitute for real life instruction, in my opinion. Furthermore, if you are serious about checking your lab work, you will have to do more plating, using different media to verify that the yeast was not contaminated during this whole process.

The downside to going to all of this trouble is that you may end up selecting a yeast colony that is atypical of the strain, for example a mutant, and/or you may end up with a contaminated starter and never know until it is too late. The end result could indeed be bad beer. What I suggest is to buy yeast from a yeast lab, propagate it before use in 1 to 2 quarts (about 1–2 L) of wort to ensure a good pitching rate, then harvest the yeast and reuse it after fermentation is complete. If you brew fairly often, you will always have a source of fresh yeast. Yeast slurry can be harvested and stored for 1 to 2 weeks before reuse, and your yeast investment can be spread over several batches.

Q What is yeast washing?

A Yeast washing, like other techniques used to handle and treat yeast, is high on my list of things to do to hone one's brewing skills. Yeast washing is useful when yeast is to be stored and reused, because it removes dead yeast cells, trub, and beer from the good yeast. The overall effect is higher yeast viability (because many dead cells are removed from the stored population), higher yeast vigor (trub interferes with yeast's uptake of nutrients when it is stuck to the yeast cell wall), and a better environment in which to store yeast, since the alcohol from beer isn't the best medium for yeast health.

The method is straightforward. Water, preferably distilled or bottled and free of chlorine, is boiled for 10 to 15 minutes to sterilize it. Water that contains at least 50 milligrams of calcium per liter works best. So when using distilled or low-calcium water, add about ⅛ teaspoon (0.6 ml) of gypsum per gallon (3.8 L) of water prior to boiling. After the water is boiled, it should be chilled to at least 38°F (4°C) before using it for yeast wash water. This process is easier if the water is boiled in canning jars, so it can be sealed and cooled after boiling. You can make enough bottles of wash water for months of brewing.

Once the water is sterilized and cold, it is time for the yeast to take a bath. Mix equal volumes of yeast and water in a clean and sanitized container, swirl the mixture gently, and allow it to sit in the refrigerator for at least 30 minutes, preferably 1 hour, before going to the next step. I typically use the same container the yeast is stored in for this step.

During the cold rest, yeast cells will settle to the bottom of the container and dead cells, beer, and trub will separate into the top layer. After these layers have clearly separated, carefully pour off the top layer while not pouring the yeast layer out of the container. If the yeast still contains a lot of trub, a second or even third wash can be used.

Care must always be exercised so as not to throw away the yeast being washed. The calcium in the water aids in this objective, because calcium helps yeast to flocculate and separate from the trub, dead yeast, and beer.

Keys to yeast washing are sanitation and care. Whenever you open the container that holds the yeast, spray the top with alcohol and flame to minimize the chance of introducing an airborne contaminant into your yeast slurry.

Q **I've heard that when recovering yeast for reuse, the yeast should be acid-washed to eliminate any possible contaminants, such as bacteria. Is there a way a homebrewer can acid wash recovered yeast?**

A Some brewers use acid washing to kill bacteria in their pitching yeast. Brewers who acid wash their yeast have different rules concerning when to acid wash. Some do it every time they use their yeast. These brewers assume that acid washing has an effect on the yeast and should be done before every use to avoid inconsistency. Other brewers acid wash only when they know the yeast has an unacceptably high microbial load. These brewers rely on microbiological examination of their yeast to gauge when acid washing is needed. The rest of the brewers acid washing yeast do it on a regular schedule based on the age of the yeast, usually somewhere between 5 and 10 generations.

The procedure to acid wash yeast is fairly simple, both in principle and in practice. The idea is similar to chemotherapy: Make the environment severe enough to kill the disease but not the patient. In acid washing, the disease is a bacterial contamination and the patient is the yeast. Luckily for brewers and our friends the yeast, beer spoilage bacteria do not tolerate low pH environments nearly as well as yeast. This fact makes pH a suitable tool for yeast chemotherapy. Like human chemotherapy, the treatment is not too good for the patient. Thus the conditions and time must be carefully monitored so that the treatment doesn't inflict undo harm upon the yeast.

Three variables must be controlled during acid washing: 1) pH, 2) temperature, and 3) time of exposure. To acid wash yeast, first cool the yeast to 32 to 36°F (0–2°C). This cool temperature minimizes the damage the low pH environment can cause. Next, slowly add food-grade phosphoric acid to the yeast while gently stirring it. Acid addition continues until the pH drops between 1.8 and 2.2. The target pH depends upon the brewer; personal experience is needed to pick a pH that works best for a particular yeast strain.

This part of the procedure requires good pH measurement. The best instrument is a pH meter that can be calibrated between uses. A good pH meter will cost more than $100, but may be more gear than the average homebrewer really needs. Unfortunately, pH papers don't give continuous readings, don't work very well with yeast slurries, and should not be used for acid washing

After the yeast slurry pH is adjusted to the target, it is time to wait. About 2 hours is typical. Shorter times kill fewer bacteria. The last step of the process is to stop. This step is done simply by adding the yeast to wort and getting on with the brew day. Personally, I would rather use clean yeast than clean up dirty yeast, and I see acid cleaning as a temporary solution. I would rather keep my yeast young and healthy with routine propagation.

Q What are yeast nutrients, and how are they used?

A Most yeast nutrient blends contain amino acids, inorganic nitrogen (ammonia), B-vitamins, sterols, unsaturated fatty acids, and often, autolyzed yeast that gives a mixture of all these components. The blends are typically used when making wine, cider, or high-adjunct beers to provide critical growth factors required by yeast. Fermentations that lack yeast nutrients are usually sluggish and have a tendency to become stuck.

Brewer's wort is a rich medium and has most everything yeasts require for a good fermentation. In fact, the practice of repitching yeast from one batch to another usually carries some autolyzed yeast with it; yeast extract is a good source of vitamins, amino acids, and fatty acids. When yeast grows, it requires amino acids and nitrogen for protein synthesis; sterols and fatty acids to build cell walls (yeast can synthesize these compounds as well as use external sources); and B-vitamins as cofactors in yeast metabolism.

Brewers typically do not add these sorts of nutrient blends unless they are brewing high-adjunct or very high-gravity brews. One nutrient often added to wort is zinc; yeasts require some zinc for growth. Wort zinc levels should be between 0.10 and 0.15 ppm. Zinc can come from copper when copper brewing vessels are used, but today most equipment is made from stainless steel and zinc additions are helpful.

One problem with adding zinc salts, such as zinc sulfate, is that much of the zinc is lost in trub. Biologically available forms of zinc can be enhanced by growing yeast in a zinc-enriched media and then drying the yeast for use as a yeast nutrient. This form of zinc has lower trub losses when added to the brew kettle.

I use such a nutrient product, called Servomyces, for every batch of beer we brew at our brewery. If wort is low in zinc, we see lagging fermentations as well as poorly flocculating yeast. A friend of mine working for a very large brewery told me that they have a target yeast density following primary before transferring to the lagering tanks.

This brewery adjusts wort zinc levels to influence cell density after primary. If the cell density is too low, they back off on the zinc to reduce yeast flocculation a bit. If the cell density is too high, they slightly increase the zinc.

In my experience with brewing all-malt beers and some beers with about 25 percent adjunct, I have never felt the need to add anything other than biologically available zinc, like that found in Servomyces, to wort since wort is really the ideal nutrient source for hungry yeast cells!

Q **What do you advise about using pure oxygen in a 5-gallon (19 L) primary fermentation?**

A The answer has to do with 1) How much oxygen is enough? and 2) How do you get oxygen into the wort?

Technically speaking, yeasts require 6 to 8 milligrams of oxygen per liter of wort to produce healthy offspring in the early stages of a brewery fermentation. This is about all the oxygen you can get into wort if using air. If you use pure oxygen, you can reach five times this level.

If the yeast don't get enough oxygen, you will have poor yeast growth during fermentation and the yeast offspring will be sickly. The results may be sluggish fermentation rates and a very fruity finished beer. If you add too much oxygen, you may get excessive yeast growth and very vigorous fermentations. So the solution is to hit it just right!

Let's address the second issue and come back to the idea of getting it just right. As far as getting the oxygen into the wort, we're up against buoyancy. Oxygen bubbles float to the surface of the wort and release their booty to the atmosphere, so only part of a bubble's cargo gets into the wort. Smaller bubbles allow more oxygen to diffuse into solution than large bubbles. That means that the large bubbles you create with your racking cane release most of their oxygen into the atmosphere.

The easiest way to get the needed oxygen into wort is to push gas through a porous device. Aeration or aquarium stones are ideal. A racking cane with tiny holes poked in it and a sealed end also works well. The smaller bubbles have a larger surface-to-volume ratio and are better able to diffuse their oxygen into the wort. They rise slower than large bubbles, too, and have more time to give up their load.

Armed with small bubbles, let's get back to just right. This figure depends on yeast strain (some require more oxygen than others), pitching rate (underpitching requires more yeast growth), and wort gravity. The yeast issues are straightforward. Basically, get a feel for your yeast's oxygen needs, meet the oxygen needs, and then pitch enough yeast.

The wort gravity issue is one of the many catch-22s in brewing. Generally, higher-gravity worts require more oxygen than lower-gravity worts for a normal fermentation, but high-gravity worts allow less oxygen into solution. That's because oxygen solubility is inversely proportional to wort gravity. Insufficient wort oxygen is a recipe for fruity beer.

So high-gravity beers are usually more fruity than lower gravity brews.

Professional brewers resolve this dilemma by getting as much oxygen into solution as possible, because a lack of oxygen causes many more problems than having too much. Too much oxygen will create a copious yeast crop during fermentation, blowing some of the yeast crop out of the fermenter. If that happens, the oxygen level is simply reduced. Most brewers use air instead of oxygen (air cannot add too much oxygen). They inject the air in-line while the cooled wort is headed toward the fermenter.

Q **At what point is wort to be aerated?**

A Although seemingly confusing, the rule about oxygen or air and brewing is to avoid it in all operations except after cooling and before fermentation. During mashing and lautering, it is possible for certain enzymes (lipoxygenases) to catalyze the oxidation of lipids to yield stale flavors. Also, the oxidation of proteins during lautering can cause proteins to crosslink with one another and impede wort collection. During transfer of hot wort from the lauter tun to the kettle, oxygen will cause the wort to darken. Most brewers making darker beers are not too concerned about color pickup, but those trying to make very pale beers are concerned.

The only time to intentionally add air or oxygen is during cooling. In the past, some brewers aerated the wort as it entered the wort cooler. This practice helped dissolve the oxygen as the wort flowed through the cooler. But most brewers discontinued the practice because it led to wort darkening. Today, it is common to inject sterile air or oxygen immediately after cooling.

If aeration of wort did not occur, there would be very little oxygen in the wort (boiling drives almost all dissolved gases from the wort) and the yeast would suffer. To reproduce, a yeast cell must synthesize all of its basic components. Lipids and sterols are two classes of compounds needed to make more yeast cells. It just so happens that yeasts require oxygen (in its molecular form) to synthesize these compounds. Most of the yeast growth occurs early in fermentation; this is why oxygen is needed. After this point, they no longer have a use for oxygen.

Now the oxidation story begins to resurface. Oxidation of beer not only causes the formation of stale, paperlike flavors, but it also can cause the beer to darken and even get hazy. So you see, brewers have a love–hate relationship with oxygen in which we hate it more often than we love it and hate the fact that we occasionally have to love it because it would be a lot easier to simply hate it!

THE RIGHT YEAST FOR THE JOB

Sometimes I am asked if Fleischmann's active dry yeast can be used to brew ales. The simple answer is no. If you want great beer, you must have great yeast. Fleischmann's active dry yeast is great for bread, not beer.

Baking yeast is grown under aerobic conditions and is chock full of glycogen. When baking yeast is hydrated in warm water, the glycogen is used by the yeast cell for energy and a byproduct is carbon dioxide. Yeast gives bread a nice yeasty smell and carbon dioxide for leavening. The beauty of baking yeast is that it works very quickly due to the large quantity of glycogen.

Baking yeast and brewing yeast share genus and species — both are *Saccharomyces cerevisiae* — but the similarities end there. Baking yeasts are living gas bags and can be replaced, minus the yeast flavor, with leavening agents such as baking soda (sodium bicarbonate) and baking powders (such as cream of tartar, tartaric acid, monocalcium phosphate, and aluminum sulfate). Brewer's yeast, on the other hand, makes beer! We make the wort, and the yeast transforms the wort into a complex mixture of alcohols, esters, aldehydes, sulfur compounds, and many other flavor-active compounds.

When Fleischmann's makes baker's yeast, it strives to make the best yeast for bread baking and gives little thought to the possible outcome of using its yeast for beer brewing. Make sure the yeast you use is intended for brewing beer, not baking bread.

Q What are some tips for fermenting high-gravity beers to completion?

A My basic philosophy with high-gravity beers is pretty simple: Pitch enough yeast, aerate the wort well, and get on with it! Most brewing strains can handle wort gravities up to about 1.080 SG without much problem and many will work fine with worts up to about 1.100 SG.

Some brewers add air or oxygen during fermentation if the fermentation rate begins to slow or hangs. Personally, I would never add more oxygen to fermenting beer — period. Adding more yeast, on the other hand, is often beneficial when fermenting a high-gravity wort.

The technique of krausening is traditionally used as a method to carbonate lagers, but it can be used to solve other problems. With or without krausening, lagers are carbonated during aging because they are aged under pressure. For this reason high-gravity lagers, like doppelbocks, are allowed to naturally clarify during their long lagering period without worrying about bottle conditioning. All traditionally aged commercial lagers employ this method, but most homebrewers treat ales and lagers the same when it comes to carbonation. If you use a traditional lagering method, there is no need to add more yeast before bottling, although you will need a counterpressure bottle filler.

Some fermentations begin to slow toward the end because of premature flocculation of the fermenting yeast. A simple technique to keep these sorts of fermentations on track is to *rouse* the fermentation. In a commercial brewery, rousing may involve transferring the beer to another fermenter or pumping the beer around in the fermenter to mix it up, but at home, rousing is simple — just gently rock your carboy or fermenting bucket and the fermentation has been roused!

■ ══════════ ■

Q **Can you explain the meaning of attenuation and the way to calculate it, as well as its relation to alcohol content?**

A Attenuation expresses the reduction in wort concentration during fermentation and is typically reported as a percentage. In other words, it tells a brewer how much the specific gravity will drop during fermentation.

Brewers actually use two measures of attenuation. The most common is apparent attenuation, properly called *apparent degree of fermentation,* or ADF for short. The apparent degree of fermentation is equal to the original wort density (in degrees Plato) less the apparent final density divided by the original wort density. Use a hydrometer to measure wort density (gravity) for both the original and final measurements. This is easy to understand if we turn it into an equation: $ADF = (OG - FG) \div OG$. For example, a beer with a wort density of 12°P and a final gravity of 3°P has an ADF of 0.75 or 75 percent.

So why do brewers care about ADF? For starters, ADF is related to a beer's body, mouthfeel, and alcohol content.

Very dry beers (which exhibit a high ADF) tend to be lighter in body than beers with a lower ADF. They also have more alcohol, assuming the beers have the same original gravity. Mash temperature profile, grain bill, and yeast strain all have an effect on ADF. For example, a long mash incorporating various rests will produce more fermentable wort than a short, high-temperature mash. Similarly, wort produced exclusively from malt will be more fermentable than wort made using specialty grains, because specialty grains contain a higher percentage of unfermentable sugars. Starting with a given wort, different yeast strains may have varying fermentation characteristics, and most yeast suppliers use ADF as one of the parameters to describe their yeast strains.

If your goal is to produce a dry beer, like Asahi Super Dry from Japan, you want to focus on those variables that increase ADF. I would choose a long mash profile using temperature rests from 140 to 160°F (60–71°C), use few, if any, special malts, and probably try to find a high-amylose rice variety. Amylose is a type of starch resulting in a high percentage of fermentable sugars in mashing. Finally, I would select a highly attenuative yeast strain.

This strategy obviously would fail if the goal were to produce a big, chewy Scottish ale with a luscious complement of unfermentable sugars. This type of beer typically uses a high, single-temperature mash, contains a substantial dose of special malts, and uses yeast known for low attenuation. In a nutshell, that's ADF.

You may be wondering why it carries the moniker "apparent." Hydrometers work as measuring devices by taking advantage of the linear correlation between buoyancy and liquid density. As liquid density increases, so does the buoyancy of floating objects. That physical property can be used to calibrate the scale of a hydrometer.

For example, two liquid samples are prepared in a liter volumetric flask. The first 1-liter sample contains 25 grams of sugar, 1 glug of vodka, and water. The second 1-liter sample contains 25 grams of sugar, 2 glugs of vodka, and water. Using a hydrometer, sample one reads 1.070 SG, or about 18° Plato. The second sample reads 1.048 SG, or about 12° Plato. Both samples contain the same concentration of dissolved solids, but the alcohol in sample two decreases the liquid density and the buoyancy of the hydrometer. The reason the term apparent extract is used is to denote that the sample measured contained alcohol.

The term apparent extract implies that there must also be an actual extract. There is, and it's called real extract. Real extract is determined by first removing the alcohol from a sample of beer or wine by distillation. Then, the sample volume is adjusted to the predistillation volume with water and the density of the sample is measured. Real extract is useful, because it indicates how much of the wort extract was fermented by the yeast during fermentation. This number is directly related to alcohol content and is a better indicator of body than ADF. When the degree of fermentation or real attenuation is calculated using real extract, the term "real degree of fermentation," or RDF, is used. Very few homebrewers or small-scale commercial brewers have the tools required to determine real extract. Instead, they rely on apparent extract and ADF for routine monitoring of their brews.

Alcohol content is another factor most brewers want to know about their beer. The alcohol content of beer can be estimated using the wort original gravity and its apparent extract. It is important to recognize that the alcohol content of beer can only be known for certain by measuring alcohol directly, usually by distillation, because calculations relating alcohol content to original gravity and apparent extract make many assumptions about the fate of carbohydrates during fermentation.

In simplistic terms, 1 molecule of glucose is converted to 2 molecules each of carbon dioxide and ethanol during fermentation. By weight, fermentation yields 0.5111 grams (0.018 oz.) of ethanol for every gram of glucose fermented. In reality, there is more going on during fermentation. Yeast cells are increasing in number, and a whole host of metabolic intermediates being spun off from fermentation follow different biochemical pathways, many of which result in the formation of flavor-active compounds. What this means in practical terms is that there is less than 0.5111 grams (0.018 oz.) of ethanol being produced per gram of glucose. Based on empirical data, brewers know that about 45 percent of the fermented extract (real, not apparent) is converted to ethanol.

CHAPTER 6

Fermentation and Lagering

Q **What is the difference between primary fermentation and secondary fermentation?**

A Primary fermentation occurs when yeast is added to aerated wort and ends when the change in beer specific gravity either dramatically slows or stops. After primary fermentation, most brewers, using carboys and other fermenter types without bottom cones, transfer the beer to another fermenter, usually called the secondary fermenter. The aging period taking place in this vessel is typically called secondary fermentation.

Commercial brewers do not use these definitions because they really don't make much sense. Some brewers add krausen beer or fermenting wort that is in the peak of fermentation to beer that has completed primary fermentation. Although this process is simply called krausening, it is a type of secondary fermentation because more fermentables are added to fermented beer.

Other brewers add yeast and sugar to beer that has completely fermented and immediately package. Some commercial brewers simply call this process bottle conditioning, while others use the term secondary fermentation or refermentation. This language makes sense because the beer really is going through a second fermentation because of the addition of priming sugar.

Brewing terminology varies by brewer or brewery, and I try not to get caught in bickering over semantics. It is helpful to know that a term, such as secondary fermentation, does not mean the same thing to all brewers.

Q What temperature should the wort be before I add yeast?

A I prefer cooling my wort to my target fermentation temperature or a degree or two less and aerating it before adding yeast. This makes fermentation temperature control easier, because all you need to worry about is dissipating the heat produced by fermentation. This process is easy to do in small fermenters. If you start out too warm, you may have a hard time getting the fermentation down to the temperature range you want without doing more than relying on air to cool the fermenter.

This is really straightforward advice, but it does require one important item: a wort cooler capable of cooling the wort down to your target temperature. Both immersion and counterflow coolers can do the job, provided that they are sized appropriately and that the cooling water flowing through the chiller is at least 5°F (3°C) cooler than the desired wort temperature.

■ ══════════ ■

Q What is the best way to siphon or rack beer between my primary and secondary fermenters?

A The proper tool for siphoning from primary fermenter to secondary is a racking cane. This device has a rigid tube usually made from PVC or acrylic. A tip on one end holds the tube off the bottom of the fermenter to get the suction of the tube above the yeast sediment. A flexible hose on the other end is attached to the secondary fermenter after priming.

Racking cane

The easiest way to start a siphon is by sucking on the flexible hose until beer is below the level in the primary, then quickly placing the hose into the secondary. This method works, but it is pretty crude. If you mouth-siphon, I suggest using a removable implement, such as a turkey baster minus the rubber ball, so that you are not putting your mouth on the siphon tube.

Another reliable method is to fill the racking cane and hose with water and start the siphon with a primed hose. This method is difficult to describe and takes a bit of practice, but is my preferred method of starting a siphon. If you don't want the water in your beer, you can easily collect the water in a small container, stop the siphon by pinching the hose, and then resuming the siphon after the hose has been placed into the secondary.

Some clever siphon starters available from homebrew supply houses make siphoning easy. Some have check valves or plungers to prime the siphon and others have sterile filters attached to a carboy cap that allow you to blow air through the filter and into the carboy to start the siphon.

Q My yeast is foaming up through the *airlock* like mad? Is it contaminated?

A It sounds like you are witnessing a normal fermentation! The foamy ferments are most likely not contaminated by bacteria during the foam-over. Foam, or krausen volume, is a function of several variables. The two most important are yeast strain and the pitching rate of viable and vital yeast. In my experience, weizen and wit beer strains of yeast take the grand prize when it comes to krausen volume. Normal ale and lager strains seem to have krausen volumes that are comparable to each other. In general, increased pitching rate results in a more aggressive fermentation with more krausen. The caveat to this statement is that the yeast pitched must be viable (alive) and vital (healthy).

Commercial brewers anticipate an aggressive fermentation because they really want to use healthy yeast and pitch enough to get a rapid fermentation. They want a rapid fermentation, in part, to minimize the time taken for primary fermentation — after all, time is money. But more importantly, rapid and aggressive fermentation is one of the best ways to reduce the risk of contamination during fermentation. A good pitching rate when using yeast harvested from a previous fermentation is about 250 mL (8.5 oz.) of thick yeast slurry per gallon (3.8 L) batch.

A slow, pathetic fermentation takes several days for pH reduction and for alcohol levels to rise. Alcohol and lower pH are two keys to suppressing the growth of bacterial invaders, especially during the early stages of fermentation. Excessive foaming and a big mess in the airlock can certainly cause problems if environmental contaminants begin to grow and make their way into the fermenter.

Another serious problem that can occur with blowoff is that the airlock becomes plugged and blows off the fermenter like a rocket or the fermenter breaks, for example, if a carboy is used. I personally do not like to see bubbler-style airlocks on fermenters during rapid fermentation. A better device is a large tube with an outside diameter that is the same as the inside diameter of the carboy opening. Make the hose long enough to place the loose end in a small bucket of water, and you now have a larger version of an airlock. This style of airlock is much less likely to become clogged, and if foam does blow off from the fermentation, you can replace the bucket of foamy water without having to remove the airlock.

Another way to minimize blowoff is to use a larger carboy or to make a smaller batch. I would rather make as much beer as I can get out of my kettle and buy a fermenter large enough to handle the volume versus allowing my fermenter to dictate my batch size. A foamy fermentation can be a very healthy sign of good beer to come!

Q Will a slightly higher fermentation temperature ruin my brew?

A High fermentation temperature alone won't ruin a beer. Temperature does play a crucial role in flavors generated from yeast during fermentation. As temperature increases, fermentation rate accelerates; with this faster fermentation come more aromatic compounds. The aromas arise because the metabolic rate is going along at such a clip that more metabolic intermediates are excreted from the yeast cell. I liken this to people getting stinky and sweaty during vigorous exercise.

Fruity is the most common type of aroma associated with warmer fermentations. This generic term includes aromas reminiscent of banana, pineapple, and pear, which belong to a class of compounds called esters. Some esters, like ethyl acetate, smell like solvent (ethyl acetate is used in acetone-free fingernail polish remover). I don't mind fruity beers, but I hate smelling fingernail polish remover when trying to enjoy a pint.

Warm fermentation also increases the concentration of higher alcohols. Higher alcohols, a class of compounds, are known for their spicy, vinous aroma and the propensity to cause headaches. Strong beers normally have detectable levels of higher alcohols, but normal gravity beers, like the one you brewed, shouldn't have a detectable level.

If you discover after bottling and aging that your beer smells fruity, solvently, and vinous, the warmer fermentation is probably the culprit.

DELAYED FERMENTATION

I get a lot of questions about fermentation problems, such as one from a brewer who said fermentation had not started 2 days after pitching active liquid yeast into cooled extract beer. There are three major problems that could delay the onset of fermentation: pitching dead yeast, pitching live yeast that is killed by hot wort, and pitching insufficient yeast (underpitching).

Because this brewer said he'd pitched active yeast, let's rule out the dead yeast explanation. It is possible that the wort was too hot for the yeast, but underpitching is the problem that I find the need to harp on frequently.

Just because you had live yeast doesn't mean there was enough for a normal fermentation. Although I prefer liquid yeast to dry yeast, liquid yeast is a lot easier to underpitch than dry yeast because most homebrewers do not have an accurate method to assess the amount of liquid yeast added to the wort. Dry yeast is easily pitched by weight, and 14 grams (0.5 oz) per 5 gallons (19 L) works very well. In my experience using liquid yeast, even the smack-pack types, it greatly helps to do a propagation step before pitching. One pack added to ¼ to ½ gallons (.94–1.8 L) of wort is a nice intermediate step before adding the yeast to a 5-gallon (19 L) fermenter.

The best advice I can give to prevent problems like this from recurring is to verify wort temperature, aerate well, and pitch a good quantity of viable yeast.

Q After 8 days of primary fermentation, I went to *rack* my beer into a carboy. But, when I opened the bucket for this brew, the beer was busily foaming away. Why was this batch fermenting so slowly?

A I am forced into an unavoidable tangent about the length of fermentation before answering this question. I have yet to figure out why so many recipes for beer include a time period for fermentation. The duration of a brewery fermentation is somewhat dependent on the wort's original gravity and hence a particular recipe. But the most important factors about the duration are the concentration, viability, and vitality of the yeast, the temperature of fermentation, the level of wort oxygenation, and the amount of certain key nutrients, such as zinc. Even breweries with very tight control over every step of the process experience variations in fermentation. I am a firm believer in the "let the fermentation go to completion" method of brewing.

In this particular case, I don't agree that your yeast was behaving oddly simply because it was still fermenting after 8 days. Suppose you underpitched the yeast, a very common occurrence. I would not be surprised at all if the fermentation took longer to begin and end than expected. Or maybe the wort was cooled to 60°F (15°C) instead of 70°F (21°C) and your house temperature was cool due to the time of year; under these circumstances, I would expect a slower fermentation.

What I recommend for all brewers is to rack the beer only after the goals of primary fermentation have been achieved.

If the goal is to ferment to completion, then racking should only occur after the beer's specific gravity is stable or the fermentation is visibly complete. The yeast head thins and usually sinks into the beer as fermentation ends. A foam-free surface is a very good visual indicator that fermentation is complete. Nonetheless, I strongly suggest verifying this observation with a hydrometer. In fermenting some beers, such as lagers that depend on secondary fermentation for carbonation, the beer must be racked before terminal gravity is reached. In both examples, the beer is not racked until the goals of primary fermentation are complete. Don't worry too much about fermentations that seem to move a little slower or a little faster than expected. As long as the fermentation finishes in an acceptable range of time, you're probably fine. I get concerned when a fermentation starts very slowly and lasts longer than about 2 weeks.

***

Q **What would cause my last few beers from not fermenting all the way to the final gravity the recipe calls for? What factors influence fermentation?**

A The final gravity of a beer is an important number to hit. Bottle a beer with residual fermentables, and you are likely to end up with over-carbonated beer and perhaps even bottle grenades. The beer is also likely to taste worty and oversweet. But how do you know where a beer should stop fermenting?

Wort fermentability refers to the percentage of fermentable sugars in wort. Table sugar, unlike wort, contains no unfermentable sugar and is 100 percent fermentable. Wort fermentability typically ranges between 65 and 85 percent. Fermentability depends on three principal variables of the mash: grain types, mash temperature, and mash time.

There is a rather broad range when you look at the finish gravity of beers at the lower and upper ends. For example, a 12° Plato wort (1.048 SG) that is 65 percent fermentable finishes at 4.2° Plato (1.017 SG) compared to 1.8° Plato (1.007 SG) when the fermentability increases to 85 percent. (By the way, I am referring to apparent fermentability gauged using a hydrometer.)

When extracts are used for brewing, you really don't know how they were made and cannot predict the fermentability of the wort, until you experiment with different brands of extract. Brewers who mash can look at a few key variables to predict how their wort should ferment. Worts with a lot of unfermentable sugars typically contain a high percentage of special malts (like crystal malts) and are made using a single temperature mash from 155 to 158°F (68–70°C). Highly fermentable worts usually contain little or no special malts and are made using multitemperature mashes with extended steps in the temperature range from 140 to 150°F (60–65°C). This is how dry beers (remember Bud Dry and Asahi Super Dry?) and some light beers are made.

One easy method of assessing the fermentability of a wort sample is running a forced fermentation. To do this, take a sample of wort from a batch, pitch a healthy dose of yeast (at double the normal rate), and proceed with a quick, warm fermentation. Most brewers who rely on this method put a magnetic stir bar in a flask and speed things up by using a stir plate to continuously stir the fermentation. At home, you can swirl the fermenter periodically. When signs of fermentation end, measure the finish gravity and you have an indicator of where your actual fermentation should end.

Let's assume your test shows that the wort has a low fermentability. Extract brewers don't have much of an alternative other than choosing a different extract. The companies that make extracts make wort the same as all-grain brewers, so the factors affecting fermentability hold true for both. Talk to your local homebrew store about their selection of extracts with respect to fermentability before purchasing.

Or your forced fermentation indicates a high fermentability, but the actual fermentation fails to finish properly. This test result would indicate a problem with the fermentation itself. My guess is that the root cause of your problem falls in this category. Factors such as wort aeration, yeast pitching rate, yeast health (viability and vitality), and yeast strain (flocculation and attenuation traits) dramatically affect the properties of fermentation. In my experience, a normal ale fermentation ferments to completion in 3 to 5 days. Sometimes fermentations that seem slow and lack vigor do not make it to the finish. The key factors are having enough healthy yeast to handle the task and properly aerating your wort. Meeting these needs should set the stage for a strong fermentation.

(See forced fermentation, page 229.)

Q How can I unstick my stuck fermentation?

A The most common cause of a good fermentation that suddenly slows, is poor wort aeration and/or underpitching. A stuck fermentation ferments for several days but the final gravity gets stuck at a higher level than the true final gravity of the wort. The only way to properly diagnose a stuck fermentation is to run a forced fermentation, during which the wort is overpitched and fermented warm. At the end of the forced fermentation, you measure the final gravity and use this number as a benchmark. Though effective, this is not a practical method for homebrewers.

Stuck fermentations are frequently caused by yeast that prematurely flocculate. In most cases, the yeast have been overused and are beginning to lose some of their basic properties. Another possible cause could be nutrient deficiency in the wort (especially low levels of zinc).

Some brewers will try to rouse a stuck fermentation by racking it, or they may krausen the beer to try to get it to the proper final gravity. Krausening involves adding a small amount of new fermenting wort to a fully fermented lagering to create a secondary fermentation.

If you think that you underpitched, review your pitching methods. A rule of thumb is 1 cup (237 mL) of thick yeast harvested from a fermenter or 1 quart (.95 L) propagation per every 5 gallons (19 L) of wort. If you simply follow this advice, your future fermentations should almost always go off without a hitch.

Q **Is it ever good to add oxygen once fermentation has started?**

A I would never aerate beer during fermentation, but this answer would be incomplete if Yorkshire stone squares were not mentioned. Yorkshire stone squares are a type of fermenter developed in Yorkshire, England. A Yorkshire square is an open fermenter with two chambers separated by a deck and connected with some tubes. The center of the deck has an opening that flares upward to allow the fermenting beer to spill up onto the deck.

One key feature of a square is a recirculation device that pumps the beer from the lower chamber and sprays it through a device resembling a showerhead onto the shallow deck that separates the upper from the lower chamber. The beer in the upper chamber flows back into the lower chamber through tubes called organ pipes. Yorkshire squares sound really strange when described — it is no surprise they were invented in merry old England. The pump-over simultaneously rouses and aerates the fermentation. This method of rousing was apparently developed to deal with brewing yeasts that are very flocculent and demand lots of oxygen. The technique works for the brewers who use it, and they make some really nice beers. One of the side effects of aerating a fermentation is abnormally high levels of diacetyl; that's a trait of beers fermented this way.

If all else fails, aerating your beer during fermentation will not be the end of the world. You may even be pleasantly surprised with the resulting beer!

Q I've currently got a Belgian white in my primary, and it's still got a pretty vigorous fermentation after 7 days. Would transferring now be a good idea, or should I wait for the primary fermentation to settle more?

A The main reason to rack the beer from primary to secondary is to reduce the yeast load for aging. This is not absolutely necessary, but it does help reduce autolysis if the beer is aged in the fermenter for several weeks prior to bottling. This method is still widely practiced by commercial brewers, but it is gradually being replaced by the uni-tank method of fermentation in which beer is fermented and aged in cylindrical tanks with conical bottoms that permit removal of yeast without racking. If the beer is still fermenting when you rack it into the secondary, you will carry more yeast over than if you wait until fermentation is substantially finished and the yeast has had a chance to flocculate. It certainly will not hurt the beer to rack it before it is completely finished . . . but if the point is to get it off the yeast, you don't want to rack it too soon.

Doing gravity checks at home can be viewed in a negative light, because each sample is equal to about a half bottle of beer and each time the fermenter is breached with a sampling device you risk contamination. I firmly believe that the pros of sampling far outweigh the cons and like to check my fermentation for completeness. If you don't test it, you really don't know if it fermented properly until it is too late. I take several samples during fermentation to track the progress. This practice gives me a chance to take a corrective measure — adding more yeast, for example, if things are not going as planned. It also produces a sample to taste. If something really bad happens early that results in a bad batch, I prefer to jump ship then instead of spending any more time than necessary on a lost cause. My advice is to test it, taste it, and rack it when the time is right!

Fast Fermentation

What causes a fast fermentation? Assuming a brewer did not ferment at higher temperatures, which would certainly change fermentation rate, the logical explanation has to do with yeast. It is my experience that most homebrewers do one of two things (and often both): 1) Use too little yeast, or 2) use poor quality (dead or darned near dead) yeast that doesn't behave properly. Fortunately, the average homebrewer can fix this second problem by switching to liquid yeast or high-quality dry yeast. The underpitching problem is still pervasive, even when good yeast is used. The best way to ensure adequate pitching quantities is to use a yeast starter for a very healthy fermentation!

Q What is a forced fermentation?

A A forced fermentation reaches completion faster than the normal batch of beer (made from the same wort and yeast), so that a final gravity value can be obtained for that particular combination of wort and yeast — the two factors affecting the final gravity. The main difference between a forced fermentation and a regular fermentation is that a forced fermentation has a higher yeast density, a higher temperature, and a smaller sample size; it is frequently stirred to accelerate things even more. The reasons for the higher pitching rate and stirring are not only to accelerate the fermentation, but also to prevent the fermentation from hanging or failing to reach completion.

Forced fermentation is akin to reading the end of a novel before the bits in between. Knowing the terminal gravity ahead of the normal fermentation comes in handy when trying to decide whether it's time to rack the barleywine when it stops bubbling at 1.020 SG. This method might not be the highest-tech method in the world but it works, and many brewers rely on forced fermentations to predict the final gravity of a brew. In fact, many professional brewers who use this method will perform a forced fermentation on every wort produced in the brewhouse.

The most important point to remember is that sanitation is as important here as in the normal batch, even though the beer is not mixed with the good stuff. The reason for the sanitation is that certain yeasts and bacteria are capable of overattenuation, or giving a lower final gravity than the normal, or uncontaminated, lot. If this happens in the test batch, then results are not representative of the larger batch — unless, of course, both lots are contaminated.

— ■ ─────────── ■ —

Q **Does fermentation activity cause increased temperature inside my fermenter? I've noticed it seems higher than my room temperature. Do I need to compensate for this difference if it exists?**

A An active fermentation does create an appreciable amount of heat energy. In small fermenters where the ambient air temperature is used for cooling, an increase in fermentation temperature is present as the brew goes into active fermentation. Most brewers compensate for this difference by setting the room temperature a little cooler than the desired fermentation temperature. If you are brewing an ale and you want to keep the beer around 70°F (21°C) during fermentation, you may choose to cool the wort to 68°F (20°C) and set your room temperature at 66°F (19°C). If you have healthy yeast, chances are that fermentation begins before your wort temperature drops down to the ambient temperature. As fermentation proceeds toward completion, the temperature will begin to fall, eventually equalizing with the ambient temperature.

Q My last two 5-gallon (19 L) batches of beer seemed to ferment to completion in about 3 days. I am worried about the effects of such a fast fermentation. Is this going to significantly affect the taste of the beer?

A I will assume that this 3-day fermentation was an ale and not a lager. In commercial brewing, ale fermentations often finish in 3 days, and many popular domestic microbrews ferment just as quickly.

One possible side effect of a very fast primary fermentation is the temptation to skip over the diacetyl rest and jam the beer into cold storage for clarification purposes, then fill it into bottles or a keg too quickly. The diacetyl rest, a 2-day hold at fermentation temperatures before going into cold storage, allows diacetyl precursors secreted by yeast during fermentation to convert to diacetyl. This process takes time and occurs more quickly at warm temperatures as opposed to cool ones. After the diacetyl rest the yeast can absorb diacetyl and turn it into compounds that have much higher flavor thresholds (difficult to smell) than diacetyl and do not smell like butter.

If the diacetyl rest is skipped and the beer is bottled with diacetyl precursors present, the precursors will begin turning into diacetyl (especially if the beer is stored warm) and will stay in the beer if no yeast is present to reabsorb it. (See fast fermentation, page 228, and diacetyl, page 331.)

Q I dry hopped with hop pellets in my second-ary fermenter, and it looked like lots of bubbles were slowly coming out of the muslin bag and filling my airlock. Were the hops causing another fermentation, or were they simply rehydrating?

A I once was a bubble watcher, too, but no longer. Tracking the course of fermentation without using a hydrometer is like hiking without a map; you may end up in the right spot, but a map makes things a whole lot easier. And without taking gravity checks toward the end of fermentation, you don't really know if fermentation is complete. In my experience at the brewery where I work, ale fermentations quickly drop to near-completion and then slowly cruise into their finish gravities over several days.

Let's assume this fermentation was indeed complete. My guess is that the hops you added were packed into the muslin bag a bit too tight and did not immediately hydrate. I assume they were packed in tightly because the bag had to be small enough to fit through the small hole in the carboy. The gas you observed was likely caused by a combination of slow hydration and the hops acting as nucleation sites for gas breakout. Even in finished beer stored at atmospheric pressure, dissolved carbon dioxide is present. Slight increases in temperature will drive the carbon dioxide out of the beer until equilibrium is reestablished.

Personally, I do not see the need to place hops for dry hopping in a muslin bag. When using pellet or whole hops, it is OK to put the hops into the secondary fermenter and to simply rack the beer onto the hops. Once the beer has been racked into the bottling bucket, you can easily remove the spent hops from the secondary. If you choose not to use a hop bag, you probably will find a nylon stocking tied to the end of your racking cane handy. The nylon will prevent hop

That Bathtub Ring

A brewer once asked if a ring at the top of a carboy, like one on beer bottles, is a guarantee that the beer has some sort of contamination. Actually, it's probably a good thing.

All beer fermentations have a "bathtub" ring at the top of the beer at the end of primary fermentation. German brewers call this *braun hefe,* or brown yeast, and it is a combination of trub, hop resins, and yeast that combine on top of the brew during fermentation. Some braun hefe ends up stuck to the wall of the fermenter, and some of it ends up in the bottom of the fermenter and looks like little bits of chocolate. If the ring you are describing fits my description of braun hefe, you have nothing to worry about. I'll say that again. A big, thick, crusty, brown, nasty-looking ring of schmoo stuck to the side of the fermenter near the top of the beer is totally normal, and it is also common for some of this crunchy stuff to end up in the bottom of the fermenter with yeast. Do not worry about it!

particles from being siphoned to the bottling bucket. The key with dry hopping is to allow the hops to fully hydrate and not be restrained after they swell up — this would be less effective. My suggestion for future dry-hop trials is to eliminate the muslin bag. (See dry hopping, page 143.)

Q **Will the lack of krausen removal have a major effect on the flavor of my beer?**

A The topic of krausen removal is not discussed much in commercial brewing circles because most modern fermenters are not designed to remove krausen. And frequently, blowover creates an unwanted mess in the brewery. This is not to say that krausen removal has no effect on beer flavor. Some brewers firmly believe that krausen removal helps smooth out the flavor of beer. Anheuser-Busch has specially designed fermenters that remove the braun hefe (brown yeast) from beer during fermentation. The braun hefe is the trub-yeast-scum that floats on top of beer during fermentation. Many other brewers in the world have their own special way of removing braun hefe during fermentation. Every brewer should taste braun hefe just for grins; most of us will agree that it doesn't taste all that good. This is one of the reasons that traditional methods of fermentation involved *skimming*.

It sounds like you removed the braun hefe by relying on an active and aggressive fermentation to blow it out of your fermenter. This method works well to push the brown crud out of your fermenter, but I doubt that it has a drastic effect on beer flavor. I think skimming is one of many techniques that are used to make subtle changes to beer flavor.

Most commercial brewers have gone to uni-tank fermenters since the late '80s. Beer is fermented — usually without "blowing over" — and aged in the same vessel. During this time, the krausen rises and falls, yeast cells grow and flocculate, and the beer goes from wort to aged beer. It makes a brewer wonder how many subtleties have disappeared because of this method of fermentation.

Q **I brewed an Imperial Stout, and after the primary fermentation was complete, probably a month ago, I racked the stout into the secondary. I got busy, and there it remains. The airlock is still in place, and there are still small bubbles rising to the top. Will I need to do anything different from the normal priming and bottling?**

A Many beers, especially big beers such as Imperial Stouts, mellow with extended aging in the secondary fermenter. It is usually best to place the secondary in a cool place for extended aging to prevent excessive yeast autolysis and to stunt the growth of bacteria that may be slowly growing and contributing funky flavors to your beer.

Your beer has only been around for a month, so it probably is still OK, but take a sample of the beer and taste it. If it tastes like good beer, then continue to the next step and don't worry too much. Depending on the type of yeast you used and the room temperature, the beer may have very little yeast left in suspension. Visual inspection in a very thin glass will show how much yeast is suspended in the beer. Another point to keep in mind is that the yeast in solution may not be in great health. If the beer seems extremely clear or if you feel the yeast may be cranky, you may want to add some yeast to ensure proper carbonation.

The actual amount of yeast required for *conditioning* is extremely small, about one-tenth the amount required for pitching. Although I recommend using liquid yeast for pitching wort when possible, dry yeast works very well for bottle conditioning. Let's face it, all you really want the yeast to do is to cough out a little carbon dioxide and then sink to the bottom and keep quiet! As long as you choose a brewing-quality dry yeast, you'll be fine.

When using dry yeast, it is always best to hydrate the yeast in boiled and cooled water before use. The easiest way to measure out a very small quantity of yeast into your bottling carboy is to hydrate a whole pack of brewing yeast in a known volume of water: 8 ounces (237 mL) works well. Then use about 1 ounce (about 2 tablespoons/30 mL) of the slurry per 5 gallons (19 L) of beer for conditioning purposes. If you decide to do this to ensure proper carbonation, be sure to mix the yeast slurry and priming sugars evenly in the beer prior to bottling. If the beer still tastes good on bottling day, your unintentional neglect shouldn't cause any future problems. (See high-gravity fermentations, page 405.)

I just switched over to brewing lagers from ales, and I am noticing the yeast is taking a long time to start up compared with my ale batches. Could I be doing something wrong?

The lag between pitching yeast and the onset of vigorous fermentation is determined by pitching rate, wort aeration, and wort temperature. When seasoned ale brewers brew lagers, they often make the mistake of simply switching yeast strains and fermentation temperature.

In my experience, lagers ferment much better when a higher pitching rate is used. For example, many commercial ale brewers use between 5 and 10 million yeast cells per milliliter of wort, while some lager brewers typically use between 15 and 20 million yeast cells per milliliter of wort. Homebrewers do not usually count yeast cells like commercial brewers, but given the same type of yeast-slurry thickness, you would need to double or triple your pitching volume to get these results. It is my experience that many brewers add insufficient amounts of yeast. Your description of the slow start sounds like a classic case of underpitching.

Wort aeration also has a dramatic influence on the length of the lag time because the yeast uses oxygen for growth. Low wort-oxygen levels translate to decreased yeast growth, lower peak-cell density in solution, and longer fermentation times. The best methods for aeration utilize some device to actively transfer oxygen into wort, such as an aeration stone. Simply splashing the wort as it enters the carboy is not as effective as an aeration stone, and relying on oxygen from the atmosphere to diffuse into the wort by briefly leaving the airlock off is the least effective method. If you are using the latter technique, your slow starts could certainly be due to poor aeration. Try a different method, then put the airlock on immediately to minimize the risk of contaminating your wort with airborne microorganisms.

Finally, there is the temperature variable. Some lager brewers like to add plenty of yeast, begin fermentation between 46 and 48°F (7–8°C) and allow the fermentation to rise to about 52°F (11°C). These brewers feel this method produces the cleanest lager flavor. Other brewers advocate beginning fermentation around 70°F (21°C) and cooling it down to around 52°F (11°C) after fermentation begins. This method compensates for lower cell densities by stimulating yeast growth. I have experimented with various methods and have found that some lager strains are more finicky than others and really don't work well with cool starts. The lager strain I most frequently use is a German Pilsner strain. It works best for me if I use a healthy pitching rate and begin fermentation no cooler than 52°F (11°C). I typically see active signs of fermentation within a day of pitching, and primary fermentation is usually complete within 14 days.

Q When I lager, should I drop the temperature quickly or gradually?

A There are several different lagering practices used around the world. The world's largest lager brewer, the one with the Eagle trademark, ferments its beer near 55°F (13°C) and holds its flagship brand at the same temperature for its 3-week krausen process. The idea behind this practice is that the yeasts still have work to do and cooling the beer to very cold temperatures will drastically slow their metabolic activity. Other brewers slowly cool the beer from around 50 to 32°F (10–0°C) over several days to allow the yeasts to finish their work and to start the beer's clarification process. Other brewers quickly cool their beer from 50 to 32°F (10–0°C) under the "don't waste time" philosophy.

One lagering method that is gaining in popularity, especially in Europe, is to warm the beer to 68°F (20°C) after fermentation for an accelerated diacetyl rest. After about 2 days, the beer is then chilled to 32°F (0°C) for lagering. In a commercial brewery, tanks are designed to cool beer, not heat it up, and this method requires special equipment. However, at home it is easy enough to carry a 5-gallon (19 L) carboy from one spot to another to change the beer's temperature, so it's easy to try this method at home. Commercial and home brewers use these methods of fermentation and lagering successfully to make good beer. The method of choice really depends on which one seems to work best for the individual brewer. When lagers are about 2° Plato (8–10 specific gravity points) higher than the terminal gravity, I suggest transferring to a soda keg and allowing the beer to naturally carbonate at 50°F (10°C) for 4 days. Then cool the beer to 39°F (4°C) for 10 days, and finally, cool the beer to 32°F (0°C) for 2 weeks.

Q What is the right temperature for a diacetyl rest?

A There is no right temperature at which to do a diacetyl rest, the process of allowing the beer to remain on the yeast after fermentation finishes to reduce diacetyl and the buttery flavors it causes. Ale brewers use a warm temperature (65–75°F/18–24°C), and some lager brewers use their primary fermentation temperature. Others warm the beer up to ale temperatures, and some high-tech, chemical engineer–brewer hybrid types heat the beer to pasteurization temperatures and pass it over an immobilized yeast column to reduce diacetyl in only a couple of hours. The most helpful thing I can do to help answer your question is to go over some facts about the rise and fall of diacetyl in beer:

- Yeast cells do not produce diacetyl but the precursor of diacetyl called *alpha-acetolactate*. This compound is secreted from the yeast cell and is converted into diacetyl in beer through a chemical oxidation reaction. The conversion of alpha-acetolactate to diacetyl can be catalyzed by numerous oxidizing compounds, including oxygen, iron, and copper.

- Yeast can reduce diacetyl only if the alpha-acetolactate has had an opportunity to convert to diacetyl. Higher temperature diacetyl rests speed aging because the conversion rate of alpha-acetolactate to diacetyl increases with temperature.

- Yeast will reduce diacetyl only if the yeast cells are alive, kicking, and have access to diacetyl (beer). Yeast that is too flocculent often produces beer high in diacetyl, because by the time the diacetyl is ready to be reduced, the yeast is lying on the bottom of the fermenter. The need to increase yeast surface area during aging is one of the reasons a certain big brewery says it uses beechwood chips.

- Diacetyl also can come from bacterial contamination. Certain *lactic acid* bacteria that spoil beer have the ability to crank out enormous quantities of diacetyl. For example, the rich butter aroma found in many wines comes from an intentional bacterial malolactic fermentation usually accomplished by adding *Leuconostoc oenos* following primary fermentation. Yeast, especially lager yeast, is a common vector of lactic acid bacteria.

- Diacetyl also can mysteriously appear in a beer following packaging if the beer still contains alpha-acetolactate. Remember that alpha-acetolactate converts to diacetyl when it is oxidized. Since bottling always incorporates some oxygen, beers that have been insufficiently aged at very cold temperatures may develop a nice diacetyl nose after bottling. This scent is a good sign that the diacetyl rest was unsuccessful.

When brewing lagers, I use a fairly specific temperature profile during fermentation. I ferment my lagers at 50°F (10°C) until the gravity reaches about 1.014 SG. At this point I transfer the beer to a keg for natural carbonation. The keg is held at 50°F (10°C) for 4 days, and the pressure is maintained at 15 psi. This gives me a naturally carbonated lager without the need for carbonating after aging. After this period, I cool the lager to 40°F (4°C) and hold it for 10 days. Finally, I cool my lagers to 32°F (0°C) and lager them for 3 to 4 weeks. This method works for me, but as I said, there is more than one way to age a lager!

Q What is the best way to approximate your final gravity when developing a recipe?

A Predicting the final gravity of a brew is very difficult for numerous reasons. Yeast strain, yeast health, pitching rate, fermentation procedure, wort aeration, mashing, the type of malts used, and the concentration of minerals (especially zinc), all affect wort attenuation. Yeast has a large influence on attenuation; suppliers cite typical attenuation rates for the strains they sell.

If all variables relating to yeast (health, pitching rate, aeration, fermentation procedure, wort aeration, and zinc concentration) are held constant, the final gravity of beer can easily be changed by altering the mash profile. Holding constant all variables relating to yeast is a monumental task, but it is possible! In general, lower mash temperatures (140–150°F/60–65°C) produce more fermentable worts than high mash temperatures (155–160°F/68–71°C). Conversely, higher mash temperatures give better extract yields, because of increased temperature and alpha-amylase activity. Certain grains also affect final gravity. Crystal malts are well known for increasing the final gravity, and starch adjuncts, like rice and corn, can decrease final gravity. Simple sugars (like white sugar, brown sugar, and Belgian candi sugar) are the most fermentable ingredients and are used by some brewers to boost the alcohol content of beer without increasing the final gravity.

There is no master calculation that can account for all of these variables to predict final gravity. The brewers who are really concerned about hitting their final gravities are the big guys. They make the same beer day in and day out and are able to focus their attention on key variables. Their yeast is consistent; they are not experimenting with new raw materials. These brewers can adjust their mash profile to gain sufficient control over their final gravity. Some add zinc to wort in the brewhouse; small changes in concentration have a pronounced effect on yeast performance.

In my opinion, the brewer can best affect final gravity during wort production. During fermentation, we can change the temperature of the beer or cause the fermentation to prematurely stop by cooling it, but this method is riddled with flaws. Yeast strain can also be changed, based on the attenuation rate and the type of beer being brewed. Although yeast strain does influence final gravity, you can't really predict yeast performance based upon typical attenuation ranges because the strain is influenced by too many environmental factors.

You have asked one of those questions that simply do not have a precise answer. In a sense, brewers set the stage and the yeasts take it from there. We can augment the grain bill, tweak the mash temperature, adjust wort aeration rates, add yeast nutrients, and play with pitching rates. After that, the fermentation takes over, and we become observers to a fascinating process.

Q **I prefer brewing German-style lagers. Although my beginning gravity is always close, my final is always two or three points higher than desired. When racking into the secondary, could I be leaving too much bottom-feeding yeast in the primary?**

A This problem is familiar, as I have struggled through developing a method to ensure that my own lagers finish around my target final gravity. I used to judge when to transition from the primary to secondary based upon fermentation activity and then allow the beer to stay in the secondary for a set number of days at the same temperature, usually around 50°F (10°C). Then I would gradually cool the beer down to 32°F (0°C) for lagering. I have found that lagers finish higher than desired because fermentation was cut short by premature cooling to temperatures below 38°F

(4°C) — at that point, lager yeast typically stops fermenting. Lager fermentations behave differently than ale fermentations as they near completion. Ales usually transition from the original gravity to the final gravity in a rapid fashion — 3 to 5 days is normal for worts in the 12 to 14° Plato (1.048–1.056 OG) neighborhood. Lagers on the other hand, will drop within 1 to 2° Plato (4–8 gravity points) in the first 5 to 7 days of fermentation and then slowly drop to the final target gravity. This period can last as long as 2 weeks.

The method I currently use is based upon "go, no-go" points commonly found in quality control programs that larger breweries use. The idea is simple, even though developing a program takes time and implementing that program requires diligence. I had lagers that were finishing all over the place, and I could detect obvious flavor differences between batches of the same recipe. This is not a good thing! To tighten the process a bit, I established target points that had to be met during fermentation and before the next step could begin.

The method I have developed to ferment most lagers has five steps:

1. **Ferment at 54°F** (12°C) until gravity is within 1.0–1.5° Plato of the finish gravity.

2. **Spund the fermenter** (a special valve that releases pressure at a defined point is made for spunding) and allow the beer to carbonate naturally.

3. **Cool the beer to 38°F** (4°C) 6 days after spunding, only if the beer has reached the target finish gravity. The beer is then held at 38°F (4°C) for 10 days.

4. **Cool the beer to 32°F** (0°C) and hold for at least 7 days.
5. **Filter the beer** and transfer to the serving tank.

I use this procedure to produce 1-month lagers (a typical duration for fermentation and aging in commercial breweries). When I brew stronger lagers like doppelbock, I extend the fermentation and cold-aging steps. The key is meeting the goal of each step before proceeding to the next. For steps 1 and 3, take a gravity sample to verify the goal. Time and temperature parameters mark completion in steps 3 and 4. The methodology is quite simple.

Frequently, recipes include vague terms, because a recipe, by nature, is only a road map that describes how one brewer made a batch using certain ingredients and pieces of equipment. Some recipes lay down times like lines in the sand. For example, "ferment for 7 days, rack to the secondary, and hold for 3 weeks before bottling." This type of instruction is great for describing the overall process but should not be used as action items on a calendar. They are not qualified with goals that can be measured. My simple yet effective monitoring method has given me lagers much more consistent in finish gravity.

The other extremely important thing with brewing lagers is yeast. Whenever I have flavor problems or lagging fermentations, the first thing I turn to is the yeast. Questions about age, pitching rate, adequate wort aeration, and propagation steps are all important to address when dealing with lagging fermentations. I don't offer too many guarantees with my advice, but I will offer this tidbit: Lager fermentations almost always lag at the end if your brew is underpitched. Since pitching rate refers to the number of living cells added to wort, underpitching can be a result of yeast viability or simply not adding enough cells.

I'll offer another assurance with respect to finish gravity and other beer specifications. Recipes give a laundry list of ingredients, procedures, and all sorts of numerical specifications that will be met at each step. The fact is, these numbers can only realistically be met if you take the time to tweak the recipe. Parameters such as wort fermentability can rarely be replicated simply following a mashing profile in a recipe. To really hone in on these somewhat illusive targets, minor adjustments to the mash profile, mash thickness, water salts, and base malt type may be required. In other words, if you get close to a target cited in a recipe, you may have done everything well and have no problems to solve!

Q My fermenting lager smells like sulfur. Will it affect the taste of my beer?

A Welcome to the wonderful and often smelly world of lager brewing! The lore of lager brewing is steeped in glorious tales of storing large wooden barrels of beer in deep earthen cellars to slowly mature, patiently awaiting consumption. These stories may be romantic, and for the most part true, but the plain fact is that lager beers usually have a strong sulfur stench that only mellows with time. Like ale yeasts, many different lager strains exist, and they each have their own character. It is safe to say, however, that most lager yeast strains produce more sulfur aromas compared with ale yeast. These stinky smells usually begin to blossom after the first 2 or 3 days of fermentation and slowly mellow from that point.

Unlike some beer flavors, such as the buttery diacetyl and the green applelike acetaldehyde, that mellow with time due to their uptake by yeast, sulfur aromas escape from the beer and pass into the atmosphere. This trait is why commercial breweries do not lager in a sealed container. Instead, they age lagers in aptly named lager vessels fitted with some type of constant pressure valve. These devices allow the brewer to carbonate the lager naturally by trapping a certain top pressure of carbon dioxide produced from fermentation, usually about 15 psi, and letting the excess carbon dioxide escape. The ability for the excess pressure to escape is critical because the vented carbon dioxide carries with it the volatile sulfur compounds produced during primary fermentation. In time, the sulfur smells will drop to an acceptable level.

Subtle sulfur aromas are a crucial part of the aroma profile of a good lager. Some factors that affect the amount and type of sulfur aromas. Pitching rate and wort original gravity play important roles in the amount of sulfur compounds produced during fermentation. Usually, lower pitching rates and/or high original gravity worts will produce more sulfur aromas.

Yeast nutrient levels also influence sulfur levels. Worts that are low in sulfur-containing amino acids, such as methionine, typically produce more sulfury aromas during fermentation. Nutrient-deficient worts are not normally encountered when brewing all-malt beers, but they are typically found when high percentages of nutrient-devoid adjuncts, such as rice and corn, are used. To combat this problem, many large-scale brewers add proprietary yeast nutrient blends to their fermentations.

When brewing lagers, a detectable amount of sulfur aromas will always be produced during fermentation. The key to controlling it is patience. If you are patient and the beer still smells too sulfury, then begin looking at other factors such as yeast strain, pitching rate, original gravity, and adjunct usage.

■ ════════ ■

Q **I can't seem to get rid of diacetyl when I brew lagers. The problem is that I cannot taste the diacetyl in the green beer; I can detect it only after the lagering period. Is there any hope, or am I an ale drinker for the rest of my days?**

A The first thing that comes to mind when contemplating diacetyl problems is yeast strain. Highly flocculent yeast strains are often associated with diacetyl problems, because the yeast drops out of solution before the diacetyl in the beer is reduced. The observation you make about detecting no diacetyl in the green beer before racking but picking it up after is important. I think you are picking up some oxygen during your racking step, and the oxygen converts diacetyl precursor (alpha-acetolactate) in the green beer into diacetyl during lagering.

Another possible cause is bacterial growth that occurs slowly and shows up later in the process. If you maintain effective sanitation practices and ferment with healthy yeast, this is probably not the problem.

Yet another possibility is that you detect the diacetyl only late in the process when some of the funky flavors associated with fermenting and young beer have mellowed; the diacetyl was present before you racked to lagering, but you were unable to taste it.

Let's get back to the late-blooming diacetyl. It is quite common, and prematurely chilling the beer causes it. What happens is that diacetyl precursor remains in the beer after the yeast has been effectively knocked out by chilling. Any oxygen or oxidizing ions, like iron or copper, later convert the precursor to diacetyl; there will not be any yeast left to mop it up. Krausening is an effective technique to correct diacetyl problems associated with rushed fermentation; however, this technique cannot mend bacterial problems.

Most brewers who krausen add about 1 part krausen beer to 9 parts finished beer. The key to the method is an actively fermenting population of yeast. The high krausen stage of fermentation is the peak of excitement — for ales this occurs about 24 hours after pitching and for lagers about 48 to

72 hours after pitching (yeast health and pitching rate heavily influence both durations).

If you are going to take the time to save your buttery brew, spend a little time making a krausen beer. I would suggest making 2 quarts (about 2 L) of wort using dry malt extract and a sprinkle of hops to get the bitterness in the same ballpark as your troubled batch. If I were doing this, I would boil the wort for 30 to 60 minutes, transfer to a gallon jug, screw on the lid, and throw the jug in the fridge or in an ice bath to cool it down. Such a small volume will be easy to cool without a wort chiller. Once cooled to about 68°F (20°C), add your lager yeast and start the propagation. At this time, move your keg out of cold storage and allow it to warm up to around 60°F (15°C) in preparation for the yeast. Keep an eye on the progress of the starter. When it kicks into high gear (approaches high krausen), transfer this to your keg. Hold at 60°F (15°C) for 1 to 2 weeks and move it back into cold storage. You may want to rack before transferring back to the cold to remove the yeast added with the krausen beer.

(See diacetyl rest, page 240, and krausening, page 214.)

Q **What would cause my lagers to taste more like ales?**

A A warmish lager fermentation sometimes produces a fruitier lager than cooler temperatures, for example, 50°F (10°C). Many brewers use the practice of warming a lager after the primary fermentation is complete to accelerate diacetyl reduction; typically it has no affect on aroma compounds related to fermentation (as fermentation is complete when the temperature is increased). Yeast strain can also make a lager smell like an ale. Many lagers have a distinctive sulfur aroma and lack the fruity esters found in many ales — this aroma profile typifies lagers. This is not true of all lager strains and some have little sulfur in the nose and can be slightly fruity (to the point that they're mistaken for ale). Anchor Steam is a lager fermented in the 65°F (18°C) range that is known for its alelike aroma. Ingredient selection is another factor that can confuse the yeast strain. For example, if you make a really hoppy wort with ale hops, such as Cascades, the finished beer may be so dominated by an aroma typically associated with ales that the yeast strain becomes a nonfactor. There are many commercially available stouts actually made using lager yeast. The typical consumer would never be the wiser because the dark grains and hopping dominate the flavor.

Q I was wondering whether or not you should 1) remove hops and 2) remove trub?

A I would advise hop and trub removal because that is how beer as we know it is made. Leaving the hops in the fermenter will have a different flavor effect, and leaving the trub in the wort will also affect flavor. Furthermore, if you plan to reuse the yeast, a practice I recommend for several reasons, trub separation is advisable because trub leaves a film on the surface of the yeast cell, leading to longer lag times in subsequent fermentations. Also, you have better chances of brewing a clear beer if you remove sediment when you can.

I view brewing as a continual process of extraction and purification. Wort production extracts sugars, colors, and flavors from grain and releases bittering compounds and a wide variety of aromas from the hops. Yeast processes fermentables into alcohol, carbon dioxide, and flavor compounds. Some flavor compounds, such as sulfur aromas, are vented from the beer, and others are retained for their pleasant aromatic properties. Clear beer is then separated from yeast solids, often by using a filter or some sort of yeast fining. Finally, our body extracts the alcohol out of the beer, and the whole process is brought full circle.

My philosophy is simple: When brewing beer, extract and purify when given the chance, especially if the action affects flavor positively. If removing something from the beer, for example yeast removal via filtration, is found to be detrimental to flavor, don't remove it.

Q Is secondary fermentation really necessary?
If the beer is done fermenting in 10 days, why
not bottle and let the beer condition in the bottle?
Some beer recipes actually state that secondary fermentation occurs in the bottle.

A Secondary fermentation is a loosely defined term
used by both homebrewers and commercial brewers
to describe several different changes that beer undergoes
after its main fermentation. Most brewers would agree that
a true secondary fermentation is used to naturally carbonate
beer, to allow the beer to clarify naturally by sedimenta-
tion, and to allow the beer to mature in flavor. Classical
examples of secondary fermentation include lagering, cask
conditioning, and bottle conditioning.

In the true lager process, beer is transferred from the
primary fermenter when some residual fermentable sugars remain. In the fermentation of a normal strength
beer, a common point for the transfer is when the gravity has dropped to about 1.016 SG. In traditional lagering
the beer is held in a closed vessel (the secondary) at cold
temperatures for a period of 3 to 12 weeks. During this
period, fermentation completes, the beer becomes carbonated, yeasts settle out of the beer (resulting in clarity), and
green flavors (such as the buttery-smelling diacetyl and
green-applelike acetaldehyde) left in the beer from primary
fermentation mellow.

The krausen process is a variation of the lager process,
except the beer is completely fermented during the primary

fermentation, and actively fermenting beer, or krausen, is added as the beer is transferred to the aging tank.

Cask-conditioned ales are somewhat similar to krausened lagers, except priming sugar, usually corn sugar, is added to the completely fermented ale instead of actively fermenting wort. Also, cask-conditioned ales are usually dry hopped for aroma and have finings added to the cask to accelerate clarification. Like lagers, cask ales mature in flavor, carbonate, and clarify during their secondary fermentation. The process is much shorter, however, lasting several days versus several weeks.

The last example of a traditional beer using a secondary fermentation is bottle-conditioned beer. Usually, these beers are allowed to settle for some period prior to bottling to remove most of the yeast. When the time is right, the beer is transferred out of the fermenter, priming sugar is added, and the beer is packaged.

Some brewers actually filter the beer after fermentation and add yeast in addition to the priming sugar. The carbonation and flavor maturation then occurs in the bottle. So does natural clarification, when the bottle is left undisturbed.

All of these methods have three things in common: carbonation, flavor maturation, and clarification. Not all beers are made using these techniques. For example, many microbreweries and brewpubs allow the beer to finish fermenting and then hold the beer at fermentation temperature for a couple of days for the diacetyl rest. This time allows for diacetyl that is left after fermentation to be absorbed by yeast and converted into a flavorless compound. After the diacetyl rest, the beer is quickly cooled, filtered, and carbonated.

Beer made using this method can be as tasty and satisfying as one made using a traditional method of secondary fermentation. Maturing flavor and settling yeast are the only differences during its short aging period. However, the beer is not clear, and it is not carbonated.

None of these methods is right or wrong; all can be used to make good beer. The method you are currently using is bottle conditioning, and it does involve a secondary fermentation. If you are happy with the results, stick with it. Personally, I like my bottled beers to contain very little yeast sediment and always allow the beer to settle for at least 1 week before bottling. Whether this is done in a separate carboy or in the same vessel the beer fermented in, the secondary fermentation still occurs in the bottle and the beer is clear, mature, and carbonated.

CHAPTER 7

Bottling, Kegging, and Carbonation

BOTTLING EQUIPMENT

Bottling requires some basic pieces of equipment, assuming that you will bottle condition your beer.

◆ **Bottles.** I suggest buying new bottles at a homebrew supply shop or selecting heavy-duty returnable bottles that can be stripped of their labels and cleaned up. Do not use lightweight, one-way glass bottles that have become the norm for 6-packs of American beer. Even the classic bar bottles that were returnable longnecks have faded into obscurity. I like flip-top bottles, because they are made of heavy glass and do not require caps. If you want flip-tops, expect to pay a pretty penny for them and make sure you get your bottles back if you give beer to friends. Keep in mind that the rubber gasket that seals the lid will require replacement every so often and also requires routine cleaning after every use.

◆ **Bottle trees.** This tool is used to air dry bottles and make the chore of cleaning bottles a little easier.

When you use your bottling equipment for the first time, remember to have priming sugar on your shopping list so that you have everything you need to complete the task.

Bottle tree

◆ **Hose and racking cane.** To get the beer into the bottle, you need a hose. The hose and racking cane you use to rack beer from fermenter to fermenter and from fermenter to bottling bucket works here as well. Little gizmos (racking tube clips) are available to shut off the flow from your siphon hose; these make it easier to transition from one bottle to the next without having to squeeze the siphon hose and risking a mess if not done properly.

◆ **Bottle capper and caps.** These are must-haves.

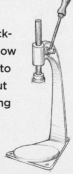

Bench bottle capper

◆ **Counterpressure kit.** A more advanced bottling technique is counterpressure bottle filling. It allows one to bottle carbonated beer that can be consumed immediately after bottling. This technique requires a keg setup with a carbon dioxide cylinder and a counterpressure *filler.* These fillers

Hand bottle capper

have a valve used to pressurize the bottle with carbon dioxide, a beer inlet to bring beer into the pressurized bottle, and a vent valve to allow gas to exit the bottle as beer flows in. If you want to filter your beer and not reyeast for bottle conditioning, these fillers are a must-have tool.

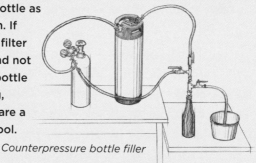

Counterpressure bottle filler

Q What are the basics of bottling?

A Bottling is very easy with the proper equipment. Begin with an elevated bottling bucket so that you are not working on the floor. To bottle a batch, all you need to do is rack the beer into the bottling bucket, mix in your priming sugar, siphon the beer into the bottle, and cap the bottle. It is important to have consistent fill heights and to leave a minimum amount of headspace of about ½ inch (12–13 mm), so that you have minimal air in the headspace. Excessive headspace can result in oxidation as well as undercarbonation.

Q Do you have to sanitize bottle caps before using them?

A Many brewers feel the need to boil their caps to sanitize them before bottling. In my opinion, this step is overly cautious if you are using clean caps that come from a plastic bag. Commercial brewers do not sanitize caps and rely on a supply of clean caps to mitigate the potential of contaminating beer with stuff on the cap. Some crowns have liners in them that scavenge oxygen; moisture activates the substance in the liner. If you use this type of crown, you do not want to get it wet before use, as moisture will render the special liner useless.

Q How can I figure out how much priming sugar to add for carbonation?

A The two most important things to consider before adding priming sugar to your fermented beer and bottling it are 1) the volume of beer you wish to carbonate, and 2) the amount of carbonation you want in the beer.

Assuming you rack your fermented beer to a bottling bucket on bottling day, determining volume is easy. I recommend fixing a vertical strip of masking tape to the outside of the bucket and calibrating the tape by adding a quart (946 mL) of water to the bucket at a time and placing a mark on the tape for each addition.

Volume is important because the amount of priming sugar depends on the amount of beer being carbonated. Even if you always brew the same batch size, the volume of beer to be carbonated varies because some beer may have been lost during fermentation through blowoff, and the amount of beer left in the primary after racking varies with the fluffiness of the yeast.

The second question is: How much carbonation do you personally desire? I can't help you on this decision, but let's just say your last brew was carbonated to your satisfaction and that you added ⅔ cup (158 mL) of priming sugar to 4¼ gallons (16 L) of beer. That works out to be 0.157 cups (37 mL) per gallon (3.8 L) of beer. One cup is roughly the same as 237 mL. Using the metric system, we get 158 mL (⅔ cup) of priming sugar per 16 L (4¼ gallon) or 10 mL per liter.

The next time you brew and get ready to bottle, you can use this figure: Suppose you have 4¾ gallons (18 L) of beer and want to know how much priming sugar to add. This is easily determined by multiplying 4¾ gallons by 0.157 cups of sugar per gallon — you need ¾ cup of sugar. This is equal to about 180 mL. In a small volume of beer, the carbonation produced by ⅔ cup (158 mL) versus ¾ cup (176 mL) is the difference between fully carbonated and undercarbonated. Find out the levels you like in your beer, and you can apply this calculation to future beers.

Q **How much carbon dioxide is produced by the different priming sugars commonly used?**

A Corn sugar (glucose) and *invert sugar* (equal mixtures of glucose and fructose) produce the same results when used for carbonation. Both types of sugars produce 0.489 grams (.017 oz.) of carbon dioxide per gram of sugar (dry weight) when completely fermented by yeast. Sucrose (table sugar) yields 0.515 grams (.018 oz.) of carbon dioxide per gram of sugar (dry weight). Dry malt extract and wort yield a wide range of carbon dioxide levels, because wort fermentability depends on the mashing schedule.

Q What are volumes of carbon dioxide?

A Beers range in carbonation levels, and one measure of carbon dioxide content is the volume. One liter of beer containing two volumes of carbon dioxide has enough carbon dioxide to fill a 2-liter balloon at atmospheric pressure and 32°F (0°C). Most beers range from 2 to 3 volumes of carbon dioxide. In simple terms, 2 volumes seems flat, 2.5 volumes is typical of most bottled beers, and 3 volumes is on the high side for most beers (some weizen beers are up around 5 volumes). Another scale is to express carbonation in terms of grams of carbon dioxide per liter of beer; 4, 5, and 6 grams/liter correspond to 2.05, 2.55 and 3.05 volumes, respectively.

Q I've been conditioning my newly bottled beer upstairs because it's much too cold in the basement. I keep it next to the heater vent, where the average temp is 72°F (22°C). My beer has been carbonated in about 3 to 4 days, whereas in the summer it takes about 2 weeks in the basement. I know that good things come to those who wait, but am I doing my beer a disservice by this method of turbo conditioning?

A This is a real world problem for commercial breweries selling bottle-conditioned beers. As you point out, storing beer in the basement or an underground cellar reduces the air temperature to the average earth temperature of the location of the cellar. In most parts of the world, the average earth temperature is about 55°F (13°C). This temperature impairs the speed of bottle conditioning and, for many ale strains, is really too cold to get much carbonation at all.

This is why bottle-conditioned beers are typically stored in warm cellars controlled to a comfortable temperature of about 75°F (22°C). This temperature is plenty warm for the yeasties to do their work in a reasonable time frame and not so warm that the beer starts to prematurely age because of high storage temperature. This practice is relatively common in Europe and the United States among brewers who bottle condition their beers. I know three breweries with warm cellars: Duvel in Belgium, Sierra Nevada in California, and New Belgium in Colorado. Sierra Nevada holds its beer for about a week before releasing it for sale.

So, in the commercial world of brewing where time is money, warm conditioning reduces the number of cases that are sitting around waiting for carbonation to happen. Bean counters like to minimize this type of inventory. At home, the economic drivers of inventory control are different, but why wait 2 weeks to sample your next tasty brew when you can cut the time to 1 week? There is no reason whatsoever not to practice this method . . . I declare open season on "turbo conditioning"!

Q **I bottled my beer with priming sugar 1 week ago, and it is still flat. Why isn't it carbonating?**

A At this stage of the game, you really have only one option, and that is to wait and see if the beer will carbonate with more time. One week is often too short for beer to carbonate in the bottle. If a batch has a relatively high concentration of healthy yeast and the bottles are conditioned at room temperature, it is common to have fully carbonated beer in a week's time.

However, if the yeast count is low or in poor condition (like old yeast from a batch that has been aged for several weeks prior to bottling), carbonation may take much longer. If this batch remains flat, a quick fix that would make the beer drinkable would be to blend it with a carbonated beer. If it is a flat pale ale, blend it with a carbonated porter in your favorite mug and have a half-and-half. The blend will have a lower carbonation level, but it won't taste quite so flat.

This batch may be a lost cause with respect to its drinking qualities, but it does present a good lesson on bottle conditioning. For brewers who put the entire batch in a keg and wind up with flat beer, I would suggest checking the keg for gasket leaks — after all, if the keg doesn't hold pressure, the beer won't carbonate! The other thing I always question when dealing with weights and volumes is accuracy. Recipes always give priming sugar suggestions based on a 5-gallon (19 L) batch, but a 5-gallon batch rarely contains 5 gallons of beer when it comes time to bottle. When you measured your priming sugar are you sure you measured out the right amount? I don't like relying on sugar volumes for priming (⅔ cup, for example), because powders do not pack or settle consistently. That's the main reason why bakers measure flour volume after sifting. I prefer working with weight measurements.

Finally, think about the yeasts. These little critters pump out the carbon dioxide needed for carbonation and can only do that if they are active. If you have healthy yeast, it really does not take much for conditioning.

■ ━━━━━━━━ ■

Q **To what extent does the use of various dry malt extracts as priming sugars contribute to the flavor or color of the beer?**

A This is a question I often ask myself when reading recipes. It seems to me that using dry malt extract or saving wort for priming is a pain in the neck. The contribution of color or flavor to beer from priming sugar is insignificant compared to the flavor and color present in wort before fermentation. Even if the priming sugar added some flavor, an argument could be made for adding it before wort boiling, for example, brown sugar.

I think the best sugar to use for priming is either corn or invert sugar because they are both 100 percent fermentable and easy to handle. The problem with using wort or dry malt extract (DME) for priming is the inconsistent fermentability of wort. If you use DME with an unknown fermentability for priming, then it's impossible to control the carbonation level. Commercial brewers who prime with wort measure wort fermentability before priming and base the amount of primings on this measured number.

The main difference between beers primed with DME or wort versus those primed with corn sugar is that the beers primed with corn sugar are not in compliance with the *Reinheitsgebot,* the German beer purity law.

Invert sugar consists of equal parts glucose and fructose. When fructose is transported into the yeasts, it's converted to glucose and enters the glycolytic pathway, where it's used as cellular fuel and ends up as alcohol and carbon dioxide. When maltose from wort is transported into the yeast cell, it's first converted to two molecules of glucose and then follows the same biochemical pathway as the glucose from corn sugar. The only difference between wort and a corn sugar solution are the nonfermentable sugars, proteins, and color compounds present in wort. These compounds are present in much higher concentrations in the original wort.

Q **I have some leftover wort with a gravity of 1.113 SG and would like to use it to prime my latest batch of barleywine (original gravity 1.018), but I don't know how much to use. I don't want bottle bombs, nor do I want undercarbonated brew. How much should I add in a 4½-gallon (17 L) batch to give the proper carbonation level?**

A Priming with wort is very tricky, because it is not completely fermentable and its fermentability varies from batch to batch. Breweries that bottle condition with wort determine the fermentability of each lot before use and have tables that enable them to consistently carbonate with it.

If you want your barleywine to be its best and want to carbonate with wort, add 1 liter (34 oz.) of the high-gravity wort to the beer, condition it in a keg, and carefully bleed off the excess pressure to fine-tune the carbonation level. If you try to bottle it using wort, the results very likely will be disappointing unless you do some trial runs to determine the right amount to add. By using a series of voodoo calculations, I estimate your 1.113 SG wort has 190 grams (7 oz.) of fermentable sugar in 1 liter (34 oz.). These 190 grams of sugar will produce about 95 grams (3.4 oz.) of carbon dioxide. A good carbonation level is 5 grams of carbon dioxide per liter of beer; therefore, to carbonate 4.5 gallons (17 L) of beer you will need 900 mL (30 oz.) of your 1.113 SG wort. This sounds convincing, but I don't have much faith in bottle conditioning unless I run some trials. So condition it in a keg or, if bottling, use plain old corn sugar for the priming.

■ ══════ ■

Q Does bottle conditioning greatly improve beer stability? Is it possible to bottle condition my homebrew so there is little or no yeast sediment at the bottom of the bottle?

A Contrary to popular belief, bottle conditioning is not the cure-all to the problems of bottling. It is true that yeast can scavenge some oxygen from bottle-conditioned beer and perhaps ward off oxidation, but the yeast is also very capable of causing flavor deterioration. This process begins when yeast cells autolyze and release intracellular enzymes and yeasty flavors into beer. Some of these enzymes, called *esterases,* break down esters (esters contribute fruitiness to beer) and alter the beer's aroma profile. Other enzymes, *proteases,* chew up foam-stabilizing proteins and reduce foam stability over time. The flavors released when yeast autolyze can make a good beer taste like dead and decaying yeast. Yum! So there are some good reasons to control the amount of yeast in a bottle-conditioned beer. The idea is to have enough yeast to allow for conditioning while keeping the level low enough to minimize the negative effects of yeast autolysis.

You want to begin by first clarifying your homebrew. Several clarification methods do not require filtration. Beer naturally clarifies if held cold, 32°F (0°C), from 5 days to several weeks. Cold storage not only gets rid of most of the yeast, but it also chillproofs the beer, which guards the beer from subsequent chill hazes caused by the coprecipitation of proteins and tannins in cold beer. Fining agents, such as *isinglass* and collagen, can be used to quickly remove yeast from the beer. These finings also provide some protection from chill hazes, although they are not as effective as cold storage.

Another useful technique is to select yeasts that have good flocculation properties. These kinds of yeast will naturally drop from the beer at the end of fermentation. Of course, flocculent yeast coupled with cold storage or finings makes for the easiest clarification, if filtration is not an option. If you do have a filter, then use it to filter cold beer. It is always best to filter beer colder than the anticipated minimum serving temperature to guard against unwanted chill hazes.

After your beer is clarified, add yeast and priming sugar to it. Remember that the quantity of priming sugar depends not only on the desired carbonation level in the finished beer, but on how much beer you are bottling. A bottling bucket with a volumetric scale is always best. The tricky part of this process is adding the yeast, because not much yeast is needed. The target concentration in the beer is about 1,000,000 cells per milliliter of beer. This is about 10 times less than the amount added to wort before fermentation. If you're using dry yeast, about 1 gram (0.04 oz.) per 5 gallons (19 L) of beer will do the trick. If you want to use a liquid yeast slurry, the amount will be a bit more inexact, because yeast concentration is not as consistent in liquid as it is in dry yeast. A rule of thumb is to use 1 mL (0.03 oz.) of thick yeast slurry per liter (34 oz.) of beer or about 19 mL (0.6 oz.) of yeast slurry per 5 gallons (19 L) of beer. I define thick slurry as the consistency of yeast harvested from the bottom of a fermenter.

Q My bottle carbonation always seems to be slightly off, even though I am following the recipe for the amount of priming sugar to add. What is going on?

A Carbonation level is one very important beer attribute that can be somewhat difficult to control, especially if the beer is bottle conditioned. Recipes that call for a volume of priming sugar per batch — for example, ⅔ cup (158 mL) priming sugar per 5 gallons (19 L) of beer — are inherently flawed.

The first problem is that ⅔ cup of priming sugar is not a constant weight because the density (weight per volume) of sugar depends on how fine the sugar is ground and how tightly it is packed into the measuring cup. Carbonation level is a function of the weight of priming sugar added to the beer, not the volume.

The second flaw with priming sugar directions is the assumption that a 5-gallon (19 L) batch actually produces 5 gallons (19 L) of beer at the time of bottling. Steps in the brewing process, such as racking the beer from the primary fermenter to a secondary fermenter or taking samples out of the fermenter for measuring or tasting, result in beer loss. Not every 5-gallon (19 L) batch will have the same losses, and so the volume of beer being primed is always different.

My preferred method for priming is to convert everything to grams of priming sugar per liter of beer. This works well if you have a carboy with a calibration strip taped to the outside. This is used to determine the beer volume to be primed. The carboy is used to hold the beer while the primings are mixed — after they've been carefully weighed on an accurate scale. Home experiments are useful to zero in on the ratio of primings to beer that suits one's personal taste. (See determining priming sugar additions, page 261.)

■ ══════════ ■

Q Is there a rule of thumb to use for the appropriate levels of carbonation for different styles of beer?

A In the United States, carbonation level is expressed in terms of volumes of carbon dioxide. A volume of carbon dioxide is defined as the volume of gas that could be removed from a volume of beer at 20°C (68°F) at one atmosphere of pressure. For example, a liter (34 oz.) of beer with 2.5 volumes would fill a 2.5-liter (84 oz.) bag with carbon dioxide if all the gas were removed at 20°C (68°F) at one atmosphere of pressure. This really is a weird unit of measure! Almost all other countries express carbon dioxide in grams per liter, a more logical measurement.

Most beers in the United States contain between 2.5 and 2.6 volumes of carbon dioxide. Beers such as Bud, Miller, and Coors fall into this carbonation range. These beers served on draft have slightly lower carbon dioxide levels and fall about 0.05 to 0.1 volumes below their bottled brethren. Bottled lagers from Europe have a little less carbonation, about 0.1 volume less than American lagers, but they seem dramatically less fizzy because most European lagers are all malt, and that has a dramatic effect on beer body.

Traditional English ales served from casks have very low levels of carbon dioxide, usually somewhere around 1.8 volumes. Since beer at 55°F (13°C) contains about 1.3 volumes of carbon dioxide when it is sitting in an unpressurized carbon dioxide environment, English ales fall at the very low end of the carbon dioxide scale when compared with other beers from around the world. Bottled ales tend to be higher in carbonation, but they still have less than most lagers. Typical values fall between 2.2 and 2.4 volumes.

The wheat and fruit beers of the world, such as Berliner weiss beers, Bavarian hefe-weizens, Belgian wit beers, and lambics, have very high levels of carbon dioxide to give them a light and refreshing palate. These beers have carbon dioxide levels ranging from 3 to 5 volumes. Like Champagne, these beers are often served in fluted glassware to present them with elegance.

Some generalizations can be drawn about carbonation and flavor. Beers that have complex palates usually have lower levels of carbon dioxide, so the beer's true identity isn't masked by carbonation. Beers with less complex palates that are meant to be served ice cold typically have more carbonation. Since carbonation stimulates the trigeminal nerve, the nerve that is also stimulated by spicy foods, some noted brewing experts have given these beers the nickname "pain beers." Pain beers often derive a significant portion of their flavor from the carbonation, and many taste downright nasty if that high level of carbonation is lost.

When microbrewed beers are dragged into the picture, things get a little jumbled. Most microbrewed beers have complex palates, leading one to speculate that they also have low carbon dioxide levels. However, many have carbon dioxide levels equaling or exceeding American lagers. When consumed, the beers don't seem to be over-carbonated because their full flavors are able to carry a higher level of carbon dioxide without seeming unbalanced.

Rules of thumb are useful guides but cannot be rigorously applied to all scenarios. It is up to the brewer to discover the level of carbonation best for him or her.

Q My lager recipe calls for adding more yeast at bottling time. Is this an accepted method, and do you recommend it?

A The problem with brewing lagers at home is that the yeast almost completely settles out during lagering. Hence, when it is time to bottle, there may not be enough yeast to carbonate the beer.

One solution for homebrew recipes is to add more yeast to the beer, usually in the bottling bucket, at the time of bottling. The method works well, but too much yeast in the bottle can lead to yeasty flavors from yeast autolysis (yeast death and decay) if the bottled beer is stored warm for long periods. If you want to bottle condition a well-aged lager beer, then adding more yeast at bottling is a good idea.

If this practice doesn't appeal to you, an alternative is to age your lager in a keg and carbonate naturally during aging. This is how commercial breweries naturally carbonate their lagers, except they age and carbonate in large lagering vessels and then filter the carbonated beer prior to packaging. To age and carbonate in a keg, rack your lager from the fermenter to the lagering vessel (a soda keg) when the specific gravity is 1.016–1.018 SG and complete the fermentation in the sealed keg. This practice will create sufficient pressure to carbonate the lager.

Age the beer in the same container. After aging, you can rack the beer under counterpressure into another keg or use a counterpressure filler to bottle. If I had to choose a method to brew lagers at home, I would lager in a soda keg, rack the beer off the yeast after lagering, and bottle it or serve it from the keg. This method avoids having to add more yeast, uses no priming sugar for carbonation, and removes the settled yeast before serving. The resulting beer would be a traditional lager beer that uses the same procedures as a commercial brewery minus filtration.

Q How can I use nitrogen to carbonate my beer?

A The process of adding nitrogen to beer is referred to as nitrogenation. This is somewhat of a misnomer, since nitrogenated beers also contain carbon dioxide and the gas blend used for the process is usually 75 percent nitrogen and 25 percent carbon dioxide. This mix is used to dispense draft Guinness Stout and is easy to find in markets that have draft Guinness.

Nitrogenated beers typically contain very low amounts of carbon dioxide, around 2.4 g/L or 1.2 volumes, and an even lower concentration of nitrogen of about 20 mg/L. Typical beers contain about 5 g/L of carbon dioxide and no nitrogen. The concentration of nitrogen is much lower than the carbon dioxide content, because nitrogen is not very soluble in liquids. When dispensed through a special faucet, the nitrogen breaks out of the beer and forms very small, stable bubbles. Nitrogen foams are much more stable than carbon dioxide foams, because the atmosphere is about 79 percent nitrogen and there is not much driving force between the gas concentration in the bubble and the concentration in the atmosphere. That's why nitro beers have such awesome, stable foam. The foam's density and creaminess also add terrific mouthfeel to the beer.

Like many brewers, I love nitrogenated beers and have some rules of thumb on the procedure. Once you have the right equipment (see page 278), follow these steps for proper nitrogenation:

1. Rack your beer to a keg after fermentation is complete (add finings if desired) and pressurize the headspace of the keg with mixed gas (75 percent nitrogen and 25 percent carbon dioxide) to a pressure of 10–15 psi. This pressure seals the keg and does not nitrogenate the

beer. Do not pressurize with 100 percent carbon dioxide because the beer will absorb too much.

2. Transfer the keg to the coldest place you can find, preferably a refrigerator set at about 34°F (1°C) and allow it to clarify for about 2 weeks. Step 2 (alternate): Filter the beer after holding cold for about 1 week. Nitro beers pour much better when they are free of yeast.

3. Make sure your beer is cold (34–38°F/1–4°C). Connect the mixed gas supply to the carbonating stone and set the pressure regulator to 30 psi. Gas will bubble through the beer until the headspace pressure reaches 30 psi. At 30 psi, slowly loosen the pressure-relief fitting on the top of the keg until you hear a very low flow of gas escaping from the fitting. Allow the mixed gas to slowly bubble through the beer for 30 minutes. (If foam begins to come out of the fitting, tighten the fitting and allow the beer to rest for 30 minutes before continuing the slow bleed.) After this 30-minute purge, tighten the pressure-relief fitting and allow the beer to rest for 30 minutes, and then do another 30-minute purge.

4. Hook up the mixed gas to the headspace of the keg and set the pressure regulator to 30 psi. Let the beer sit still for a few hours before pouring.

5. Pour yourself a pint of nitro homebrew! If the foam seems excessive, you should use a lower pressure the next time around. If the beer seems a bit flat, you can repeat Step 3, using a higher pressure.

Equipment for Nitrogenation

Don't bother nitrogenating any beer unless you have the proper faucet. There are many stout faucets on the market that are based on the Guinness faucet. These faucets have a disc with small holes inserted in the beer flow path and a device called a flow straightener placed after the disc. As beer flows through the holes in the disc, pressure drops, causing the nitrogen and carbon dioxide to break out of solution. If the gas blend is just right, you get a great glass of milky-looking beer that settles out with a perfect head.

The other piece of equipment that is very important is a carbonation stone. I recommend the type of stone that can be connected to a stainless-steel rod and attached to the out fitting on a Cornelius soda keg. The stone is important because nitrogen is essentially insoluble and it really helps to have small bubbles dispersed in the beer during the nitrogenation procedure. The key is getting the right gas blend. Too much carbon dioxide results in a large foamy head that doesn't settle properly; too much nitrogen results in wild beer that will foam uncontrollably. Too little dissolved gas produces a pint that just seems flat.

Q **Is it true that only certain styles of beer work well with the nitrogenated draft system?**

A I do love a good pint of mixed-gas beer dispensed from stout faucets: the rich creamy head, the smooth, full mouthfeel, and the amazing drinkability of beers like Murphy's or Guinness. It just so happens that both of these beers are stouts, but any beer can be made to dispense like these, and there are no special recipe requirements.

Q **What determines how long a beer will need to age?**

A Aging. The word alone conjures images of perfection, like a fine wine that has spent a couple of decades in a dank cellar. Aging beer is much different from aging wine because most beers do not benefit from long aging. There are obvious exemptions to this blanket statement; certain Belgian ales, barleywines, and some strong lagers (e.g. bocks and doppelbocks) can change for the better during aging. Usually the beers that benefit from aging have high original gravities and high alcohol contents. The changes that occur during aging are numerous and complex, but two key changes with big effects on flavor are oxidation reactions and yeast autolysis, the latter occurring only in beers containing yeast (bottle-conditioned beers).

Oxidation reactions all require the presence of oxidizing compounds. The most common oxidant is oxygen, but certain metal ions, such as iron (Fe^{3+}) and copper (Cu^{2+}), are potent oxidizers that will quickly change beer flavor. The presence of oxidizing metal ions is never favorable. The most common cause of oxidation is headspace air from bottling. This problem can be minimized if the beer is foamed immediately before capping, but this foaming requires some dissolved carbon dioxide. Oxygen reacts primarily with alcohols (both ethanol and higher alcohols or fusel oils) and lipids in beer to form a class of organic compounds called aldehydes. Aldehydes can give rise to a range of flavors including green apple (acetaldehyde), paper or cardboard (trans-2-nonenal), and sherry (sherry is the quintessential oxidized wine). When lipids are oxidized, cheesy flavors are also produced because the lipids are broken down into volatile fatty acids (cheesy) and aldehydes. In dark beers, certain malt-derived compounds oxidize to lend sweet, malty flavors to the finished beer.

Yeast autolysis also occurs during aging and can really cause some nasty flavors to show up in beer. However, in small quantities these flavors can lend complexity to some beers. One of the key attributes to sparkling wines employing bottle conditioning (method *champenoise* as opposed to tank carbonation) is yeast autolysis. The yeast is removed at a certain point in the process to prevent excessive yeast bite and to allow further aging. To help prevent excessive yeast bite, beers meant to age should contain very little yeast.

In general, beers begin to lose their edge upon aging. Hop notes, fruity aromas, and alcoholic flavors begin to fade. As these fresh beer flavors become more subtle, dark beers will gain sweet, caramel-like, honey, toffee, and cheesy aromas. In lighter beers, wet paper aromas are the most obvious oxidized flavors, and their fresh flavors become dulled.

The types of beers that typically benefit from these age-related mellowing changes are robust, dark, and highly alcoholic beers; kind of like an overenergetic teenager chilling out with age and becoming a little more tolerable. Barleywines and Trappist ales are examples of beers that mellow gracefully with age. Thomas Hardy Ale from England — reported to improve for up to 25 years — begins to show pruney, raisiny notes after a couple of years that meld into a mellow and complex mélange of rich fruitiness after further aging.

Q I overcarbonated my bottled beer. Can I bleed off some of the carbonation by lightly tipping the cap and resealing when the gas escapes? Is there another way to blow off some of the carbonation to even the beer out?

A I suppose you could open all the bottles, allow them to degas for a while and recap them to help salvage the batch. The potential risk I envision is that if you keep the beer around for much time, the beer will become notably oxidized. Good luck with your rescue attempt, and be careful when opening the bottles. Wear safety glasses when uncapping the bottles and point the top of the bottle away from people (including yourself!).

Q **How long does homebrew bottled by a counter-pressure filler remain good?**

A Every brewer who bottles beer wants a definitive answer to this question, but it depends on bottling techniques. When carbonated beer is bottled, the shelf-life clock starts ticking. (Bottle-conditioned beers age differently, so this answer is only for counterpressure-filled beers). With few exceptions, dissolved oxygen increases when beer is transferred to a bottle. Even commercial brewers with the most modern fillers equipped with bottle preevacuation features worry about oxygen pickup at the filler.

Oxygen is public enemy number one when it comes to beer stability, be it bottled or kegged beer. Most counterpressure fillers are designed so that carbon dioxide can be purged through the fill tube and out of the top of the bottle prior to filling. This helps reduce the oxygen in the bottle and oxygen pickup during filling. During filling, it really helps to minimize splashing, because beer foams when splashed and also picks up more oxygen. Most counterpressure fillers have long fill tubes that extend to the bottom of the bottle to minimize splashing.

Once the beer has been gently transferred to the bottle, the fill tube is removed and the bottle prepared for capping. This step is critical. The idea is to get the beer to foam controllably so that the air in the bottle headspace is displaced with foam, and only then is the bottle capped. This is easier said than done. Sometimes the beer sits in the bottle and does not foam and other times it gushes out of the top like a geyser at Yellowstone. I like the former situation because it is easy to make beer foam, either by knocking the bottle on the counter or by rapping gently on the side with a plastic screwdriver handle. Geysers can be avoided by properly cooling your beer prior to bottling. The last protective measure to ward off oxygen pickup is to use bottle caps with an oxygen-absorbing liner. These caps can make a good system better, but they are not able to prevent oxidation without other preventive measures in place.

Beer bottled using a counterpressure filler under ideal conditions should remain fresh for at least 2 months and typically will stay fresh for 4 months. This is assuming the beer is kept cool or cold, is unfiltered, and is not some high-alcohol behemoth — these giant beers will last much longer and some of the changes brought about by aging affect these beers positively. In general, darker beers have a better shelf life than light beers because compounds responsible for beer color also play an antioxidant role. The most difficult beers to bottle are the really light styles, like Pilsners and American-style lagers. If bottled improperly, these lighter beers can show signs of oxidation within days of bottling, especially if stored warm.

CONTROL FOAM UNDER COUNTERPRESSURE

Follow a few rules of bottling and you can use a counter-pressure bottle filler without having the bottles overfoam.

The first thing to check is the length of the fill tube. One of the most important rules of bottle filling is to gently fill the bottle. There are two types of filler-tube designs used in commercial breweries: long-tube and short-tube fillers. Short-tube fillers fill the beer by directing its flow to the inside walls of the bottle, and the beer cascades down the sides of the bottle during filling. Long-tube fillers extend all the way to the bottom of the bottle and allow the beer to fill from the bottom up without excessive turbulence. If the tube ends farther from the bottom, the beer will start to foam as it falls from the bottom of the fill tube to the bottom of the bottle. If your fill tube is too short, extend it.

The next rule of bottling is that beer foam breeds more beer foam. This is because gas is released from beer when nucleation sites are present. Nucleation sites include rough spots on a beer contact surface, such as an etched glass, crystals in beer (for example, when salt is added to beer), and beer foam. Toward the end of filling the bottle, leave some space at the top and do not allow any beer to squirt out of the gas vent valve. If the bottle is filled all the way up, beer will squirt out of the vent tube during the depressurizing step and foam will form. So it is important to stop filling before beer comes out of the vent tube. This rule applies not only to filling beer bottles at home, but it is also used in commercial bottle machines. In fact the fill tubes on a commercial filler are designed so that beer cannot be filled all the way to the top of the bottle.

On the same line of reasoning, the beer bottle itself is often the culprit of foaming, especially when returnable bottles are used for bottling. Glass is not always smooth; imperfections in glass make beer foam. When beer bottles are cleaned and reused at the brewery, the surface of the bottle becomes etched, and this problem is exacerbated. Filling a wet bottle is easier than filling a dry bottle because a film of water on a bottle's surface is smoother than a dry surface and, you guessed it, results in less foaming. Commercial filling lines have a bottle rinser preceding the filler to ensure that beer is filled into wet glass.

When these rules are followed on most beers, things usually go pretty well. If I sound a little unsure, it's because bottling provokes brewers to swear a bit more than do other operations. Bottling beer is never a sure thing. Two variables that often throw a kink into the mix are beer carbonation level and beer temperature. I prefer to choose a pressure and temperature combination that results in the carbonation level I am after and allow the beer to carbonate over several days. This method is more predictable and reproducible than high-pressure carbonation followed by a reduction in keg pressure.

Q What could cause my beer bottles to break if overcarbonation doesn't seem to be an issue?

A Bottles breaking due to age and diminished strength is not only possible but quite common. Although domestic breweries recycle very few beer bottles through returnable glass programs, returnable containers are standard in many other countries. Returnable glass comes back to the brewery in a wide range of conditions. Some of the bottles have been emptied by their borrower, rinsed with water, and carefully placed back in the carton from which they came. These bottles simply have to be delabeled, cleaned, sterilized, and inspected before reuse. Other bottles have not had it so good. They have been emptied, dropped on the floor, and stuffed full of half-burned cigarettes.

Many homebrewers, including me, intercept returnable glass by buying cases of empties at the local dive bar with the largest selection of cheap beer in bar longneck glass (12 oz./355 mL). Through careful rinsing, cleaning, and delabeling, these grungy, stinky bottles can be readied for duty.

The problem is that no homebrewer I know has an in-line glass inspector to see hairline fractures in the bottles the way commercial breweries do. Damaged glass is dangerous, plain and simple. If bottles fracture during capping, especially with gooseneck cappers, it is very easy to slice your arm on the fractured bottle. I know a person with permanent nerve damage caused by such an accident. If the bottle does not fracture on filling, pressure created during carbonation can cause failure. Again, if this occurs near somebody, injury can ensue. I remember an accident involving an exploding beer bottle that resulted in blindness in one eye of the injured person. I don't want to create unnecessary fear regarding bottling, but I want to be realistic. With the large number of microbreweries around the country, new glass is fairly accessible at reasonable prices at many homebrew supply stores. Given the potential risks involved with used glass, new glass is not a bad deal.

Q How does a counterpressure bottle filler work?

A A counterpressure bottle filler is designed to deliver a carbonated product into a bottle without excessive foaming. The idea behind these devices is to pressurize the beer bottle to the same pressure as the keg holding the beer. After the bottle is pressurized and the beer valve allowing beer to enter the bottle is opened, the beer will only begin to flow if the keg is placed higher than the bottle.

The beer flow will stop quickly as the forces pushing it from the keg and those slowing it from entering the bottle become equilibrated. When this happens, the bottle vent is opened and the beer flow will continue until the bottle is full. Then, the pressure in the bottle is slowly relieved and the filler is removed from the bottle. If everything went right, there is little foam coming out of the bottle and a cap can be quickly placed on the bottle.

Q What causes carbonation in my bottles to be uncertain, often stuck? When this happens I move the bottles to a warmer location for a week, shaking occasionally. This seems to do the trick.

A It may simply be related to the temperature at which you have been holding your bottled beers during conditioning. For fast and reliable carbonation, especially with ale yeast, it is best to hold the bottles at room temperature for 7 to 14 days before cooling them down.

Another possibility is that your conditioning is working well; it clarifies the beer during the process. The result of good gravity clarification may be a beer that contains insufficient yeast for carbonation purposes, or at least insufficient to carbonate the way you originally were accustomed. Although insufficient yeast for carbonation can happen, it is very difficult to really remove that much yeast without filtration. It is, however, fairly easy to change the yeast concentration enough to affect the rate of carbonation.

The last resort to this sort of problem is to add fresh yeast at bottling time. This method works very well, and there is nothing wrong with the practice. It provides healthy, fresh yeast that usually carbonate beer much more quickly compared with the old, cranky yeast carried over after aging. I consider this a last resort because most homebrewed beers have plenty of yeast to carbonate beer in the bottle and adding more yeast will only increase the yeast load.

If the finished beer is very clear, then a small addition of yeast, about 10 percent of a proper pitch for primary, will provide plenty of yeast for carbonation. A proper pitch for primary is about 14 grams (0.5 oz.) of dry yeast or about 1 cup (237 mL) of thick slurry harvested from a previous fermentation.

■ ══════════ ■

Q **Do you have any suggestions for finding the right kind of corks for bottling my Belgian-style beers?**

A Your attempt to recreate the entire package at home is admirable, and more challenging than using crown caps on normal beer bottles. Fortunately, the challenge has more to do with finding the proper tool for the job than honing a delicate technique. The type of cork used to seal bottle-conditioned beer bottles is virtually identical to a champagne cork — the market for the cork is the only thing that really differs!

Making this type of cork begins by forming high-quality granulated cork into a high-density composite with uniform mechanical properties. Often, two to three discs of fine natural cork are then laminated to the end of the cork that ends up on the inside of the bottle. Their mushroomed tops make beer and champagne corks easy to recognize; the shape forms when the cork is inserted into the neck of the bottle with a special type of corker. The wire cage covering the cork is very important, because it holds the cork in place and prevents the bottle pressure from ejecting the seal.

Pretty simple . . . If you want to create the ultimate in package presentation for your Belgian-style ales, you need to purchase the proper tools for the job. A quick Internet search will yield numerous suppliers of champagne corkers as well as the special corks and required wire cages. Plastic corks should work quite well, unless you are using recycled tops or are mismatching the cork with the bottleneck diameter.

Here are some other keys to using corks as a closure for beer: Keeping the cork in the bottle is just as important as getting it out. Not all corks for beer and champagne have the same diameter before cramming them into the neck of the bottle. This can lead to carbonation issues.

Another occasional problem that haunts winemakers is the dreaded corked off-flavor caused by the compound trichloroanisole (TCA) that is associated with a combination of mold growth in the cork and bleach used to sanitize the cork. This compound has an incredibly low threshold of detection of about 5 parts per trillion — that's 5 nanograms per liter, or the equivalent of 5 gallons per trillion gallons . . . a trillion is a thousand billions, in case you're wondering. A very small concentration indeed!

The recommended cork for your mission is a 27 mm (1 in.) Sabaté Altec composite cork from France equipped with a solid disk end. This cork reportedly has good memory, will seal your bottle for a long time, and will free itself when beckoned. You do need to buy the special corking tool to get this bad boy into its temporary home.

Q **Is it possible to successfully use twist-off style bottles for homebrews with success?**

A If a brewery like Sierra Nevada can add yeast and sugar to beer and package it in a bottle with a twist-off cap, then it follows that the same practice can be used at home. The key here is recognizing a few things about bottles, caps, and cappers.

There are two types of bottles sold for use by brewers: one-way and returnable. One-way bottles are intended for only one use and are lighter in weight than returnable glass. In this country, returnable glass has just about vanished.

One-way bottles are designed for one use and are much lighter than their returnable cousins. This means that the first thing you need to find is a source of one-way bottles with a twist-off neck.

When you put a cap on a twist-off bottle, you can use a standard style crown rather than finding special twist-off crowns. Commercial brewers do like the printed caps with the "Twist Off" arrow on the crown to assure consumers that twisting will indeed permit consumption!

You do need a capper that doesn't grab the neck of the bottle. Most handheld cappers grab the small ring around the perimeter of the neck, using it to hold the crowner tight to the bottle. This ring on the one-way, twist-off bottles often breaks when capped with a handheld capper. The ring is simply too thin and too weak for use with hand cappers. Benchtop cappers do not grab onto this ring and are preferred to put crowns on twist-off bottles.

The last thing to consider about bottles is carbonation level. One-way glass is designed for normal carbonation levels. If you want to do a beer with high carbonation, such as a Belgian-style or hefe-weizen, you should use a stronger bottle. This is where a collection of returnable half-liter bottles or an investment in flip-top bottles is handy.

The Demise of Returnables

Returnable beer bottles — in the form of longnecks — have just about vanished. The reason is logistical.

If a bottle is imprinted with the name of the brewery or has a special shape, like the now extinct Michelob hourglass, the end user must somehow get this bottle back to the correct brewery. The most common reusable beer package in the United States is marketed to bars that can reclaim empties. The distributor picks them up and returns them to the brewery. The brewery then has to verify the glass is what they expect (rather than some other brewery's bottles) remove the label, wash the bottle, inspect for cracks, and refill any bottles that can be reused. These bottles show wear over time and can get downright ugly — not the best thing from an image point of view. The pressed shirts in marketing probably view this package in a negative light.

The long and short of returnable glass is that the bottles are becoming more difficult to come by as the popularity of one-way glass continues to grow.

Q What equipment do you need for a basic homebrew keg setup?

A Keg setups are great because they eliminate bottling, which can become a chore if you brew regularly. Plus, beer can be ready to drink within 2 to 3 days of kegging.

The only things you need for a basic keg setup are a keg, carbon dioxide bottle, two-stage regulator, and some type of tap. Most homebrewers use Cornelius kegs, which are available from several companies that refurbish used Corneliuses to sell to homebrewers.

Basic keg setups come with a hose and a plastic tap, just like those you get when you buy a keg of beer for a picnic. You can make this basic system fancier by adding a bar-style beer tap and drip tray to the door of a refrigerator. Although the cost of this setup is a bit more, it is really nice to have. Just toss the keg in the fridge and when you want a beer, you simply pull the tap on the door. If you want to really go wild, you can build your own bar and run a draft line between the refrigerator holding the keg and the tap at the bar. This adds another level of complexity, since the beer line between the refrigerator and the tap should be cooled in order to prevent the beer in the line from becoming warm.

The great thing about the state of the homebrewing hobby is that there are numerous equipment suppliers. In the old days of homebrewing, if you wanted

Kegging setup

a keg setup you had to do a lot of digging around for parts and pieces and do a lot of the design work on your own. Many homebrewers would buy equipment from bar and restaurant supply companies and modify things intended for use with standard commercial beer kegs to work with their homebrew setup. Today it's really easy to find kegging packages that have everything you need to get started for less than $200.

——————

Q **What is your preferred method to force-carbonate a keg?**

A Using bottled carbon dioxide to pressurize kegs of beer is a carbonation method that works well. Be patient. I usually begin by selecting the combination of temperature and pressure that will provide the desired level of carbon dioxide that I want in the beer. Charts provide this information if you know what carbonation level to select. (See page 272.) Suppose 13 psi of carbon dioxide pressure at 38°F (4°C) is the right combination for your beer. The best way to get the beer to the chosen level of carbon dioxide is to pressurize the keg to 13 psi and hold it in a 38°F (4°C) refrigerator for about 3 days, giving the keg a good shake once or twice a day. At the end of the period, the beer should be equilibrated with the temperature and pressure in the refrigerator and be properly carbonated.

Q My keg containing naturally conditioned ale loses pressure over time and I was wondering what causes this?

A When using a soda keg and carbonating with priming sugar, it is important to apply a top pressure of carbon dioxide from a bottled source to initially seal the keg. If you don't do this, the keg might never seal. Instead, it will slowly vent the products of conditioning to the atmosphere. This happens if the keg lid is not firmly smashed to the top of the keg with gas pressure to get it to seal. The other common pitfall with kegs is a loose lid that never really seals, regardless of pressure. Obviously a leaky keg lid will always let your beer go flat and should be fixed or replaced. Check on the O-ring gasket on the top of the keg if you have a leaker.

Q How long will my beer stay fresh in a keg?

A The topic of beer shelf life and freshness after packaging does not have any hard and fast rules, because beers differ in their ability to stay fresh after packaging. In general, beer flavor changes much more slowly over time when stored cold. Freshness is affected by numerous variables, but the key factors for unfiltered beers are microbiological contamination, oxidation, and yeast autolysis.

Microbiological spoilage is a concern of all brewers. Off-flavors associated with wild yeast and wort spoilage bacteria can manifest themselves very rapidly and may be detectable within a week after wort production. These beers are frequently surrendered to the porcelain god and never make it to the bottle or keg stage of their lives.

Other contaminants, such as lactic acid bacteria (*Lactobacillus* and *Pediococcus* species), grow much slower and can take weeks or months to rear their ugly heads. When they have grown enough to be detected, the contaminated beer may taste sour and have a very noticeable diacetyl aroma. Clean yeast, short fermentation lag times, and excellent sanitation practices greatly reduce the risk of having beer contaminated with these sorts of organisms.

Homebrewers are in a much stronger position to monitor freshness than commercial brewers are because we have absolute control over our beer. Use clean yeast, keep the brewery clean, and minimize air pickup during bottling and you will be well on your way to producing a beer that will stay fresh for at least 60 days after packaging. Store it hot and this period will be reduced, store it cold and it will become longer. Refrigerated homebrew can taste excellent as much as 4 months after packaging. Taste your beer and develop your own opinion on the subject. You can then extend shelf life by simply focusing on those techniques in your process that can use improvement.

Q **How long can I safely store my kegs at room or refrigeration temperature before the flavor is affected?**

A The answer to your question has plagued brewers since beer was first conceived or however it came into being. Many famous scientists studied the spoilage of beer and wine, and Louis Pasteur developed the heat-preservation technique now called pasteurization for beer, not milk. If brewers only knew how long their beer would last after packaging, distribution and packaged beer control would be so much easier.

The homebrewer and the pub brewer do have it pretty simple, however, because the palate can tell when the beer no longer tastes good. The simple answer to your question is that your beer's flavor will remain unaffected by storage until your palate is able to detect that it has changed! At this point, you may want to have a party and drink the rest of the beer before it becomes bad. Or if you detect the change in flavor at the same time it becomes bad, then you probably will want to dump the beer. This advice sounds crude but it works. Most pub brewers use their palate as the best indicator of freshness.

Q What is the best way to separate an ale from the yeast before I transfer beer to a keg? I want to do this to cut down on any off-flavors that the dead yeast might add to the beer.

A One of the best ways for homebrewers to clarify beer is to simply move the carboy to a refrigerator and hold it cold for at least a week; 38°F (4°C) is ideal, but anything colder than the final serving temperature should work. Chilling your beer will accomplish several important things. The most obvious effect of chilling is that a big portion of the total yeast in suspension will flocculate, or drop to the bottom of the fermenter. Chilling your beer will also help promote a reaction between proteins and tannins or polyphenols that results in chill haze. The great part of having chill haze at this stage of the game is that it will settle to the bottom of the fermenter. In a commercial brewery, the settling time takes weeks, but luckily for homebrewers, the beer depth in a carboy is about 2 feet and the settling time is measured in just days.

Depending on the flocculation characteristics of the yeast strain, this method may produce very clear beer or it may do very little to improve clarity.

A more active approach to yeast removal is to use a fining agent, such as isinglass. Isinglass finings are a very pure form of collagen and are derived from fish swim bladders. When hydrated in an acid buffer solution, the collagen protein becomes positively charged. When you add this solution to beer, the collagen will act like a big net to bind yeast cells and drag them to the bottom of the fermenter. There are some isinglass preparations available today that are treated with the acid buffer and then dried. They can simply be rehydrated in water before use to make preparation easier. I have always wondered how this practice first got started!

The last common option available is filtration. Few homebrewers filter their beer because filtration equipment is usually on the expensive side and, if done improperly, filtering can quickly ruin great beer. When filtration is carefully and properly performed, the result can be very gratifying. I have heard countless brewers, both commercial and hobbyist, bash filtration. Detractors of filtration claim that it strips flavor and color from beer and makes beer taste watery. While this can happen if certain types of filters are used, especially membrane filters, it is the exception. Most commercial beers are filtered to produce a brilliant beer. Some styles, like hefe-weizen, cask ale, and bottle-conditioned beers, are unfiltered, but you will find that most other styles are typically filtered.

Whether you rely on cold storage, isinglass, or filtration, you can reduce your yeast load. By doing so, you can worry less about autolysis (yeast death) and will also have a clearer beer that better displays the colors of the malts used in the brew. One factor that you should be mindful of is that bottle conditioning becomes difficult when too little yeast is present and impossible when there is none! Some brewers who bottle-condition actually filter their beers "bright" and then add a small dose of healthy yeast along with priming sugar just prior to bottling. (See fining agents, page 309.)

Q **Does it matter if my ales are primed, carbonated, and aged in the keg at room temperature and then put in the fridge when ready for dispensing?**

A Bottle- and keg-conditioned ales must go through several key steps before they can be refrigerated and enjoyed. The first step is to estimate the volume of beer and to add an appropriate amount of priming sugar for carbonation. Most brewers use less sugar to prime an equivalent volume of beer in a keg compared with bottles.

After the beer is primed and the container sealed, it should be transferred to a suitable environment for the carbonation or conditioning step. The normal temperatures for conditioning range from 60 to 70°F (16–21°C) for ale and 40 to 55°F (4–14°C) for lager. During conditioning, the yeast produce carbon dioxide from the priming sugar and also mature the beer flavor by absorbing butterlike diacetyl and green-applelike acetaldehyde molecules and converting them into flavorless compounds. These changes are good changes and will occur in 7 to 14 days in ales that are stored in the 60 to 70°F (16–21°C) range. Lagers will take longer and use a different procedure, but your question is about ales, so I will stick to ales!

Once the good changes brought on by conditioning have occurred, other changes begin that may have a negative effect on your beer's flavor. The first bad thing to come will be yeast autolysis (yeast death and decay). Autolyzed yeast not only has an unpleasant flavor, but the intracellular goo that is excreted during autolysis is rich in enzymes and *nutrients.* Some of the enzymes secreted, such as proteases, damage beer foam. Others, specifically esterases, change the aroma of fresh beer.

Another change that will eventually occur in beer is oxidation. Although minimizing oxygen pickup during beer transfers and beer packaging will reduce the rate of oxidation, it is inevitable. In the early stages of oxidation, beer takes on a wet paper or wet cardboard aroma that some Americans who drink imported beer have learned to love! As the beer oxidizes more, it begins to smell like honey and eventually takes on aromas typically found in sherry and over-ripened dried fruits, such as raisins and prunes. Beer drinkers fond of the rich flavors found in aged barleywines, Belgian strong ales, and the like are responding positively to oxidation, but in most beers it is definitely considered a defect.

Brewers can delay these negative changes by minimizing the amount of yeast that is transferred into the bottle or keg, minimizing oxygen pickup, and using cold storage temperatures. If you store your kegs at room temperature before tapping, they may taste great for 2 to 3 weeks then begin going downhill. If they are refrigerated after conditioning, they can last for months and still taste great. In a nutshell, after your beer has been aged, it is best to cool it for longer-term storage.

Q **I have one soda keg that has produced three batches in a row of different beer with a strong chemical taste. What can cause an iodine or strong chemical taste in my kegged beer?**

A Chemical off-flavors are frequently encountered in beer and can be caused by numerous factors. The most obvious cause is traces of cleaning or sanitizing chemicals. Chemicals containing chlorine and iodine are well-known contributors of chemical off-flavors if the compounds remain on the equipment. Of the two, chlorine is the worst because it can combine with malt phenols to form a class of compounds called chlorophenols, which have a pronounced medicinal aroma. Iodine sanitizers usually cause no problems, if used at their recommended concentration.

Some brewers encounter problems with chlorine even without using chlorinated sanitizers. These problems are often traced to chlorinated tap water, such as that used for rinsing brewing equipment. One well-known craft brewer had problems with chlorophenols in his fruit beer that were eventually traced to the fruit. The fruit source had been rinsed at the farm with chlorinated water, and the chlorine was being introduced to the beer at the time of fruit addition. This problem took some good detective work to solve.

Medicinal aromas can also come from wild yeast contamination. In fact, the classic indicator of wild yeast contamination in beer is a distinct phenolic aroma. This aroma is often likened to cloves or the smell of standard bandages.

These are all possible explanations to your problem, but I don't think they are the real culprit. All of your beers from all kegs would taste off if it were due to your chemical selection or city water, and wild yeast attacks probably would not be limited to one keg, although that is certainly possible.

I think the most probable cause of the off-flavor is leftover flavors in the keg gaskets. I think you have an old root beer keg on your hands, and the aroma in beer is not iodine or medicinal but root beer. The most notable aromas in root beer are phenolic by nature and do smell somewhat medicinal. They are also next to impossible to completely remove from rubber gaskets they contact. Many a pub brewer will tell awful stories of contaminating beer lines, gaskets, hoses, and beer fillers with root beer where the only solution was to replace all soft parts. This can be expensive in a commercial brewery! The lesson for them is to keep their root beer away from everything else. In your case, you inherited the taint but the solution is the same.

Take your suspect keg apart and remove all rubber O-rings and gaskets and replace them. Most homebrew stores selling kegging equipment will carry or have the ability to order replacement parts. Even if the problem is not from root beer, your problem is most likely associated with the keg's previous resident!

The Gift of Beer Foam

Beer foam affects the mouthfeel of beer and increases the creamy sensation of beer when consumed. It also has a very appealing appearance on a freshly poured beer. If it leaves a nice lacy pattern on the glass, it's considered truly superior foam.

Most brewers like foam for these reasons; they want to produce a beer that has a nice foam volume with good stability and lacing. To many consumers, however, foam occupies space in their glass that could be filled with beer. This is where the brewer and the beer consumer often run into arguments. I explain to people who drink my beer that the foam is a gift from me. It makes the beer visually appealing and improves the mouthfeel. I like to use beer glasses with a fill line to establish the volume where the beer stops and the foam begins.

Q **What concerns should one have when doing cask-conditioned ales and serving with a beer engine?**

A The concern many have with traditional cask ales is leaving the cask vented to the atmosphere for prolonged periods, resulting in beer oxidation. This begins to change the beer's flavor, which some people like in a cask ale, but the oxygen also allows for the growth of aerobic beer spoilage organisms. These bugs only grow in oxygen-containing environments and are not a problem for beers dispensed with carbon dioxide.

However, cask beers can and do spoil due to aerobic bugs. The most notable example is spoilage from *Acetobacter* species, which convert ethanol in beer to acetic acid (vinegar). A slight overpressure of carbon dioxide or a mixture of carbon dioxide and nitrogen will prevent the problems associated with oxygen in the headspace of your keg. Care must be taken not to use too much pressure as the beer can over-carbonate, just as it can lose its carbonation with too little pressure.

Q Can I do anything to salvage an over-carbonated keg of wheat beer?

A I prefer to package beer in kegs for several reasons. Besides being convenient, it's very easy to change the carbonation level in a beer. In your case, you either added too much priming sugar or went overboard with your carbon dioxide pressure during the carbonation step. Whatever the reason, the problem can be solved simply by releasing the top pressure on the keg. This method works to drop the carbonation level.

If you drop the head pressure in the keg, it will slowly return as the carbon dioxide in the beer reequilibrates with the headspace in the keg. If you have a Cornelius keg, make sure the lid reseals properly or you could lose a lot more carbon dioxide than planned.

After a few hours, you can hook your gas supply back up to the keg at your normal dispense pressure and check the level of carbonation. You may need to repeat this method a time or two, depending on how badly you over-carbonated your wheat beer! Although this is a nuisance, it is definitely a solvable problem. That's the beauty of kegged beer. If the beer were bottled instead of kegged, then you would be out of luck.

CHAPTER 8

Homebrew Trouble-shooting

Q How can you improve head retention?

A Beer foam is pretty neat-looking stuff and is one of those topics that brewers can only discuss with other brewers. Start talking about the merits of good foam among nonbrewers and people will think there is something fundamentally amiss! I have spent a lot of time looking at and thinking about beer foam — in fact, I did my master's thesis on beer foam — and have developed a simplified approach to brewing beer with great foam.

The key to my approach involves malt selection. This means going all-grain. All-grain brewers really have a leg up on extract brewers when it comes to foam for a few reasons. First of all, foam is primarily a function of wort or beer protein content and type. Protein (or more correctly polypeptide) content decreases when wort is heat-treated, because proteins come out of solution (the wort) when heated. Extracts are heated and sometimes boiled when produced, and the brewer again boils the wort at home (unless you're making a no-boil beer). Another key factor affecting beer foam is the type of malt used. Extract brewers can select different specialty malts but have no control over the type of malt in the extract, which typically comprises more than 85 percent of the recipe. Plus, some extracts contain adjuncts, for example sugars, which

Beer foam

dilute the protein content even more and have a negative affect on foam.

When selecting extracts look for all-malt, low-color types. These will give you the best shot at good foam. I prefer dried malt extract (DME) over liquid extracts because most DME receives less heating in the process. Some extracts describe the wort it will produce. If you can find unhopped, all-malt extracts that use the descriptors "light color" or "lightly modified malt," you will be in good shape.

KISS Approach to Killer Foam

I believe great beer has great foam. So here is my simplified approach to achieving killer foam:

1. Begin with undermodified malt if you really want killer foam (use special malts as normal for color and flavor).
2. Avoid using protein-free adjuncts like corn, rice, and sugar.
3. Never use any soapy cleaner or sanitizer without a very thorough rinse.
4. Use really clean beer glasses.

 Would fining with gelatin have an adverse effect on naturally conditioned beer?

Fining is one of those brewing practices that takes some touch and feel to perfect. Not all beers respond equally to finings, regardless of the type. That's because the components in the beer affected by finings, primarily protein, yeast, and polyphenols, vary in composition. This is especially true of yeast because different strains vary in flocculation and respond differently to collagen finings (gelatin and isinglass).

Irish moss is used to help remove protein from wort, which ends up in the trub and is separated from the wort prior to fermentation. Another step in the brewing process where finings are used is post fermentation. Cask-conditioned ales are racked into a keg where isinglass finings and priming sugar, and often dry hops, are added before the keg is sealed for conditioning. Isinglass is made from the cleaned and dried swim bladders of certain fishes and contains a very pure form of collagen. Gelatin is also rich in collagen, but it is not as pure as isinglass and is not as effective at removing yeast. Both can be used in brewing.

The preparation of isinglass involves stabilizing the protein in an organic acid (tartaric or malic, for example) at a pH of about 2.5. When added to beer, isinglass casts a large open net with positive charges on the surface of the molecule. These charged sites act like little magnets and electrostatically bind yeast cells, due to the overall negative charge of yeast. The pH of beer is usually around 4.5, and at this level, the collagen begins to precipitate from solution, falling through the beer and pulling yeasts to the bottom of the fermenter. It is also important that you store and use your finings at a temperature range of 42 to 55°F (6–13°C), or they will not fine your beer correctly.

Not all yeasts respond the same to this method of fining, because not all strains have the same density of negative charges on the cell wall. Trial and error will tell you if the yeast strain you use is effectively removed by isinglass. Most serious users of finings perform benchtop tests to avoid over fining. A good starting point with isinglass is 1 mL isinglass solution per liter (0.03 oz./34 oz.) of beer.

Finings remove compounds from beer and wine and the compounds removed are not singular. Add too much isinglass and you may end up stripping more than yeast from your beer. The philosophy with fining is to add just enough to accomplish the primary goal. The concentration of yeast after fining with isinglass can be quite low. Ales fined with isinglass typically contain less than 100,000 cells per mL, sometimes as low as 10,000 cells per mL. Most commercial breweries I know that bottle condition like to see about 1 million yeast cells per mL of beer. Anything significantly lower than this density causes problems with carbonation.

This takes us back to cask-conditioned ale. These beers carbonate during the same time that the yeast is being pulled down to the bottom with the isinglass. The other key to recognize with fined cask beer is that the cask has a belly where the yeast can collect without flowing to the *tap*. Since isinglass forms a fluffy yeast layer, it is important not to disturb a cask that is being dispensed.

Bottled beer is another animal. You cannot use the cask technique to fine, prime, and condition beer in the bottle. The floc would never stay at the bottom of the bottle during those necessary movements (transferring to the fridge, drinking from the bottle, or decanting to a glass). You can fine your beer with isinglass (or gelatin), rack the clear beer off the yeast, and add yeast and sugar to the beer prior to bottling. This allows you to have clear, fined beer and sufficient yeast for carbonation.

■ ━━━━━━ ■

Q I have chill haze in all of my ales and in some of my 6-week lagers. I add Irish moss during the last 15 minutes of the boil. I keg and force carbonate. How else can I prevent chill haze?

A I will assume your problem is chill haze and not a yeast haze commonly seen in beers fermented using a yeast strain with poor flocculation properties. Chill haze occurs when certain proteins and polyphenols (tannins) loosely bond at low temperatures and cause beer to appear hazy. Chill haze disappears when beer is warmed and reappears when chilled. Given enough cycles, a chill haze may become permanent and fail to disappear upon warming. This same thing happens in wine and iced tea.

Battling chill haze involves removing the protein or the tannin from the beer, thereby minimizing the concentration of the problem compound. Some brewers try to remove both parts of the equation. Irish moss is effective in removing proteins, and as it turns out, somewhat selectively removes the sort of proteins that are most often implicated in hazes. (For those protein geeks out there, haze proteins are typically rich in the amino acid proline.) Irish moss must dissolve into wort and this requires time. The conventional thought is to add it during the last 15 minutes of the boil. Adding it too late can reduce its efficacy. I have seen 40–60 ppm as a recommended addition range in text books. This equates to roughly 1 gram (or about 1 teaspoon) per 19 liters (5 gallons). As with most chemical interactions, the ability of Irish moss to bind proteins is pH-dependent — but luckily for us, it works well at wort pH (5.2–5.4).

Other brewers focus on removing tannins from beer. The most common tannin fining is PVPP (polyvinylpolypyrrolidone — say that three times fast, or even once without taking a breath, and you may be a wizard yourself). PVPP is a fast-acting adsorbent. Some brewers add it and allow a few hours for PVPP to work prior to filtration. Others inject it in-line as the beer is being filtered. At home, PVPP can be separated through racking, since it is a granular powder that sinks in beer. Textbook addition rates for PVPP range from 7.5–25 grams per hectoliter (approximately 0.01 to 0.04 ounces per gallon).

An alternate method is cold filtration. This method works great for brewers who prefer not to use finings. Basically, beer is chilled down to near-freezing temperatures and held for at least a few days if not longer (much longer at times). The cold temperature encourages haze and some of the haze actually settles out — this practice can be accomplished at home. The next step involves filtering the beer at the same cold temperature and removing the haze. In order to obtain satisfactory filtration results, it is important to select a filter that is tight enough to remove these particles. In my experience, a filter pore size of 2 microns or less works well for producing very bright beers. Although yeast can be removed by pore sizes up to 10 microns, haze removal requires a tighter filter. Using multiple sizes (coarse, then fine) is common in larger breweries trying to get more efficient use of filtration materials. Many pub brewers, however, only use one pore size for filtering.

One of these methods will probably work to clear up your hazy brew!

Q **I was told by a friend that my beer was "skunky." What causes this?**

A Skunky beer, also called light-struck, is cause by ultraviolet light affecting iso-alpha acids present in all beers. This reaction, called photolysis, causes iso-alpha acids (originating from boiled hop iso-acids) to break into two parts. One of the parts goes on to react with sulfur, found naturally in all beers, to produce the unmistakable stench of isopentyl mercaptan.

Avoid skunky beer by using brown bottles, not clear or green. Brown glass filters out the ultraviolet light that does the damage. Clear and green glass bottles allow these wavelengths access to the beer inside and will produce skunky beer if exposed to light. That's why many commercial beers with green bottles smell so distinctive.

REDUCE YEASTY OFF-FLAVORS

The best way to reduce yeasty off-flavors in beer is to minimize the amount of yeast carried forward into the bottle. This can be done by long, cold storage (which helps yeast to settle), the use of finings (such as isinglass or gelatin), or by filtering your beer. Since most home-brewers do not have access to a filter, finings and/or cold storage provide a good start.

Yeastiness does not always come from excess yeast in the package; it can come from too many dead cells going into fermentation with the yeast pitch or too many cells being carried forward from primary fermentation into secondary fermentation. Less common, too many cells remain in solution during fermentation.

Suggestions to deal with these sorts of problems are:

◆ Use a good, highly viable pitching yeast. Fresh yeast will help minimize dead cells in the pitching yeast.

◆ Reduce the yeast cells in your secondary by chilling the primary for 2 days before racking. This will cause more yeast to settle from solution.

◆ Avoid overpitching. Adding too much yeast is hard to do, especially when using liquid yeast, so this is not a common problem in homebrewing, but it can happen.

Try these techniques and continue critically evaluating your own beer. Part of being an excellent brewer is being an excellent taster. Combine good brewing knowledge with careful tasting and you will succeed in brewing!

Q What are the best fermenting and storage temperatures to avoid a ripe banana aroma?

A The banana aroma is associated with the ester iso-amyl acetate. In general, ester production increases when wort aeration is low. Some weizen brewers actually limit aeration intentionally to get more banana aroma. You can do the opposite and aerate your wort more aggressively than normal.

Another factor is temperature. Generally, higher temperatures lead to more esters in the finished beer. Yeast strain also has a great influence on aroma; some yeast strains are known to produce more isoamyl acetate than others, for example, weizen strains.

Finally, there is wort original gravity. Ester levels increase with wort gravity. Aerate the wort well and try to keep your fermentation temperature less than 75°F (24°C) for ales. Aging temperature has no effect on ester production.

■ ━━━━━━ ■

Q Every time I brew a light Kölsch or Pilsner I get a massive dose of dimethyl sulfide (DMS) in my beer. The DMS does not show up until the beer carbonates, and everything else about these brews goes well. Help!

A The great thing about DMS problems in beer is that they are easy to identify and easy to rectify. DMS, or dimethyl sulfide, is derived from a compound found in malted barley called *S-methylmethionine* (SMM). When SMM is heated, it is converted to DMS. DMS has that wonderfully aromatic property that reminds one of canned corn . . . mmmm, canned corn.

Malted barley is heated in two key steps during malting and brewing. Malt is first heated during malt kilning and heated again during mashing and wort boiling. SMM is converted to DMS during these hot processes. Much of the DMS can be removed with vapor if the duration of heating is sufficiently long.

Very pale malts are exposed to as little heat for as little time as possible during kilning to prevent darkening. The goal with these very pale malts is to dry the grain, but not to toast or roast it. Consequently, pale malts may contain a lot of SMM, since they have not had sufficient time at high temperatures to convert the SMM to DMS and drive the DMS from the malt.

Darker malts — like pale ale malts, crystal malts, Munich malts, and roasted malts — contain much less SMM, and much of the DMS formed from SMM has been driven off the grain during kilning. Very pale malts will have more DMS than darker malts. It's the malt color that is the real factor with DMS, not the barley variety. The problem with pale malts can show up in the brewhouse when SMM is converted to DMS during mashing and boiling, and deficient evaporation during boiling leaves enough DMS in the wort to be detected in the finished beer. If this is the case, increasing boil vigor and duration helps.

Another frequent cause of DMS is prolonged exposure to high temperatures after boiling. These holds will permit SMM to convert to DMS, but since the wort is not boiling, the DMS is not driven from the wort. This is one of the reasons why brewers like to rapidly chill wort. Mash pH and water salts, while very important for other reasons, do not play a role in the DMS equation.

In your particular case, you are using a pale-colored malt to make lightly flavored beers. Lightly colored beers typically have more DMS than darker beers because of the light malts and because DMS is not masked by the strong malty aromas typically found in darker beers. It is very common for two beers to have the same measured levels of DMS but very different perceived levels — for example, a stout may have no detectable DMS aroma, while a Pilsner with the same measured level will have an obvious DMS smell.

So what is a brewer to do? Some do nothing different and buy into the notion that pale beers have a detectable DMS aroma. In fact, some brewers take the idea further and make the argument that DMS should be present in certain styles. Other brewers see this as a cop-out for not being able to reduce the levels. The brewers who do not like DMS in their beers because they think the aroma is offensive aggressively take measures to minimize DMS in their beer.

Methods of minimizing DMS include more vigorous wort boiling, resulting in better conversion of SMM to DMS and greater evaporation of DMS. Some commercial brewers are using film-type evaporators in which a thin film of wort is pumped over a hot surface to further reduce the levels of

DMS in the wort. Anheuser-Busch has for many years used a device they call a wort stripper to reduce the levels of DMS in its beers. Other brewers have turned to changing how the wort is handled after boiling.

Some brewers deal with DMS problems by reducing its source. In other words, they replace malted barley with adjuncts, like rice, that do not contain SMM and do not contribute DMS to beer.

No DMS answer would be complete without mentioning that certain wort spoilage bacteria can contribute DMS aromas to beer. Equipment, like wort chillers, in which wort is allowed to sit too long after use when not properly cleaned can also cause DMS issues.

<hr>

Q **My Pilsner is 12 days old and it has a very unripe, somewhat sour taste to it. Kind of a "green" peach or something. Will this subside? Does it just need more time to age?**

A One thought comes to mind, and that is acetaldehyde. Almost all homebrewers know about diacetyl and are often taught to dislike diacetyl with vigor. Acetaldehyde and diacetyl are two flavor compounds frequently associated with insufficient aging time. Both flavors are easily reduced by allowing a rest period between fermentation and cooling. (Diacetyl is also associated with bacterial contamination, and time will not cure that problem!)

Acetaldehyde is a metabolic intermediate and is leaked from the yeast cell during fermentation. After vigorous fermentation is complete, yeast cells will absorb acetaldehyde and reduce this "green" aroma compound to ethanol. Most commercial lager brewers monitor the level of diacetyl, diacetyl precursor (alpha-acetolactate), and acetaldehyde before cooling beer and moving forward in the process. When beer is prematurely separated from yeast and crash-cooled (which effectively halts yeast activity), the likelihood of having a beer smelling of apples and butter increases.

If there is sufficient yeast in your bottled Pilsner, the problem may subside. I would suggest taking a few bottles of your green beer, gently rolling them around to re-suspend the yeast, and storing them warm for a week or two. If the flavor intensity does not drop in this time frame you are probably stuck with it. In the future, especially when fermenting lagers, make sure you hold the beer at fermentation temperature for at least 4 days prior to cooling.

Q **My last two batches of beer that I brewed tasted kind of like Anbesol. What went wrong?**

A Two of the keys to problem solving in brewing are having a good palate and having the ability to describe what you are detecting with your senses. Anbesol is a phenol-based local oral anesthetic (like Chloraseptic). There are several things that can make a beer taste phenolic.

Certain malts can impart phenolic flavors to beer. The most notable example is peated malt. Peated malt is intended for Scotch whiskey, not for beer, but some clever brewer started a wave of "Scotch" ales brewed with peated malt. Some highly roasted malts also have a phenolic flavor, but the intensity of the flavor is nowhere near that of peated malt.

However, the most common source of phenolic flavors in beer comes from yeast. Some yeast strains produce phenolic flavors as a normal part of their metabolism. These strains have enzymes that other brewing yeasts lack. The phenolic flavors originate from phenolic acids naturally found in malt, especially ferulic acid. Strains of yeast with the right enzymes transform these phenolic acids through a decarboxylation reaction into aromatic phenols, such as 4-vinyl guaiacol. These compounds are often described as possessing clovelike and vanilla aromas. Yeast used to brew Bavarian weizen beer is supposed to produce these aromas, and weizen beer is the best beer to buy if you want a standard for the phenolic flavor. Some Belgian and English ale yeasts also produce detectable levels of phenols in beer. Phenolic aromas are not associated with most lager yeasts.

In general, brewing yeast strains do not produce enough phenolic aromas to be detectable. Phenolic beers are usually a sign of wild yeast contamination. Wild yeast can get into a brewery fermentation through poor sanitation practices or can be dumped in the fermenter in high numbers if the pitching yeast is contaminated. Contaminated pitching yeast is not uncommon, even if you use "fresh" yeast from a packet. In general, dry yeast contains wild yeast more often than liquid yeast, but both forms are capable of being contaminated. If I had to pick a likely cause of your problem, I would nominate your pitching yeast as the culprit. Try using a different strain or use yeast from a different company. If the problem doesn't go away, then you need to work on the other causes of the dreaded phenolic aroma.

Q **What would cause a smoky flavor in my beer, even though I didn't use any *smoked malts*?**

A The smell associated with smoked beers comes from phenols that arise during malt kilning. The phenols in smoked malts are derived from either peat or beechwood, but phenols can also be derived from phenolic acids present in malt. Phenolic acids are not aromatic, but when chemically modified into phenols, they are very aromatic. Certain yeast strains can convert phenolic acids found in wort into phenols and impart a phenolic character to beer. Most beers with a phenolic character have been contaminated with wild yeast strains. The phenolic character is a clear indicator of improper yeast handling.

Some beers, such as Bavarian weizens and Belgian ales, intentionally use yeast strains that are able to convert phenolic acids to phenols. These beers are considered normal when they have this particular aroma.

Another way that phenols can make it into beer is through intense roasting. During malt roasting, and coffee roasting for that matter, intense heat can and does convert phenolic acids to phenols, and very dark malts and coffees can take on a smoky aroma. The easiest way to solve the problem is to switch your roasted malt supply or to decrease the amount used. I have found more of these smoky aromas in roasted barley and black malt than other dark malts.

If you really want to eradicate this flavor, I would focus on selecting dark malts that do not have it. Tasting malt and making hot water extracts ("teas") of the malts you want to use will help to identify this flavor before using the smoky malt in your beer. Most likely you will be able to smell the smokiness in the malt if the malt is indeed the source.

Because yeast can also lead to phenolic flavors, you may want to evaluate your yeast by switching to a different strain for comparison. Many people describe the clovey, spicy character in weizen as smoky. If you have a yeast strain capable of producing these flavors (some ale strains produce the same compounds, only less), the yeast may be the culprit.

Q Every batch of India Pale Ale or other highly hopped ale that I have brewed has a distinct iced-tea flavor. Could it be from dry-hopping?

A Hoppy beers often have a bite from the tannins in the hops. This is similar to the astringency of strong tea and young red wines. However, not all hoppy beers are overly astringent and the true hop connoisseur will come to appreciate big hop flavor in time. The source of the iced-tea flavor in hoppy beers is obviously the hops. Hops contain bittering acids, aromatic oils, and plant matter. It is the plant matter that imparts this potentially unpleasant flavor. If the quantity of plant matter added to the beer is reduced so is the astringency in the finished product. You might think I am suggesting that you avoid brewing hoppy beers — but that's not my point.

The classic ideas about hopping are really quite limited when brewing some of the aggressively hopped beer styles found on the market. The basic notion is that high alpha hops are used early in the boil for bitterness and that any hop used for imparting aroma is a lower alpha variety. The problem with this rule of thumb is that the aromatic oils in hops are produced in the same place (the lupulin gland) that the bittering acids are produced, meaning that the concentration of aromatic oils typically decreases somewhat proportionally with alpha acids.

Using high alpha hops is one way of adding a good deal of hop oil while minimizing the addition of the hop plant matter. The notion that high alpha hops in general have poor aroma is totally false. Anyone who has ever rummaged around in the hop room of a brewery that uses whole hops has likely smelled many nice high alpha varieties. Historically, alpha acids were simply not "wasted" as aroma hops, and any hop varieties with appreciable alpha were used for bittering. Today, most beer brewed in the world has little hop aroma, and the vast quantity of hops grown in the world are produced for alpha acids. In fact, most statistics on hop production equate yields in terms of metric tons of alpha produced, because that remains the most important stat to the commercial brewer.

Another way of minimizing the plant material added to the brew is through hop pellet selection. Two types of hop pellets are produced by hop processors: type 90 and type 45. A type 90 pellet contains 90 percent of the weight of unprocessed hops. This means that 100 pounds (45 kg) of raw cone hops yield 90 pounds (41 kg) of pellets. The missing 10 pounds (5kg) is from stems, strigs, and the like. Type 45 pellets are made by separating much of the leafy matter from the lupulin glands that contain the stuff brewers want from hops. 100 pounds (45 kg) of hops yields 45 pounds (20 kg) of type 45 pellets. Using type 45 pellets for aroma will reduce the amount of plant material added to your beer by 50 percent.

Let's go a step further and essentially eliminate plant material from the equation and use a liquid hop preparation — not sexy, but functional. If you want hop aroma without bittering acids and plant material, there are hop oil extracts available. There are even hop tablets that are kind of like Alka-Seltzer tablets infused with hop oils that make measuring a no-brainer.

Q **The head of my beer has a very strong, bitter taste like concentrated hops, but the actual beer tastes great. What causes the phenomenon?**

A What you have discovered is that hop bittering acids are concentrated in beer foam! This is the same empirical evidence that led brewing scientists of the last century to hypothesize that hops are related to beer-foam stability. More than a century later, scientists are still studying the effects of hops on beer foam. Beer is one of very few beverages intended to maintain a persistent foam, and the foam on beer adds to the overall sensory experience. If a beer's foam is too bitter to drink and must collapse before consumption, the beer drinker is denied one of the pleasures of the malt tipple. An excellent beer should taste excellent when served properly. A properly served beer is cool enough to refresh the palate but warm enough to smell. Beer should always be evaluated from a glass to best release the beer's aroma qualities. Finally, a properly poured beer should have a foam that adds to the sensory experience.

Q Is it possible that a clove flavor in my beer is from wild yeast rather than bacteria, and assuming that it tastes good, is it all right to drink?

A The clovelike flavor you describe is a relatively common flaw in beer and usually comes from one of two places. Some brewing strains are termed phenolic off-flavor positive (POF+) and are capable of converting ferrulic acid in malt to 4-vinyl guaiacol, a compound that smells like cloves. Ale strains used in German weizens are POF+, as are many Belgian ale strains. Lager strains, on the other hand, are always POF-. Some ale strains are slightly POF+ and produce just enough 4-vinyl guaiacol to be detected.

Many wild or nonbrewing yeast strains produce this clovey flavor and many brewers associate this problem with wild yeast. Most brewers these days use closed wort coolers (as opposed to the cool ships of yesteryear) and really do not operate in an environment at risk for yeast drifting in from the environment. If you told me you used an open fermenter, this possibility would certainly be a prime candidate.

The other common cause of phenolic off-flavors comes from wort-spoilage bacteria. One commonly implicated bug is *Obesumbacterium proteus*. This critter can be picked up from wort coolers or any contact of boiled and cooled wort with nonboiled wort. I have brewed beers that I was convinced were contaminated with this bug because the intensity of the off-flavor was extremely high — this is a trait of the bacteria, as is a healthy dose of dimethyl sulfide (DMS). Beers spoiled by *Obesumbacterium proteus* taste extremely foul and, in my opinion, are totally undrinkable — prime candidates for the sewer.

If your beer is drinkable with a lower intensity of the clove aroma, I doubt that *Obesumbacterium proteus* is the culprit. If your palate is biased and tends to be a bit forgiving, you may be understating the aroma.

Q About a year ago, I suddenly started to get beer that was thick, syrupy, and very disgusting. It seems to take 2 or 3 weeks after bottling to start to show up, a little at a time. I suspected sanitation, but I have been extra careful and it still happens. I now suspect my water, which is from a well. Help!

A The problem you describe sounds like the phenomenon called *ropiness,* or the development of a complex polysaccharide slime in beer produced by certain bacteria. The slime produced by rope-forming bacteria is thixotropic in nature, which means the *viscosity* of the beer will drop when it is stirred or shaken and will increase once the beer is left still. The famous Belgian brewing scientist Jean De Clerck wrote in his *Textbook of Brewing,* published in the 1940s, that ropiness is "the most unpleasant infection which can be encountered in beer."

Ropey beer is caused by two different kinds of bacteria. The aerobic, vinegar-forming acetobacter are known to secrete slime — that has such a nice sound to it! Ropiness from the acetobacter species is only common in beer exposed to oxygen, like cask ale and beer left in beer taps. Your bottled beer does not have enough oxygen for acetobacter to grow and form rope.

The other bacteria known to form rope in beer are the varieties *viscosus* and *limosus* of *Pediococcus damnosus.* Unlike other strains of *Pediococcus,* these guys do not produce diacetyl (buttery or butterscotch flavor). *Pediococcus* is a common spoilage organism in beer and grows best under anaerobic conditions, like those found in a bottle. Like other beer spoilage bacteria, *Pediococcus* is commonly found in the environment and is often carried into beer through yeast or other ingredients added after the boil.

In general, your problem is most likely a result of poor sanitation. This does not necessarily mean that you are using dirty brewing practices. It simply means that you are contaminating your beer somehow. Good sanitation after the boil requires all implements that touch beer or wort to be cleaned with a detergent and sanitized before use. Make sure you are using a recognized sanitizer and that its concentration is correct. If you are using hot water, make sure the water is hotter than 180°F (82°C) and that you allow at least 20 minutes at this temperature before considering your tools sanitized. This includes carboys, hoses, spoons, bottles, and bottle caps.

Good sanitation also means that any ingredient added to beer should be properly treated before its addition. If you are adding well water to beer after fermentation, the water should be boiled. This rule also applies to priming sugar and other postboil additives.

Q **I found bugs in my new bag of wheat malt! Would the brewing process neutralize any bug-related contamination?**

A Insects in malt are actually a fairly common problem. I am not suggesting that this is by any means acceptable, but it is common. In my experience, flour weevils are the most commonly found bugs in malt. Weevils can cause major problems for commercial brewers if they infest a malt silo. These little critters eat malt, robbing brewers of the important carbohydrates that they have purchased from the maltster. As a by-product of metabolism, bugs, like other creatures, produce heat, carbon dioxide, and water. Insect infestation — and the fecal matter that comes with it — can lead to an increase in the malt moisture content, which in turn can lead to other problems, such as mold growth.

Steeping at 160°F (71°C) does not kill harmful bacteria, but boiling does. With that said, I wouldn't worry too much about the occasional flour weevil in the malt. Since these bugs spend their entire lives in flour, malt, or whatever else they are infesting and are not rooting around in nasty environments, as are flies and roaches, they do not fall into the "vector" bug category. A vector is something that spreads bad stuff around, like a fly that lands on your grilled Spam sandwich right after it was sunbathing on a stinky pile of . . . well you get the point.

I have seen the odd weevil in malt, as well as flour, and personally believe that a couple of weevils per pound are not a big deal. Other bugs, like roaches, are totally unacceptable since they travel around and spread filth. I have also had several bags of raw wheat arrive at our brewery that had numerous insect larvae on the outside of the bags — the wheat was obviously infested. I certainly did not want to spread this problem into my storage room and destroy the rest of my grain. My malt supplier happily replaced the wheat for free. I expect a refund for malt containing bugs, and I would never buy again from a shop that refused one.

■ ══════════ ■

Q **Is diacetyl only associated with lagers or is the fermentation temperature more of a key factor?**

A The real question at issue is not whether diacetyl is only associated with lagers, but rather if it is only unacceptable in lagers. Diacetyl is naturally found in all beers during fermentation; some beers can contain perceptible levels of diacetyl after aging. Diacetyl, also known as 2,3-butanedione, is produced outside of the yeast cell when the compound alpha-acetolactate is oxidized by metal ions or dissolved oxygen. During aging, yeast cells absorb diacetyl, use it as a hydrogen receptor in biochemical reactions, and in the process, convert into a flavorless alcohol called 2,3-butanediol.

Style gurus agree that diacetyl should never be found in lagers. Its presence is a sign of insufficient aging and is simply not acceptable in a type of beer named after its long, cold storage! Diacetyl can also originate from beer spoilage bacteria, especially *Pediococcus,* and any off-flavor associated with bacterial contamination is bad, regardless of the fermenting strain. (Wild beers, such as lambics, are of course held to a different set of rules.)

Oddly enough, if you asked the question, "What is the easiest type of beer to brew without having to worry much about diacetyl?" I would answer, "lager." In a classic lager fermentation, there is plenty of time for diacetyl to be produced from alpha-acetolactate and for yeast to absorb diacetyl and reduce it to 2,3-butanediol. The fact that lager yeast strains are typically less flocculent than ale strains also helps, since contact between the yeast cell and beer is essential for beer–yeast interactions to occur. Some ale strains and brewing methods, like those used for alt for example, make these beers more similar to lagers with respect to yeast behavior and fermentation technique than ales. In other words, I would not worry much about diacetyl in these types of ales.

Because of advances in brewing science over the past few decades, diacetyl is very well understood. The underlying biochemistry has allowed brewers to accelerate the aging process by manipulating beer temperature after fermentation.

Diacetyl is one of those compounds some people really like in small doses, because it adds to the complexity of some beer (and wine) styles. Most brewers see it as a defect because of its association with beer spoilage organisms, as well as its satiating effect on the consumer. If you want to get more diacetyl in your beers, take the opposite route of alt brewing. Use a flocculent yeast, room temperature fermentation, short aging, and good racking techniques to minimize the amount of yeast carried into the bottle. (See diacetyl rests, page 240.)

Q I tried to make a double IPA and added Champagne yeast after primary fermentation to give it some extra kick. I can already tell that it is too dry for my liking. How can I add malty sweetness back to my brew without starting all over?

A Your problem is yeast selection. Champagne is a yeast strain that tends to be highly attenuative and creates a very dry finished product. I am not a huge fan of extremely strong beers and typically brew with an original gravity of 18° Plato (1.072 SG) or lower. I have never had fermentation problems with these beers using my brewery's standard ale and lager strains. In fact, I have brewed a barley-wine with an original gravity of 25° Plato (1.100 SG), and it fermented to completion with our standard ales yeast.

I have never understood why Champagne yeast is so popular for strong beers. Most brewing strains can ferment strong worts, as long as the yeast is healthy and you pitch enough. Some of the whacked out, super-strong beers being brewed are simply too strong for these conventional methods. Brewers must do things such as change their yeast strains and slowly feed their fermentations to successfully make their odd tipples. Imperial IPAs, however, do not fall into this category of beers and the Champagne yeast is not required.

So you have this really dry, fairly bitter beer and wish it had more balance to it. There are several things you can consider here, and they involve adding something sweet to replace what the Champagne yeast took out. One method I like is to add a different beer and do a little blending. Blending is a really great tool used by winemakers, distillers, and a few brewers to take two or more products whose sum is greater than the individual pieces. With this beer, you could blend in some sweet stout to create a weird beer that may not have an identifiable style but may have a satisfying flavor — maybe you could call the concoction Imperial Brown Ale and invent a new style. You could add extract to the beer for sweetness, but you probably would be jumping from the pan into the fire. You might end up wanting to get rid of the worty flavor in your new creation.

Of course, both of these methods have one problem — Champagne yeast. If your beer still contains viable Champagne yeast cells, which it probably does and will continue to for quite some time, the added beer or wort will be dried out like your original beer. Depending on the population of viable Champagne yeast, this can happen relatively quickly or take a very long time.

This is somewhat of a double-edged sword. If you are able to correct the dryness issue and drink the beer before the Champagne yeast dries it out again, you'll be in good shape. However, if you bottle your new creation and let it sit around too long, you will begin to see over-carbonated bottles of beer and quite possibly explosions. Kegging your beer and keeping it very cold is a possible alternative to bottling and eliminates the explosion issue. The cold storage temperatures will also slow down the yeast action.

CHAPTER 9

Extract Brewing

Q **What are the basic steps to making an extract beer from prehopped kits, *nonhopped* extract, and extract with specialty grains?**

A Brewing beer using extract kits is a great way to begin homebrewing, and many homebrewers are happy to continue to brew beer from extracts. The most basic extract kit for the homebrewer includes prehopped cans of extract. To brew beer from prehopped extract, all that is required is to dissolve the extract in water, give it a boil according to the instructions with the kit (some require more boiling than others), cool it, and add the yeast. Since wort boiling drives aromas — including hop aromas — from the wort, prehopped kits can and do benefit from the addition of late hops if you want more hop aroma than the kit provides.

Adding hops to hopped kits is somewhat contrary to the notion of using prehopped kits. So many brewers who want hop independence use nonhopped extracts as their starting point. This option skips the mashing step, and the brew day begins by diluting extracts and beginning at the wort boiling stage. All of the hop additions used to brew all-grain beers are used to add bitterness, midpalate hop flavor, and a finish-hop aroma. The last addition can be in the kettle (late-kettle hopping) or in the fermenter (dry hopping), depending on the type of beer being brewed and the desired hop aroma. Although full volume wort boiling is not required when adding hops to extract brews, I recommend this practice when possible. (See wort boiling volume, page 400.)

Finally, there is the practice of adding special malts to malt extract. Adding special grains allows the extract brewer to add his or her own flair to the base malt extract, be it dry or liquid extract. Hopping-in this wort in the kettle gives the extract brewer quite a bit of leeway in the brew. The key with adding special malts to extract using this partial-mashing method is to select grains that do not require starch conversion to use. Crystal malts and roasted grains work well for this process, and these grains produce a wide array of colors and flavors. Unfortunately, malts such as Munich, pale ale malt, amber malt, rauch malt, and wheat malt all require mashing to convert starch into fermentable sugars. Even small amounts of starch in finished beer contribute to starch hazes and can lead to certain types of microbiological problems.

■ ══════════ ■

Q How is extract made? How are the hops added to prehopped extract kits?

A Extract is made the same way an all-grain brewer makes wort: Mashing grains, sometimes adding adjuncts, to produce fermentable wort. After mashing, the wort is separated from the spent grains, the grain bed is sparged with hot water to maximize yield, and the wort is concentrated. There are two main classes of malt extract: dry and liquid. (See page 341.)

Hopped extracts, both liquid and dry, have hops added sometime during extract production. The type of hops used and the time of addition varies by production. Hop extract is the most convenient hop preparation to use when making malt extract, because the hop solids do not need to be separated. Pre-isomerized extracts contain the wort/beer soluble iso-alpha-acids and can be added for hop bitterness after the wort has been concentrated and before packaging. Hop-aroma oils can also be added at this point. Bittering acids and oils could be added before the extract, but losses, especially of the hop oils, would be unacceptably high.

The thing about some extracts that many brewers don't like is what they don't know. For example, what types of malts and special malts are used? What type of mash profile was used? What, if any, adjuncts, simple sugars (sucrose and/or corn syrup), or other ingredients are present? Kits give a basic list of ingredients and some suppliers give some pretty good product specifications about their extracts, but the unknowns about these kits make some brewers feel like they lack control over their brews. These brewers usually end up wanting to go all-grain for complete brew dependence.

If you are an extract brewer who does not want to have the hassle of all-grain brewing but wants to know as much as possible about the extract being used, go to the Web sites of various extract producers and read about their products. Many companies that sell extracts to homebrewers also sell malt and certain extracts to commercial brewers and extracts to bakers and have really good information available online.

Getting Sticky Extract Out of Cans

Malt extract, like honey, corn syrup, and molasses, has a very high viscosity when cool. This makes it likely to cling to the can. Commercial operations keep malt extracts at around 120°F (about 50°C) so that they can be pumped. There is nothing worse than having a huge tank and process pipes full of sugary syrup that is too cool for smooth pumping and mixing.

Fortunately, with a bit of planning, malt extract syrups are easy to handle at home. The easiest technique? Begin with a warm can of extract.

Put the closed can in a saucepan and fill it with water until the can is half submerged, making a water bath. Set the bath on the stove over low heat or in an oven set at 200°F (93°C). In about 30 minutes, the syrup will be warm enough to pour freely from the can. Periodically rolling the can to mix it will speed the heating time.

Q **My extract always seems to get stuck on the bottom of my brew pot and make a mess. Am I doing anything wrong?**

A Concentrated liquid malt extract is one of those ingredients used in the kitchen that is prone to burning when handled improperly. If you simply pour malt extract from a can into your brew pot, add water, and stir with a spoon while heating, it is quite likely that some of the high density extract will sit on the bottom of the kettle where it will potentially burn.

Diluting concentrated syrups is best done in a series of steps. Begin with a warm can of extract. (See page 339.) Pour this extract into a medium-sized saucepan and rinse the can out with some hot brewing-quality water, pouring the hot water from the extract can into the saucepan. Be sure to keep track of how much water you have added. Once the extract can is rinsed out, stir the contents of the pot so that the syrup is evenly distributed.

Next, add the remaining volume of water (less about 2 quarts) to your empty brew pot. Turn on the heat and bring this water to a boil. Turn off the heat but leave the pot on the burner. It is now time to add the extract: An extra set of hands makes this step a little easier. While gently stirring the brew pot of water, slowly pour the contents of the medium-sized saucepan into the hot water. This will help adjust the free-flowing, partially diluted malt extract to your desired preboil gravity without the dense masses of extract quickly sinking to the bottom of the kettle. After transferring the extract into the brew pot, use the remaining 2 quarts of water to rinse any extract clinging to the medium-sized pan.

This may sound like an extra step, but it beats having the bottom of the kettle coated with baked-on wort. It also helps to ensure that your finished beer is free from burnt flavors that arise from wort caramelization and burning when extract is not properly mixed.

Q For an all extract brew, is it ok to only use dried malt extract (DME) without liquid malt syrups?

A There is no reason not to use dried malt extract exclusively for your recipes, although there are fewer color choices than with liquid extracts. You will need special malts to add various colors and flavors. The exclusive use of dried malt usually requires the extract brewer to add hops to the wort, as there are few prehopped DMEs available.

The way I view this scenario is much like all-grain brewing, where the pale malt is used as the backbone of the beer and various special malts build upon the base. Hopping techniques further build upon the base. The brewer selects the variety used for bittering and aroma, the time of addition, and the amount added. I see nothing wrong or problematic with exclusively using DME as the base extract for brewing and have made many, many brews this way.

The one thing to bear in mind with extract brewing in general is that any grain added to a steeping bag should be compatible with the method. These ingredients include crystal, or caramel, malts and roasted grains. Grains requiring mashing, such as pale malts, Munich malt, rye malt, and wheat malt, and adjuncts, like rice and corn, must be mashed to convert their starch to fermentable sugars.

If you choose to use this method, you can easily convert an all-grain recipe to a DME-based recipe by multiplying the weight of pale malt by 0.7 and substituting the pale malt with DME. This only works for beers that do not use other malts — such as wheat or Munich malt — in the formulation.

Q **If my tap water tastes okay, can I just go ahead and use it to make my extract beers?**

A The rule of thumb that most homebrewers use is to worry only about treating their water when they use grains that require mashing or steeping. The taste of water is certainly a very important quality to consider as an extract brewer. The mineral composition is another important feature, even though we are not talking about mashing. Waters that have high sulfate content produce beers that taste drier and more bitter than beers made using waters low in sulfate. Yeast can also metabolize sulfate, so beers from high-sulfate water can take on sulfury aromas. Chloride has an opposite effect on beer flavor, leading to beers with a fuller, sweeter mouthfeel. These beers also have a decreased perceived bitterness compared to beers with lower chloride levels. Many brewers intentionally add minerals to their water, choosing a calcium source from calcium sulfate or calcium chloride with the flavor effects of sulfate and chloride in mind.

My short advice is to use your taste buds and follow your instinct. Rate the taste of your tap water on an imaginary scale based upon all the different water you have drunk. I really wouldn't worry too much if my tap water tastes great and would start thinking more about this issue if my rating was below par.

Q **What exactly is the difference between mashing and steeping? Don't both procedures basically involve soaking grain in hot water?**

A Mashing and steeping are very similar processes at first glance. Both involve soaking crushed grains in hot water. However, if you look more closely, there are some sharp contrasts between the two methods.

Mashing is a technique in which malted grains are soaked and amylase enzymes from the grains convert their starch to fermentable sugars. Some mashing methods combine malts that are very high in enzymes with starchy grains lacking enzymes. Other mashing methods only use malted grains. Mashing methods using adjuncts, such as rice or corn, work because enzymes from malt are able to move freely about in the mash once the malt has been crushed and wet. The amylase enzymes cannot differentiate starch from malt or rice, and they go about their merry way breaking down (hydrolyzing) starch into fermentable sugars. The key to mashing is that the starch is broken down into fermentable sugars and special attention is given to controlling the mash environment — I'll get to that later. Grains that are mashed include any pale malt, lightly toasted or kilned special malts (such as Munich malt), and raw cereal grains.

Steeping, on the other hand, is a method used to extract colors and flavors from certain types of specialty grains. Although the grains are soaked in hot water, the idea is not to have enzymes acting upon starch. Rather, steeping merely extracts compounds contained in the malt. The types of specialty malts ideal for steeping already have the starch converted to sugars during the malting process. These include the family of crystal, or caramel, malts and grain or malt that is roasted to such a high level that the starch molecules have been modified by heat to the point where malt enzymes don't do much to them. Roasted grains and malts include chocolate and black malt, roasted wheat, roasted wheat malt, roasted rye, and roasted barley. Specialty malts, such as Munich malts, pale wheat malt, pale rye malt, and flaked cereal grains like barley, oats, corn, and rice are not well-suited for steeping, because these ingredients all contain a lot of starch.

The key differences in the actual processes of steeping and mashing lie mainly in the thickness, temperature, duration, and method used to separate the grain from the liquid. Mash thickness, or the ratio of malt to water, is important in mashing because enzymes are affected by the concentration of starch. If it's too high, the amylase enzymes lack the water needed to hydrolyze starch (hydrolysis is a term used to refer to breaking chemical bonds by adding water). If the mash is too thin, the enzymes are less heat-stable and are more susceptible to denaturation (enzyme destruction). Most mashes use between 1 and 2 quarts of water per pound of malt (about 2–4 L/kg). When it comes to steeping, thin is good, and it is common to use ratios as high as 6 quarts per pound (about 12 L/kg). The thin steep not only improves the efficiency of steeping, but it is also convenient since the steep water is usually used to dissolve malt extracts after the steeped grains are removed.

When it comes to mashing, the most critical variable to control is temperature. Different enzymes have peak activities at different temperatures, and some enzymes denature at just a few degrees higher than their activity peak. Brewers have named the various mash temperature *rests* for enzymes or their substrates because of this critical connection. We have the acid or phosphatase rest, protein rest, beta-glucanase rest, beta-amylase or fermentability rest, the alpha-amylase or conversion rest, and the mash-off step. Few brewers include all of these temperature rests in their mash profiles, but mash temperature is always associated with enzymatic activity. These terms are moot when it comes to steeping, but temperature remains an important consideration. Most agree that grain-steeping temperatures should be kept below about 170°F (77°C) to avoid the extraction of astringent tannins from the malt husk.

Enzymatic reactions take time, and most mashes last at least 60 minutes. Steeping does not require such a long time, because the only thing happening is the dissolution of the malt solids. Fifteen minutes is more than enough time for steeping.

The final step is separating the grains from the liquid. Most steepers use a nylon bag (like a tea bag) that is easily removed from the steep. Depending on the amount of grain steeped and the amount of water used, the bag is rinsed with hot water. Mashing requires the more involved method of separating the wort from the grains. This process is called lautering. Wort is separated from the solids in some sort of straining device — for example, a lauter tun — and is thoroughly rinsed with hot sparge water to extract as much wort as possible. This step is required in mashing because of the mash thickness. Without sparging, the specific gravity of the wort would be around 1.080 SG, as compared to sparged gravities ranging from 1.040 and higher.

These are the key differences between mashing and steeping. To the extract brewer who uses steeping for specialty malts, mashing probably sounds very involved. However, the method of mashing is really not much more involved than steeping. It's just that there is a lot more going on, and more variations on brewing to explore, when mashing is entered into the homebrewing equation!

Q Is there some formula that will help the homebrewer determine how long a particular type of grain should be steeped when using an extract-based recipe?

A As difficult as it is to admit, brewing is a whole lot like cooking, and there are many ways to get the job accomplished. Steeping is one of these tasks. When using malts as color and flavor additives to extract brews, there really is no exact science. For example, grains like crystal, chocolate, and black malt do not change when they are mashed, the way pale, Munich, wheat, and Pilsner malts do. Most specialty malts contain either fermentable sugars (crystal malts) or roasted starches (chocolate malt). Neither type is enzymatically altered when soaked in hot water. This is as true for brewers who steep these malts as it is for brewers who mash them.

In practical terms, this means that steeping temperature is not terribly important in the grand scheme of brewing. A good cooking analogy is tea. Some tea bags intended for iced tea suggest using hot water while others suggest cold water. Increasing the water temperature used to brew tea may extract more tea color and flavor per unit weight of tea leaves — but not much more. When tea is brewed using very hot water, excessive tannins are extracted and the tea has an astringent, harsh character.

The same holds true in brewing with steeping grains for extract beers. Beers made from steeping grains in the temperature range from about 120 to 160°F (49–71°C) will taste very similar. Steeping temperatures greater than 160°F (71°C) will produce beers with progressively more astringency, but this difference in flavor will likely be marginal. All-grain brewers need to be much more cautious about mashing temperature because enzymes are involved and these enzymes are irreversibly deactivated at temperatures above their denaturation point.

If I were brewing a beer made from extracts and specialty malts, I would steep my grains at 150 to 160°F (66–71°C) for 15 to 30 minutes and sparge or rinse the grain bag with water at about the same temperature. This method is a very good starting point. Only if the resulting beer had odd flavors attributable to steeping temperature or time would I consider changing the temperature.

Q When steeping crushed grains, what is a good method to keep the husks from escaping from the steeping bag?

A All grains used for steeping should be placed in a bag unless you plan on straining the steeping grain and water mixture prior to adding your extract, be it dry malt extract or liquid extract. I would not worry too much about a few pieces of husk escaping from the steeping bag, but if you are getting a large amount of leakage, you may want to find a bag that has a finer mesh. Steeping should be performed between 150 and 170°F (66–77°C) to reduce the chance of astringent flavors.

Q What kinds of grains can I steep when making an extract-based beer?

A The only grains I would use for steeping are crystal malts and dark roasted grains like roasted barley, black patent malt, and chocolate malt. All other grains should be mashed in order to convert the starches contained in the grain to fermentable sugars.

Q Should I crush my specialty malts? If not, does this apply to all specialty malts or just the darker ones, such as chocolate and black patent?

A I must admit, not milling your specialty malt is strange, if not directly contrary to the milling practices used by commercial breweries throughout the world. It is common to completely pulverize very dark malts such as chocolate, roast barley, and black malt prior to mashing. Unlike pale malt, these grains do not have the type of husks that benefit lautering. They are very brittle and usually turn to powder when milled. In fact, many malting companies sell roasted products that are prepulverized. The rationale behind the practice is to maximize the yield of color and flavor compounds in order to use less of the stuff per unit volume. The method you mention would do just the opposite.

Q I like the toastier (or nutty) tasting ambers. I was hoping that you could tell me how to achieve this taste with my extract beers. Do I use *toasted malt* or is there some additive?

A Toasty, nutty, and burnt flavors are typically associated with malt selection. This rather broad range of flavors can be attributed to one type of malt: crystal. I think the wide range of colors and flavors of crystal malt (also known as caramel) is underappreciated by many brewers. Most recipes that use crystal malt use only the midrange types that hover around 50° Lovibond. These crystal malts (40–60°L) have nutty, malty, and caramel flavors. This type of crystal malt is essential for pale ales and other amber styles. So if you want to add nutty flavors to your extract brews, I would look at some of the midrange crystal available on the market. Crystal malt is perfectly suited for extract brewing as a steeped grain. For the extract brewers who want to add some flavor and color with no worries about starch and steep temperature, crystal is the obvious malt to consider because of its diverse range of flavor and color.

Q Is there a benefit to adding your extract late in the boil?

A Brewers who have brew pots too small to boil the entire wort volume sometimes add dry and/or liquid malt extracts late in the boil. These partial-mash brewers boil the wort extracted from malt to do all the things that are required for wort boiling, and then at the end of the boil, add the remaining extract in liquid or dry form per their recipe. A short hold at high temperatures is sufficient to kill any bacteria carried in the malt extracts, since they have already been heat-treated during manufacture and do not have high bacterial loads. After the high-gravity wort has been cooled, the gravity is adjusted with water.

The benefit to this method is that wort produced from grain is boiled with hops at a normal gravity, just like an all-grain, full wort volume brew, and all of the requirements of boiling are met. So the simple answer is that this is a sound method and has no obscure pitfalls that may end up causing disappointment.

Calculate Evaporation during Your Boil

You can track your evaporation by calibrating your brew kettle and noting the pre- and postboil volumes. Here's the formula to use:

Evaporation percent =
100 – (postboil volume x 100 ÷ preboil volume)

For example: Say you collect 5.5 gallons of wort and boil it down to 5 gallons. This would be 100 – (500 ÷ 5.5), or 100 – 90.9, which equals an evaporation rate of 9.1 percent.

Most commercial brewers target between 8 and 10 percent evaporation during the boil. For home-brewers, a good evaporation rate is 6–8 percent per hour. A kettle that evaporates 6 percent per hour will evaporate 8 percent of the volume in 80 minutes. If another kettle evaporates 8 percent per hour, then a 60-minute boil will evaporate the same wort volume. As you collect more data, you can adjust your flame to fine-tune your evaporation rate.

Q Can I hold off the addition of malt extract (in an all-extract or partial-mash recipe) until the end of the boil? Or can I just boil the hops in plain water in some smaller volume (like 1 gallon or 3.8 L) in an all-extract recipe? Or does something else in the wort (like pH levels) play a part in extracting bitterness from hops?

A The late extract method was designed for partial mashers. It suggests boiling the small volume of homemade extract with hops for about 45 minutes, then adding the dry or liquid malt extract to bring the gravity into check during the last 15 minutes of the boil. This method also appeals to the homebrewer who cannot easily boil large volumes of wort and who does not want to boil highly concentrated wort. The reason most seasoned brewers wish to avoid boiling concentrated wort and diluting later with water is that color and flavor are sacrificed and hop utilization goes down.

The method you suggest is not new. A version of this practice is unknowingly used by many homebrewers. Your idea is to essentially skip wort boiling, except for a few minutes for wort sterilization. And the hop bitterness and flavor would be added from a little pot of boiling water and hops.

Q **In extract brewing, does the length of boil affect the color of my brew?**

A Length of boil affects wort color in all types of brewing. In extract brewing, the effect is sometimes even more pronounced due to the practice of boiling a small volume of high-density wort and diluting it up to 5 gallons (19 L) after the boil. This causes more wort darkening, since the components that react to form colored compounds are more concentrated in this method of boiling and the reaction leading to color proceeds at a faster rate when the reactants are concentrated.

Q **I have read references to whirlpooling to help separate the trub from the wort. Can you elaborate on how this is done?**

A Whirlpooling is a common method used in commercial breweries to separate hop pellets and trub from wort after the wort boil. Essentially, the wort is pumped into the whirlpool vessel at rapid velocity, usually about 15 feet (5 m) per second, to cause the wort to start spinning like a whirlpool. Sometimes the kettle doubles as the whirlpool vessel and the wort is recirculated to the kettle.

Homebrewers can use whirlpools just like the big guys. Instead of pumping the wort after boiling, use a big spoon to stir persistently in a circular motion in one direction, generating a mini-whirlpool. Continue stirring for 1 to 2 minutes and allow it to rest for 10 to 20 minutes before draining the wort into your wort cooler. Watch as the wort level gets low. If you really want to separate as much hops and trub as possible, stop the flow when the trub pile starts to suck into your wort chiller.

The whirlpool is a simple device, but many variations on its basic design are used in commercial breweries. The most common design is a flat-bottomed vessel with a slight pitch toward the drain. This gives a great trub pile, but also allows the trub to slide toward the outlet if the pile is loose. Some designs have a low point in the center and an outlet drain that is a little higher than the low point. This prevents trub from leaving with the wort. Your keg/kettle will behave like this system.

Q **When you put the hot extract wort into a primary fermenter that already has 3 gallons (11 L) of cold water, doesn't that cool the wort enough to pitch the yeast? I have made several batches this way and haven't noticed any off-flavors yet. Is there something I am missing here?**

A As long as the cool water sitting in the bottom of your primary fermenter has been boiled to kill any bacteria that may be present and cooled, then you won't have any problems. A wort chiller will become a necessary part of your arsenal of homebrewing tools when you begin boiling all of your wort. This usually occurs when extract brewers jump into the arena of all-grain brewing. Until then you will do just fine cooling your wort with cold dilution water.

Q I bought some malt extract in 10-pound (4.5 kg) pails. I recently noticed that mold has developed on top of the malt. Has this ruined my extract or will the mold be eliminated in the boil? Can I scrape the top layer off and use what is left? Will refrigerating the malt prevent mold?

A Malt extract and damp malt will grow mold. Moldy grain certainly should not be used for brewing, and I personally would not use malt extract with mold on the surface, though some brewers do. Removing the mold from the surface of the extract may completely remove the mold from the container, but then again, it may not. Mold is bad for two main reasons.

Moldy grain is a known cause of gushing in beer. Certain molds, for example, the *Fusarium* species, excrete proteins that act as nucleation sites for carbon dioxide breakout in finished beer. In simple terms, this means that when a bottle of beer is opened, the carbon dioxide uncontrollably breaks out of solution and a huge foamy mess gushes from the beer bottle. This is why it is called gushing. The same thing could possibly result from using moldy malt extract.

Another reason to avoid using moldy malt or malt extract is that certain molds produce mycotoxins (toxins from mold) when they grow. Although many mycotoxins are completely destroyed when heated, some mycotoxins become more toxic when heated, as is the case with certain types of aflotoxin. This concern applies to eating moldy foods. Not all molds are bad, and some add a very nice flavor to food, such as *Penicillium roqeforti,* which is used to make blue cheese.

The mold growing on your malt extract is most likely an airborne mold that came into contact with extract when you first opened it for use. Refrigeration will certainly slow the growth of mold and will extend the shelf life of pails that are opened and only partially used. However, molds will grow in the refrigerator, given enough time. Prevent mold growth on grains by storing grain in a dry environment.

CHAPTER 10

All-Grain Brewing

Q What would you recommend for my maiden voyage with all-grain brewing?

A Keeping your mash simple the first several times around the block is the best way to go. Use 3 quarts (2.8 L) of water for every 2 pounds (.90 kg) of malt, hold your mash temperature at a constant 152°F (67°C) for 60 to 90 minutes, and sparge with 165°F (74°C) water. Use an infusion mash with no mash-off and you'll be fine. If your malt is at room temperature and your mash tun is preheated, then your mash water needs to be at about 164°F (74°C) to reach your mash temperature of 152°F (67°F). Just make sure your mash tun is preheated! Mixing room temperature malt with your hot water will get you right in the ballpark.

Now you're probably wondering about that water chemistry stuff; a most ugly topic. Water is, without question, extremely important. However, all great beer cities of the world used their natural waters. I recommend trying out your town's water and determining the type or types of beer for which your homebrewery should become famous. Once you have the basics down, start experimenting with more fancy systems, if it suits you. Just remember that some of the most well respected microbrews and British ales use a single temperature with no mash-off for all of their beers.

One of the real advantages to starting off simple is that you get to concentrate on the important details of mashing. For example, remembering to cover your false bottom with water before mashing in, perfecting the lautering process, knowing when to stop adding sparge water, hitting your target gravities, and so on. These skills are required for all types of mashing and are easier to focus on when you don't have a triple decoction cooking away!

Mashing Methods

Infusion mashing is a traditional method using an unheated mash tun, resulting in a single temperature mash. In reality, the temperature drops slightly over the mash rest and increases during sparging. Step mashing uses a heated mashing vessel, frequently called a mash mixer (or *maisch böttich* in Germany), and incorporates a number of rests. The rests in many step-mash profiles coincide with the rest temperatures of decoction-mash profiles. Step mashing is really a descendant of decoction mashing.

Step mashing allows for rests at the optimal temperatures for beta amylase and alpha amylase as well as a controlled temperature ramp from the beta rest to the alpha rest. This, to me, is the real key to step mashing, because it gives the brewer the ability to increase wort fermentability. Most dry beers have a long rest at 140°F (60°C) for beta amylase and then a slow ramp up to 158°F (70°C) for the alpha rest. The result is an increase in wort fermentability as compared to infusion mashing at a single temperature.

Q **Is it true that step mashing is necessary when you don't use well-modified malts?**

A My brewing professor and mentor always said that mashing is really an extension of malting — what does not happen in the malthouse must be completed during mashing. Well-modified malt is great for infusion mashing. Well-modified malt has had significant enzymatic degradation of the barley endosperm during malting, and the starch granules are easily hydrated, gelatinized, and broken down in size by alpha and beta amylase during mashing to produce wort. Well-modified malts typically make for easy wort separation because they do not contain large molecules that are found in the endosperm of unmalted barley.

Malts that are not well modified are usually called undermodified or poorly modified malts. This terminology is vague, but the important thing to remember is that the malted grain still retains some of the barley endosperm character. In other words, the endosperm still contains large molecules of protein and carbohydrate gums that make the endosperm very hard. In extreme cases, poorly modified grains contain a steely end that looks like the steely gray endosperm of barley. Fully modified grains do not have a steely tip and have a uniform white endosperm color. This is one reason why malt is evaluated by chewing.

Poorly modified malts do not work too well in an infusion mash because these gums make for difficult lautering. Low temperature rests of 118°F (48°C) allow the enzyme beta-glucanase to degrade beta-glucan gums (a type of carbohydrate) into smaller pieces. This is important, since long beta-glucan chains dramatically increase wort *viscosity* and make wort separation difficult.

■ ══════════ ■

Q **In beginning the mash, is it better to add the hot water to the grain or the grain to the water? Or does it really make any difference?**

A At home, I have always added malt to hot water in my mash tun. This method works well because it is easy to stir the mash and avoid clumping as the malt is dumped into the mash tun. It also allows for the water temperature to be adjusted precisely before adding the grain. This is especially useful if the mash tun is stainless steel and needs to be preheated so that it doesn't cool the mash. I suppose a nifty gadget could be made to emulate a commercial grist hydrator at home, but on such a small scale I think it would be technology overload.

Some brewers use a technique that prevents exposing the enzymes to high temperatures while also allowing for a comfortably paced mash-in process. The technique is to start off the mash cool and thick, for example using 1 quart (.94 L) of water per pound (.45 kg) of malt and starting the mash around 120°F (49°C). This gives time to mash-in at a relaxed pace and for the mash thickness and temperature to stabilize. After mash-in is over, slowly add boiling water while stirring to hit your desired mash temperature. This technique can be used to hit several temperatures between 120°F (49°C) and the conversion temperature, or you can go straight to the conversion temperature. In either case, it resolves the mashing-in dilemma.

■ ══════════ ■

Q What are the main goals I should try to achieve with my mashing?

A The brewer's goal in mashing is twofold. The primary goal is to convert starch from the variety of starchy ingredients into fermentable sugars, so that yeasts may gobble them up and transform wort into beer. This goal is crude, and we can accomplish our primary goal and produce beers with a very high residual extract as well as those with virtually no remaining carbohydrates.

The secondary goal of mashing, and arguably a much more important one, is to take control of the transformation of starch.

■ ══════════ ■

MASH CONSISTENCY

How thick or thin should your mash be? When you mash-in, you want to use anywhere from 2 to 4 parts water to 1 part grain (weight to weight basis). As with everything in life, the metric system is much more convenient than the goofy system of measurements we use in the United States, once you get accustomed to the numbers.

Using the metric system, this mash thickness is equal to 2 to 4 liters of mash water per kilogram of malt. Converted into English units (not to be confused with Imperial units) this comes out to be 0.24 to 0.48 gallons per pound (0.96–1.92 quarts). The mash resembles oatmeal, except in the case of brewing it's maltmeal. The mash changes as the enzymes convert starch to sugar. This causes the mash to thin over the course of time and changes the appearance of the wort from cloudy to clear.

Wort may appear really thick or viscous in photos, but in reality it is really not much more viscous than water and flows freely from the grain bed. Depending on the mash thickness, the wort density ranges anywhere from 16° Plato (1.064 SG) to 25° Plato (1.100 SG) at the beginning of wort collection and decreases upon sparging.

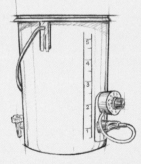

Mash tun

Q

What factors influence enzyme activity in my mash?

A

It is important to understand mash reactions themselves if you want to take full advantage of your all-grain brewing. This means boning up on mashing biochemistry — also known as enzymes. Here's a quick rundown on enzymes in the mash.

Enzymes are most active when their temperature optimum and pH optimum are both met. If the mash temperature exceeds the optimum temperature of a specific enzyme, say beta-amylase, the enzyme irreversibly denatures and permanently loses activity. The various relevant enzymes active in malt have a range of temperature optima from about 104 to 158°F (40–70°C).

The rate of enzymatic reactions is highest when the concentration of enzyme and substrate are high. This means that reaction rates drop off as time passes: There becomes a point of diminishing return where extending the mash time does not have any real effect on the mash. It also means that if the concentration of a certain enzyme group is very low in malt, for example proteolytic enzymes, there will not be much change in the wort attribute by the enzyme group. In other words, if they ain't at the party, they can't contribute to the fun!

Q What generally causes low yield in an infusion mash?

A Extract yield is simply defined as the weight of solids extracted into wort during mashing compared to the weight of ingredients added to the mash (or kettle if doing a partial mash with a grain bag). All ingredients added to the mash will contribute to wort specific gravity and are included in the calculation. Extract yield is affected by many variables, including the mashing type, malt quality, equipment design, and technique.

When conducting a mash, it is key to get the big items in line. Mash temperature, pH, and mash thickness are the variables that most concern me. For an infusion mash, I want my mash temperature between 149 and 158°F (65–70°C), the pH to be between 5.2 and 5.6, and the mash thickness to be between 2.5 and 3.5 L of water per kilogram malt (0.3 to 0.5 gal. per pound). As long as these parameters are okay, there should be no big problems in the mash. When sparging begins, as long as the sparge water is between 160 and 170°F (71–77°C) and wort collection takes at least 30 minutes, I am not worried.

Malt milling is the most common and likely cause of low yield. The appearance of properly crushed malt changes depending on the type of wort separation system being used. For example, if you have a false bottom or copper manifold system with wide slots, you will have to use coarser grist. But you should never find whole malt kernels after milling. Whole malt kernels will not yield any extract.

I use a lauter tun for wort separation, and it has a false bottom with 1-mm (0.04 in.) slots. My grist mainly consists of broken pieces of endosperm (the white stuff inside the malt kernel) that look like little pebbles and large pieces of malt husk. The grist also has some finer particles of endosperm, some flour, and some bashed-up pieces of husk. If I mill finer, I will get more of the small particles and the result will be cloudy wort. If my lauter tun had 0.7-mm slots instead of 1-mm slots, I could mill finer and still produce very clear wort. I get about 35 points per pound in my system, and I attribute this to proper milling and a nice false bottom on my lauter tun. If you try milling finer and the husk is getting really beaten up, you may want to try a different mill. If the husk looks good but you are having clarity problems, your slot width may be too wide.

Q I started to mill my grain differently and now my all-grain batches have low original gravity readings. What is going on?

A Low yields can be tracked to three general areas: milling, mashing technique, and wort separation method. Typically, decoction mashing gives the highest yield, followed by temperature-profile then infusion-mashing methods. The difference in yield among these mashing styles may be about 5 percent — really not a huge difference. Wort-separation method is also an important consideration, but this issue deals mainly with commercial breweries because homebrewers don't have too many options with respect to lauter tun design. This leaves milling.

There is no doubt in my mind that your problem is a direct result of coarse grist. In order for malt starch to be converted to sugar, by amylase enzymes, it first needs to dissolve. Generally, most malts have a laboratory extract yield of about 80 percent. This means that, under laboratory conditions, 80 percent of the weight of the malt will end up in the wort as extract. Laboratory conditions are quite different from brewery conditions, because wort clarity and ease of wort recovery are not important. The laboratory yield is simply the maximum yield possible. Most systems can easily yield about 90 percent of the laboratory number. This number is most commonly referred to among brewers as the brewhouse yield.

Using a more finely milled grist can increase brewhouse yield. I like to use the finest grist possible without creating cloudy wort or slowing wort collection. This choice is simply a matter of gradually reducing the gap on your mill until you get to the point where the grist is too fine and then backing up a step. This point is where your problem could get a bit more complicated.

You may have found that the only way to produce clear, easy-flowing wort is by using very coarse grist. If this is the case, your mill may be chewing up the malt husk or the design of your false bottom may be inadequate.

Experiment by milling samples while using different mill gaps and visually examining the grist. Ideally, you should see chunks of white endosperm (malt starch) and nice, big, fluffy pieces of husk. If you don't see nice pieces of husk, you may have an inadequate mill. If that's the case, I suggest finding a homebrew supply store that has a good mill and buying milled malt, or if you like milling your own grain, then you should buy a different mill.

Your mill, however, may not be the problem. If you have a false bottom with large holes or slits, you will be forced to use very coarse grist to produce a clear wort. Changing your false bottom will address this problem. I have always liked the copper manifold wort-collection device that can be assembled in the bottom of a cooler. The width of a hacksaw blade produces a narrow gap that works well with relatively fine grist. This system produces very bright wort, gives a good flow rate, and has an excellent brewhouse yield.

Q How can I calculate extract efficiency in my all-grain brewing, and is it even important?

A Professional brewers strive to brew the same wort day after day to achieve the most consistent beer possible. At least that's the plan. One of the many things required to brew a consistent beer is knowledge about extract efficiency or extract yield. Malts change from lot to lot and brewhouse efficiency may change with time, so commercial brewers naturally want to account for these natural variations.

Almost every batch of malt produced in a commercial malthouse is analyzed for the maximum amount of solids that can be extracted in a laboratory mash. The number produced from this analysis is called the laboratory yield. When brewers produce wort using the same batch of malt as a lab, they almost always get less extract. This is because brewers use a coarser malt grind than the lab method and they collect less of the weak last runnings from the grain bed. The relationship between the brewery yield and the laboratory yield is called the brewhouse yield and it reflects how efficient a brewery is. To calculate brewhouse yield, you need to know three numbers: wort volume after boiling, wort gravity after boiling, and the laboratory yield.

This is easy to calculate if you have a hydrometer and a way to measure wort volume. Suppose you produce 5 gallons (19 L) of a 1.040 OG wort. If you multiply 5 gallons by 40 gravity points (the number following the decimal in the OG reading), you can determine the number of gallon-points in the wort. In this example, there are 200 gallon-points. Although this is a strange unit, it works well.

Next, compare the gallon-points actually produced with the number theoretically possible. Suppose you used 7 pounds (3.2 kg) of malt that had a laboratory yield of 36 gallon-points per pound. Theoretically, you could produce 252 gallon-points of extract (7×36). Comparing the 200 gallon-points produced with the 252 gallon-points theoretically possible gives a brewhouse yield of 79 percent.

This calculation is easy on paper. However, calculating it at home is another story because very few malts purchased at homebrew supply stores state their theoretical yield. Even if the malt comes with a laboratory yield number, the number can't always be trusted. Malts settle and small samples may not have the same properties as the whole batch, bags get mixed, and many malt suppliers give typical lab results to homebrew suppliers. Falling short of analyzing the malt yourself, you probably won't know the laboratory yield of the malt you are using.

Most homebrewers (and many pub brewers) make educated guesses at the theoretical yield of different malts. This works reasonably well because the modern maltster is pretty good at being consistent; after all, we brewers demand it! Pale malt usually has a lab yield of about 78 percent, crystal is about 72 percent, rice is around 98 percent, and black malt is near 65 percent. Malt labs typically report yield as a percentage, and these numbers can be converted to gallon-points per pound by multiplying by 0.46.

The great thing about knowing your brewery efficiency and your malt yield is that they help you become consistent and are very helpful when trying to hit a target original gravity with grains you have never used. Those are really the only brewing issues related to efficiency, unless you brew commercially.

The other hobbyist aspect of efficiency is machismo. I mean, what good is 95 percent efficiency if you can't brag? Kind of like the guy with the imported sports car that goes from zero to 60 in 4.9 seconds. All of his friends surely know his car's prowess, but has he needed that acceleration lately, let alone used it? Give me a system that is reliable and predictable, and most important, makes great beer!

MR. WIZARD'S TIPS
TO AVOID A STUCK MASH

Needless to say, there are no foolproof brewing methods: Simply too many things can and do go awry. To minimize the chances of a stuck mash, focus on five key points.

1. Remember that the first step of the brewing process is milling. Malt that is milled too fine or in a manner that destroys the integrity of the husk can cause problems when it comes time to lauter. Start the day on the right foot. Buy premilled malt, use a mill at your local homebrew store, or buy a mill designed to mill malt. Blenders, flour mills, and coffee grinders are not the way to start the day. Some brewers use rolling pins or beer bottles to crush the malt, but these methods are extremely tedious. Impatient brewers like me give up quickly on such awkward tools and break out the margarita blender to finish off the task. This is not recommended!

2. Every process requires a tool. The first time you brew all-grain is not the time to be too creative with tools. Colanders, coffee filters, and the like will probably cause problems. Use a proven tool for your lauter. The double-bucket method, a picnic cooler with a copper pipe manifold, and a large pot with a false bottom are three that work well. If you take the time to build a good tool, you will greatly reduce the chances of a complete disaster.

3. Cover the bottom of your lauter tun with foundation water before filling it with mash. If air bubbles form beneath the false bottom, they will greatly impede the flow of wort out of the lauter tun. If you make this mistake once, you probably will never forget to cover the bottom again!

4. Don't let the top of the grain bed get dry. Grain in an infusion mash is buoyant as long as there is water to keep it floating. If the grain bed runs dry, it will fall onto the false bottom and the chance of a stuck mash increases. Pay close attention during sparging. Add more water when needed or increase the flow of water if you are using a sparging device.

5. Don't get greedy! If the wort flow is nice and steady and the wort is clear, don't try to make things easier by turning the lauter process into a race. Not only will your yield decrease if you collect wort too rapidly, but your chances of sucking down the bed will greatly increase. Take it easy and collect the wort over a 45- to 60-minute period.

Q I hear a lot about gravity points per pound. What is this magical mathematical formula?

A To calculate the "points per pound" of yield, you need three numbers: 1) the gravity points in your wort (this is the number behind the decimal in the original gravity; for example, 1.048 specific gravity equates to 48 gravity points); 2) wort volume; and 3) pounds of malt used in the brew.

The formula is simply:

(Points × Gallons) ÷ (Pounds of malt)

Let's assume you used 7.5 pounds of malt to produce 5 gallons (19 L) of wort with a specific gravity of 1.048. The yield comes out to be: (48 × 5) ÷ 7.5 = 32

Most malts have a maximum or theoretical yield of about 36 points per gallon, but a yield of 32 points per pound is a good yield.

Q How can I increase my efficiency when using plastic buckets for my mash?

A If you are using the double plastic bucket mash-lauter system, the problem is the holes in your bucket may be large enough to allow mash particles to escape with the wort. Plastic buckets are cheap and you could make a new bucket with smaller holes if this is an issue for you. An alternative is to use a large grain bag as a bucket liner.

Another very important parameter that affects yield is temperature. If the mash cools off during mashing and wort collection, the viscosity of the wort increases and efficiency suffers. This problem can be remedied by insulating your setup and minimizing heat loss. You can insulate with a cooler, or you can wrap the bucket with insulation or a blanket. Or, you may find that using hotter sparge water will improve yield. Many brewers are afraid of extracting undesirable compounds, such as tannins, from the husk and sparge with water that is no hotter than about 170°F (77°C).

In the case of infusion mashing with no mash-off step, you can use hotter water since the mash will significantly cool the sparge water. You can use water as hot as 190°F (88°C), as long as the temperature of the wort exiting the lauter tun doesn't exceed 170°F (77°C). Much of the conventional wisdom about sparge water temperature comes from commercial breweries that heat their mash to about 168°F (76°C) before transferring it to the lauter tun. These brewers don't worry about their sparge water being cooled by the mash since the two are at the same temperature and commercial lauter tuns are very well insulated.

Mashing-off, or heating the mash to about 168°F (76°C), improves efficiency since it lowers wort viscosity. You can mash-off in your system by stirring hot water into the mash to bring it to the desired temperature. If you use this technique, you should let the mash settle for 10 or 20 minutes before beginning your wort recirculation. Many small brewers have systems with the same limitations as the double-bucket method and increase their yield using this technique.

Q I'm looking for the best protein rest time and temperature for my all-grain mashes. What is your favorite time and temperature profile for good head retention?

A Mash profiles mean different things to different brewers. Many brewers employ low-temperature mash rests and their reasons differ. If you have read any brewing literature over the last century, you will find references to the protein rest. Historically, European malts were undermodified and required an extensive mash profile to yield the extract from these malts as well as separate the wort from the mash solids. The low-temperature rest, around 122°F (50°C), used in these long mash profiles was given the name protein rest because the by-products of proteolytic activity were observed during this time. Indeed, the protein rest does increase the concentration of free-amino nitrogen, or the amino acid ends of proteins, polypeptides, and amino acids.

Recent literature indicates that most of the proteolytic activity in the mash increases the concentration of amino acids but does not significantly alter the molecular weight spectrum of proteins and polypeptides found in wort. The molecular-weight spectrum would change significantly if high molecular proteins were broken up in size.

Some believe that the products of protein degradation are foam-positive and increase foam stability in the finished beer. I don't believe that significant changes in the molecular weight distribution of proteins and polypeptides occur during mashing at any temperature. Most of the demonstrable changes in protein size and solubility are seen in malting, where proteases are active. Protease activity dramatically declines during kilning, because proteases in malt are rendered unstable by heat and proteolytic activity in finished malt is very low.

However, there are enzymes that degrade beta-glucans (beta-glucanase enzymes) that do survive malt kilning and are active in the mash. Beta-glucanase activity is at its peak around 118°F (48°C), about the same temperature as the protein rest. Beta-glucanase activity can be very beneficial, especially when using under- and lightly modified malts, which still have enough viscous beta-glucan gums to cause wort separation problems during the lauter process.

This beta-glucanase activity is a more compelling reason for low-temperature mash rests than protease activity. I use a low-temperature rest for beers that contain under-modified or unmalted grains. For example, I use unmalted wheat for my unfiltered, American-style wheat and mash-in at 120°F (49°C) to cope with the unmalted wheat. I'm sure some will disagree, but those are my beliefs.

No hard and fast rules exist for enzyme activity because it is governed by both enzyme and substrate (what the enzyme is specific to, for example, starch) concentration. If you have a "hot" malt that is full of amylase activity, you can use a lot of adjunct grains, like rice, because the malt has more than enough enzymes to get starch conversion completed in a set time. If you have malt that is low in amylase activity, you may have a hard time converting the rice starch, even in a long mash.

The same holds true for proteases and glucanases — the duration of the rest depends on what you hope to accomplish, how much enzyme is present, and how much substrate is present. One of the reasons I'm not a big believer in the protein rest is that there's not much protease activity after kilning, and without proteases, you don't have much chance for proteolysis.

Now onto foam. Foam is affected by numerous variables. It is most greatly affected by proteins, especially higher-molecular proteins and one low-molecular weight native protein called Protein Z. It's also affected by carbon dioxide content, presence of fats and oils, and in the case of nitrogenated beers, dissolved nitrogen content. Certain beers bottled in clear glass use light-stable hop extracts that have their own foam properties, but these compounds are not widely available to the homebrew community.

I believe the key to producing a beer with a good foam is to keep adjuncts to a minimum, thoroughly rinse soapy cleaners from equipment, carbonate your beer enough to create a foam, and use extremely clean glassware. The beers I brew with the best foam are my unfiltered wheats, which use a portion of unmalted wheat, and my *porter,* which is nitrogenated. Unmalted wheat boosts the high molecular protein content, and the nitrogen in the porter is the best weapon for creating thick, creamy foam like draft Guinness. Long live beer foam!

Q **Does a low mash temperature create a dry beer? Does a high mash temperature create a sweet beer? Can you explain the cause and effect of mash temperature?**

A There is more to mash temperature than finished beer flavor. Mash temperature has an effect on wort viscosity and ease of lautering, it affects the gelatinization of starch (melting of the bonds that make starch a crystalline structure), it influences wort fermentability, and it has an effect on proteins. There are more factors that can be thrown in if decoction mashing and double mashing (the type used for beers like Bud) are considered, and if you want to know about the addition of industrial enzymes.

Unfortunately, questions about mashing usually end up with lengthy explanations of all of this stuff, and the replies often raise more questions than they really answer. The sweet beer/dry beer question focuses the discussion to one area, and that is the activity of two enzymes: alpha- and beta-amylase. The important thing to know about these enzymes is that they both attack starch, but in different ways. Starch comes in two forms. One form is called amylose (about 25 percent of barley malt starch) and contains no branches; it is simply a string of glucose molecules connected like links of a chain.

The second form is called amylopectin (about 75 percent of barley malt starch), and this form does contain branches. Imagine a chain where one of the links is connected to two links and each one of these links is then connected to one other link. Now imagine this scheme where a new branch pops up after every 25 to 30 unbranched segments. The result is a complex structure originating from a single point. It might help to understand what follows if you sketch a stick drawing of amylose and amylopectin.

Amylose and amylopectin have ends called reducing and nonreducing. The names are not that important, except that the ends of the branches in amylopectin are all nonreducing ends and its "trunk" is the only reducing end. Amylose is easy because it only has two ends, and one is reducing and the other is nonreducing. When either one of these molecules is split, there is a reducing and a nonreducing end formed. Amylose and amylopectin are made up of chains of glucose, a simple sugar. They are the only two molecules that alpha- and beta-amylase do battle with in a mash. To get to the heart of the question, I need to give some basics on the two enzymes.

Beta-amylase 1) has optimal enzyme activity between 140 and 149°F (60–63°C); 2) attacks chains of glucose from the nonreducing end only to form maltose, a simple sugar made up of two glucose molecules (beta-amylase chews through a chain of amylose like Pac-Man eating dots two at a time); 3) can't break a branch point in amylopectin; and 4) is nicknamed the "fermentability" enzyme.

Alpha-amylase 1) has optimal enzyme activity between 155 and 158°F (68–70°C); 2) randomly attacks chains of glucose and converts large molecules into a bunch of little chunks; 3) can't break a branch point in amylopectin; and 4) is nicknamed the "liquefaction" enzyme.

If you want a full beer with a low fermentability, steer your mash away from beta-amylase. Mash-in toward the upper end of the alpha-amylase temperature window and keep the mash as short as possible while still achieving a negative iodine reaction (no black-blue). Although alpha-amylase does manage to produce some fermentables due to its random activity on starch, the higher temperature minimizes the likelihood of rogue molecules of beta-amylase running around whacking off chunks of maltose from the nonreducing ends of starch molecules.

This is kind of like chopping veggies. If you don't like small bits of evenly sliced carrots in your soup, don't invite the local chef who goes chop-chop-chop at 120 chops a minute; instead invite the Boy Scout who goes whack-whack-whack and moves on to the next carrot.

One technique that will further cripple beta-amylase is a thin mash. Enzymes are more stable when they are latched onto their substrate (the substance they act upon), and a thin mash leaves a higher proportion of the enzymes floating around looking for their substrate. This is one of the reasons enzymes don't have a single optimum temperature. In any case, if you use a thinner mash, you will produce fewer fermentables than in a thicker mash (up to a point — you gotta have water to make wort!).

If your objective is to make a very fermentable wort for a dry beer, things get a little more complex. For starters you really want beta-amylase to be a happy camper. Mash-in cool, say around 140°F (60°C), and give your mash a good long hold. This will allow beta-amylase to chop up all the amylose and the tips of the amylopectin branches. This is a good start, but there are still a lot of glucose molecules tied up in amylopectin. The only way for beta-amylase to make more maltose is for alpha-amylase to open up amylopectin molecules (the starch that has branches) with a few random whacks.

If you wait around long enough, alpha-amylase will start to open up amylopectin. Remember, its optimum activity is around 158°F (70°C), but it still is active at cooler temperatures, though it's much slower. As alpha-amylase opens up amylopectin, beta-amylase starts tearing into the new nonreducing ends and freeing more maltose. At the end of the fermentability rest, the mash should still be heated to around 158°F (70°C) to achieve a negative iodine reaction. Bud Light is made using this type of mash profile, and the mash lasts for more than 3 hours. Unlike many other light beers, Bud Light does not use exogenous enzymes (store-bought enzymes) in the process.

Another way to get alpha- and beta-amylase working together is to slowly increase the temperature from 140°F (60°C), after your initial 30- to 45-minute rest, to 155–158°F (68–70°C). This is easier said than done at home because small batches are harder to control than larger ones; in commercial breweries using steam-heated, stirred mashes, this process is easy. The most common way of slowly increasing the temperature is to heat from 140–142°F (60–61°C) and rest, then from 142–144°F (61–62°C) and rest, and so on. This stair-step process is much easier to control than a continual rise from A to B because most mashing vessels are designed to heat at a constant rate and simply heating slower is not an option.

Stair-stepping can be done at home by carefully adding hot water a little at a time or alternating between heating steps and rests. The hard part is getting a good temperature reading while stirring and heating. If you are using gas or electric heat, don't crank the burners up too high, because temperature overshoot will most likely follow.

Some brewers do a bit of both. They mash-in for a beta-amylase rest and then rapidly raise the temperature to the alpha-amylase rest to avoid too much dryness in the finished beer. Other beers mash-in even cooler for beta-glucanase or limited protease activity. This is where the topic of mashing starts to get big.

One word of caution: Many brewers, when first starting out, get what seems like an ingenious idea that will not work. The idea is start out at 158°F (70°C) to let alpha-amylase do its thing and then cool the mash down to let beta-amylase do its thing. This won't work because heat denatures enzymes at temperatures above their optimum, and denaturation is permanent. This idea does work in a decoction mash and in the American double mash because only a portion of the mash is boiled, but I'll save that topic for another day!

Q I recently read an article regarding first-wort hopping that advises steeping a large portion of bittering hops in the wort before boiling. I am

trying to get better hop flavors from my ales and wonder if this might be the way.

A First-wort hopping involves adding a portion of the hops — often the additions typically added late in the boil — to the kettle as soon as wort from the lauter tun begins to flow to the kettle. The first-wort hops steep in the hot wort for the entire period of wort collection preceding the boil.

The general consensus about this method is that the beer has a smoother bitterness compared to beers in which later hop additions are used. The reasons for this are unknown, however. Also, if first-wort hopping is used without either late-hop additions or dry-hop additions, the finished beer has — as one would expect — very little hop aroma because hop aroma is lost when these compounds evaporate from a pot of boiling wort.

As it relates to first-wort hopping, most articles refer to an improvement in hop flavor. Hops do add tannins to wort, and hop tannins are known to add flavor to beer, especially when added late in the boil or as dry hops. One of the characteristics of late or dry-hopped beers is a grassy astringency coming from the plant portion of the hop cone. First-wort hopping may reduce the amount of tannins making their way into the finished beer because they react with proteins in the wort and precipitate.

Q When do you need to worry about hot-side aeration?

A Hot-side aeration (HSA) is a loose term referring to oxygen pickup in the hot-side operations of brewing. These include mashing, lautering, wort boiling, and hop separation at temperatures ranging from about 120 to 212°F (49–100°C). Since the early 1990s, researchers have presented evidence that hot-side aeration — especially prior to wort boiling — decreases the shelf life of beer by increasing the concentration of oxidized fatty acids. These compounds are carried forward into the beer and impart classic stale flavors such as the infamous wet cardboard–type of oxidation.

I am a skeptic by nature, but I find that the data demonstrating the negative effects of hot-side aeration during mashing and lautering are convincing. I am still skeptical that deleterious HSA occurs in the boil, however. The temperature range during mashing and lautering is low enough that oxygen can indeed dissolve into the liquid and cause oxidation. In contrast, boiling wort (and wort immediately after boiling) is so hot that very little oxygen can be dissolved in it.

Enzymes that oxidize lipids are present in lightly kilned malts and form staling compounds when oxygen and lipids are present. (Lipoxygenase enzymes are one example of these enzymes.) There has also been data presented demonstrating the presence of nonenzymatic lipid oxidation during mashing. This oxidation forms staling compounds and free radicals that carry on this cycle of fat oxidation, commonly known as rancidity.

Hot-side aeration can be demonstrated in medium and large commercial breweries because the brewing equipment is so big that splashing is a really dramatic event. Think of liquid flowing through a 6-inch (15 cm) pipe at 400 gallons (1514 L) per minute and cascading 12 feet (4 m) through the air before hitting the bottom of a tank. This — not roughly stirring a 5-gallon (19 L) mash with a wooden spoon — is what commercial brewers are trying to minimize.

For a homebrewer, the most likely time for aeration to occur during mashing is while you are mashing-in. One procedure to address this concern is the following: Add 2.5 quarts (2.7 L) of water out of 10 quarts (9.5 L) to the mash tun, then carefully add 2 pounds (0.9 kg) of malt out of 8 pounds and gently mix malt into water. Add 2.5 more quarts (2.7 L) of water and 3 pounds (1.4 kg) of malt and gently mix, then 2.5 quarts (2.7 L) water and 3 pounds (1.4 kg) malt and mix, and finally add the last 2.5 quarts (2.7 L) of water. As this process may take longer than your usual mash-in, it is important to make sure that your water stays hot enough during this suggested procedure.

If you use a separate vessel for wort collection and transfer your mash from the mash tun to a lauter tun, develop a procedure to minimize splashing. This is not always easy and the solution to this concern may be to mash and lauter in the same vessel. (Sometimes the solution is found by subtracting steps and pieces of equipment rather than always adding that new tool.)

I think the thing to remember about hot-side aeration is that it is not that hard to avoid at home. The real question that will probably spark heated debates for years to come is this: How good is good enough when it comes to warding off potential risks of hot-side aeration? There are some commercial brewers who have addressed all the obvious issues and now are looking at purging their mills and brewhouse vessels with nitrogen. I am anxious to hear if these aggressive methods improve the beer.

It must be remembered that oxygen pickup after fermentation (for example, from racking, filtering, and bottling) also causes oxidation and staling of beer. In fact, the effects of oxygen pickup after fermentation are more apparent and severe than the effects of hot-side aeration. This is partly because there are a wider variety of compounds in beer susceptible to oxidation than there are in wort. The point here is that if you are thinking about changing your brewing procedure to avoid oxidation, you should begin addressing oxygen pickup from the end of the process and work your way forward toward mashing.

Q Should I be concerned with mash temperature fluctuations within 10 degrees of my target? If so, do you have suggestions for controlling the temperature?

A Mash temperature in all-grain brewing has a significant and demonstrable effect on beer flavor. In general, multi-temperature mash profiles with temperature rests between 120 and 160°F (49–71°C) will produce more fermentable worts than single-temperature mashes held between 152 and 154°F (67–68°C). In flavor terms, beer produced from highly fermentable wort tends to be drier, crisper, and perhaps lighter in body than those made from less-fermentable worts. Concerns about precise temperature control are very real to commercial brewers, because the ability to repeat mash temperatures directly affects beer consistency. And consistency is an important key to commercial quality.

When most homebrewers think of quality, we think of the sensory qualities of the beer. Does it taste, look, and smell like intended on brew day? If it does, then all is great, and we will have a quality brew. However, if you only want to brew that one beer, then you should attempt to be as consistent as possible with your mash temperature, along with every other key variable in the brewing process. On the other hand, if you want to brew a wide assortment of great-tasting homebrewed beer, I would not be overly concerned. If your mash stays in the desired range for most of the time, and when it does cool off, you heat it up in a reasonable time frame. I would be more concerned if you were getting the mash too hot and then trying to cool it back down, because that can destroy enzymes.

One easy solution to your problem is to insulate your mash tun. You don't want to insulate the bottom because the vessel would be difficult to heat if the insulation was doing its job and the insulation might burn (unless it is resistant to flame, like rock wool, or glass fiber). If this were my project, I would buy a nonflammable insulation material and insulate the sides of the mash tun and make some type of simple, insulated lid to prevent heat loss from the top.

Q Why would my wort be cloudy before I boil?

A Clear wort is a function of proper milling, false bottom design, and smooth, uninterrupted wort collection. Malt milled too fine is a frequent cause of cloudy wort that no amount of recirculation will completely rectify. Fine milling bashes up the husk so much that it can no longer serve as a filter. Some brewers start with properly milled malt and have problems because the holes or slots in the false bottom are too large. The slots used in commercial lauter tuns are usually 0.7–1 millimeter wide; these narrow slots produce the brilliantly clear worts frequently referred to in recipes. Larger holes or slots will naturally let more solids through the grain bed. This is okay if the amount of solids passing into the wort is not excessive.

Sporadic wort flow can also lead to cloudy wort because the pressure differential across the grain bed goes up and down as the flow changes. Every time the flow rate slows and the pressure differential decreases, the grain filter bed coughs up bits of fine particles. If you want clear wort, controlling wort flow rate is another technique that you can work to improve.

Cloudy wort has more stuff that comes out in the boil, and may cause the wort foam to have a different appearance. The dough that forms in the mash tun has a distinctive brown-gray pasty appearance. Dough transferred to the kettle (when you're dealing with very cloudy wort) will rise to the surface and look funky. Beers brewed with a proportion of wheat frequently have a similar appearance in the kettle because of the higher protein content of wheat malts.

■ ══════════ ■

Q **After my sparge water runs through a plastic hose and a sparging arm and sprinkles onto the mash, it has cooled significantly, sometimes as much as 30°F (16°C). Are there recommended sparging devices to use that allow a more predictable grain-bed temperature?**

A Like many practices used by homebrewers, sparging techniques are typically scaled-down versions of what goes on in a commercial brewery. The basic idea is to use water hot enough to extract all of the desired compounds (mainly malt sugars) from the grain bed while leaving the undesirable stuff, such as polyphenols and starch.

One difficulty is heat loss — small-diameter hoses lose much more heat to the environment than large-diameter stainless steel pipes. This is one reason your sparge water is cooling off between your hot liquor tank and the sparge arm. Another problem is heat loss from the top of your lauter tun.

Brewers have different things that bug them; it sounds like this issue is one that bugs you. I have three recommendations to help ease your mind:

1. Heat your mash to 168 to 172°F (76–78°C) before transferring to your lauter tun. If this is not possible because you use an infusion mash/lauter setup, add boiling water to your mash while stirring to raise its temperature.

2. Compensate for heat loss by increasing the temperature of your hot liquor tank. Don't worry too much about extracting tannins. Think of sparging as taking a shower — it's the temperature flowing from the shower head that matters. You've estimated your heat loss at 30°F (16°C), which would put your hot liquor tank at roughly 200°F (93°C). Make sure your hoses and sparge arm can withstand this higher temperature.

3. Instead of idea number two, consider batch-sparging instead of a sparge arm to reduce heat loss. Batch-sparging is the practice of adding three or four additions of sparge water to the lauter tun instead of a continuous flow. Many brewers use this method, and it works very well. The key is to avoid letting the top of the grain bed get dry. In any case, batch-sparging will significantly cut down on your heat-loss problem. And you don't have to worry about overheating the grain

bed because you can assume minor heat loss, less than 10°F (6°C). (See batch-sparging, page 396.)

━━━━━━━━━━━━━

Q **To increase mash efficiency, I mash overnight. I do this with beers of low to average original gravities, but especially with high-gravity beers. I will start the mash at 155 to 160°F (68–71°C) around 11 p.m. and sparge in the morning around 9 a.m. By then, the temperature of the mash is around 145°F (63°C). I have found this method to be successful at conversion, and the beers have been good. Is there any reason why I should not be doing this?**

A I am a great fan of methods that make things easier, and this method is certainly a time-saver when it comes to scheduling those precious weekend hours. To me, saving time is the best way to improve efficiency. Very long mashes also will improve the extraction of wort-soluble solids from malt and improve your mash efficiency, although mash efficiency is primarily a function of milling and wort separation techniques. I toured a small brewery in California that brewed a batch of stout, then mashed-in the second batch and returned the next morning to finish the batch. There are no major problems with this method, but there are a few things to keep in mind to avoid potential problems.

Mashing is all about enzymes. The two key enzymes in mashing are alpha-amylase and beta-amylase. Beta-amylase produces maltose from starch and is most active between 140 and 149°F (60–65°C). The thing about beta-amylase is that it stops working when it runs into a branch in the starch molecule. That's where alpha-amylase comes to the rescue. Alpha-amylase randomly reduces big starch molecules into smaller pieces. Its temperature optimum is right around 158°F (70°C).

When enzymes run out of their substrate — starch, in the case of amylases — the reactions just stop. No big deal. Brewers typically stop mashing when the mash is complete because they want to efficiently utilize their brewing equipment. In your case, the mash is over at midnight and you are more concerned about utilizing your bed than your mash tun — so you let the mash wait for you to awaken.

The key to your method is keeping your temperature high. If you used this very long mashing method with a low mash temperature, say around 140 to 145°F (60–63°C), the result would be very fermentable wort because this temperature range is ideal for beta-amylase activity and also is high enough to get some alpha-amylase activity. When these two enzymes work together, the result is an increase in wort fermentability.

Dry beers and light beers typically begin with this sort of wort. If you want to brew something like Michelob Ultra, a very long mash-in in this temperature range is the ticket! Just make sure that you achieve complete conversion by using the iodine test before sparging. If you get a black iodine test result, you should heat the mash up to 158°F (70°C) for about 20 minutes for complete conversion. Most homebrewers don't want to brew super-dry beers and should keep the temperature above 150°F (66°C) for the mash.

Keeping the temperature high is also critical for pest control! Wort bacteria don't mess around and will quickly begin growing if the wort temperature falls into the 120°F (49°C) range. Malt is chock-full of bacteria that cause souring of wort, such as *Lactobacillus,* and other bacteria that can lead to some really rank off-flavors. In fact, the most common application to overnight mashing is for sour mashes where the temperature is intentionally allowed to drop into the realm of these bugs that so effectively turn mash sour. Perhaps the best method to guarantee that the mash stays in the 150°F (66°C) range is to put the mash into an oven set at its lowest temperature. I strongly suggest you verify that the lowest temperature is not too hot for the mash before chucking your mash into your oven for a 10-hour bake! However, it sounds like you have a very well-insulated mash tun if the mash only drops 10°F (6°C) over 10 hours. As long as the mash temperature is adjusted to address concerns about overly fermentable wort and bacterial spoilage, your method is a real daylight time-saver!

■ ━━━━━━ ■

Q **If I have a single infusion mash that starts high at 155°F (68°C) (alpha-amylase range) and cools back down to 148°F (64°C) (into beta-amylase range), do the beta enzymes reactivate or do the high temperatures cause them to remain denatured?**

A Denature is one of those words that is often thrown around with little explanation. An enzyme, by definition, is a protein that catalyzes a biochemical reaction. The amylase enzymes catalyze the degradation of starch into smaller molecules. Enzyme activity is affected by temperature and the rate of a specific reaction increases until the temperature causes the enzyme to denature. In simple terms, the protein or proteins that comprise an active enzyme irreversibly uncoil when they denature.

Common examples of denatured protein are found in the kitchen. The cheese-making process begins by denaturing milk proteins to form curd. Once milk is converted to curds and whey, there is no turning back. Another example of denatured protein is a cooked egg. The solid white material in any cooked egg is denatured egg white, which cannot be restored to its native (not denatured) state.

Enzymes may be in their native states without being active, and environmental factors such as pH, mineral cofactors, and substrate concentration do affect enzyme activity. The amylase enzymes active in a mash are most effective around pH 5.2. If the mash pH were increased to, say pH 7, by adding a base like sodium hydroxide, the activity of the amylase enzymes would dramatically reduce and become inactive. If the pH was then reduced to pH 5.2 by adding acid, the enzymes would again become active. This is because pH affects the electrical charge on the various ionizable groups associated with proteins. These groups include carboxylic acid and amino functionalities, to use the scientific language. The charge on a functional group is affected by pH, and this reaction has a profound affect on enzyme activity, but pH changes do not necessarily cause an enzyme to denature (although radical changes in pH can cause an enzyme to denature).

The practical message is to be careful with your mash. When in doubt, it is always safest to start off a bit cooler than desired and to move the temperature up to the target. Enzyme denaturation does not occur instantaneously. If you intend on mashing-in at 140°F (60°C), for example, and accidentally come in at 162°F (72°C), you can quickly add cool water and retain the activity of some beta-amylase molecules that have yet to be cooked by the high temperature.

Q **Can I use a grain bag when mashing for easier cleanup of the grains?**

A If all they had to do was dunk the grains around in water, brewers wouldn't take the time to lauter. Beer has basically been made the same way for a few thousand years, so I tend to believe that there is probably a good reason behind most common practices. You need to lauter in order to separate the good from the bad. During mashing, wort is extracted from the malt along with a bunch of protein and some tannins. Most of the tannins and a lot of the protein coagulate in the mash. The goal of lautering is to produce a clear wort comprised of soluble carbohydrates and proteins and to leave the coagulated proteins and tannins, insoluble starch particles, and small husk fragments behind. If you use the grain bag method, much of these undesirable materials pass into the wort. The results range from hazy beer to grainy and astringent off-flavors.

◼ ══════════ ◼

Q What are your thoughts on batch sparging versus using a rotating sparge arm?

A My thoughts on batch sparging vs. continuous sparging are like my thoughts on the hundreds of other issues in brewing. There's more than one way to remove the integument from a feline. I have used both methods on large and small scales, and each has its merits. Batch sparging is easier, because it is done only two or three times during the lauter process. If sparge water temperature and sparge water volume are important to a brewer, then batch sparging allows for the simple delivery of a certain volume of water at a specified temperature to the lauter tun. The down side to batch sparging is that the added volume of water on top of the grain bed induces more head pressure than continuous sparging and may compact the mash bed, which will extend the time required to collect the wort.

Continuous sparging minimizes the head pressure due to sparge water but requires more equipment and more attention to the sparging process. To sparge continuously, the flow of wort leaving the lauter tun and the flow of sparge water entering the lauter tun should be the same. Since the flow of wort leaving the lauter tun changes with time, so must the flow of sparge water. Unless a homebrewer invests entirely too much money into his system, this balance of wort and sparge water flow requires careful attention. This attention should have a payoff, and some argue that the lauter process time is decreased by the method. If homebrewing is about fun and relaxation, then I question the importance of shaving 10 or 15 minutes off a brew day.

Continuous sparging also requires an insulated vessel to hold the sparge water at sparging temperatures during the period of time required for wort collection. Batch sparging, on the other hand, requires nothing more than a pot to heat the water to sparge temperature and a ladle or small pitcher to gently pour the water over the grain bed. At the end of the day, both methods work to rinse sugars produced in mashing from the mash bed.

Q I'm trying to lower my water pH and wonder if adding acidulated malt might help. The pH of my tap water is 7.9–8.1. How do I determine the amount of acidulated malt to use, when do I introduce it into the mash, and what effect will it have on my water treatment?

A Acidulated malt is a product designed for the easy use of biological acidification. This practice is a Rheinheitsgbot-approved method of adding organic acids to the mash for the purposes of buffering the pH of the mash. A buffer is a system of weak acids or bases, such as lactic acid or sodium bicarbonate, which resists changes in pH. All buffers can tolerate additions of acids or bases without substantial swings in pH within the buffering capacity. This is due to the equilibria between the various species in the buffer, typically called the weak acid and weak base (or proton donor and proton acceptor to chemistry folk).

Biological acidification is another method, and brewers can use lactic acid naturally produced by bacteria. The simplest way to do this is to make a sour mash. Lactic acid bacteria are present on malt (both wheat and barley malt) and thrive at temperatures hovering around 122°F (50°C). After 24 to 48 hours at this temperature, a mash will sour and have substantial lactic acid.

Traditional German brewers will make a full mash, for such beers as Pilsners and helles lagers, containing up to 10 percent of a biologically acidified or sour mash for the purpose of adjusting pH. The sour mash is added to the main mash at mash-in. This requires special equipment and takes time. Acidulated malt makes this method easier to use as the biological acidification occurs in the malthouse and the lactic acid is sprinkled over malt in the kiln. The resulting grain is normal pale malt with a coating of lactic acid produced by a Rheinheitsgbot-approved method. When this grain is chewed, one gets the sensation of eating a Sweet-Tart. The sweet comes from the malt and the tart comes from the lactic acid. The Weyermann malting company produces an acidulated malt and it is called *sauer malz,* or sour malt, in their literature. One percent added to the grain bill reportedly reduces the pH of the average mash by about 0.10 pH units.

The key thing to understand here is that the goal is adjusting mash pH, not water pH. Mashes comprised of very pale malts and soft brewing water may have higher-than-ideal pHs and require some sort of acidification. Many brewers prefer the addition of either calcium sulfate or calcium chloride to lower mash pH, and others opt for the addition of biologically produced lactic acid. Both have merit and focus on the adjustment of mash pH.

I use sour malt in a Kölsch that we brew as a seasonal, and it comprises about 5 percent of the total malt bill. The sour malt is milled with the rest of the malts and goes into the mash at mash-in. Many brewers argue that lactic acid softens the palate of beers when added in small amounts to adjust mash pH. Personally, I think that the important thing is adjusting the mash pH to between 5.2–5.4 and to avoid collecting last runnings with high pH (above 5.8–6.0) and low gravity. This is where you begin to run into problems with astringency.

If you have a pH meter, use it to tune in on how much sour malt you need. If you are making really pale beers with water containing carbonates and little calcium you will need more of the lactic acid from the malt than you will if your water is very low in carbonates or if you are using dark malt. If you are adding calcium to lower mash pH, you probably will want to cut back on the amount.

GUARANTEE 5 GALLONS AFTER THE BOIL

All brewing recipes give a volume of wort to collect before boiling as a guideline. But the volume that really matters is the wort volume after boiling. Wort volume is very important, because it directly affects the concentration of everything dissolved in the wort. Specific gravity, bitterness, and color are all affected by changes in volume. All brew kettles are different with respect to their evaporation rate during boiling. Evaporation rate varies with the shape of the kettle, the material of construction (stainless, aluminum, copper), the thickness of the material, and the heat source.

I try to nail my wort gravity coming out of the kettle. The easiest way that I've found to hit a target gravity is to measure the specific gravity after the boil and add hot water to the wort to adjust the gravity. The wort gravity must be a little higher than the target gravity for this method to work. If the wort volume after adjustment is much different than the target volume for the recipe, the bitterness may be higher or lower than projected, but you can't worry about nailing every parameter. In most cases the adjusted wort volume is close enough to the target batch size and bitterness is not significantly changed.

To apply this technique you must:

1. Accurately measure the volume of your wort.
2. Calculate how much extract is dissolved in the wort.
3. Calculate the adjusted wort volume.
4. Add hot water to the brew kettle.

The easiest way to measure wort volume in a kettle is by using a calibrated dipstick made of hardwood. I like to cut notches in the stick at convenient intervals, for example, every 250 mL (metric is much easier to use in the brewing calculations).

Here's an example: Suppose you have a recipe that should yield 5 gallons (19 L) of 1.048 SG (12° Plato) wort and you determine that you actually have 4.3 gallons (16.3 L) of 1.055 SG (13.5° Plato) after the boil.

Step One: How much extract is present?

Kg extract present = (L of wort) × (specific gravity) × (° Plato) = (16.3) × (1.055) × (0.135) = 2.32 kg

Step Two: What is the adjusted wort volume?

Adjusted volume = (kg extract present) ÷ {(target SG) × (target° Plato)} = (2.32) ÷ {(1.048) × (0.12)} = 18.45 L

After crunching a few numbers, you can simply top your kettle up to 18.45 L by adding 2.15 L of boiled water. There is one notable detail in the calculation shown above. Plato must be expressed in decimal form, because degrees Plato is a weight/weight percentage (12° Plato means the wort contains 12 grams of solids per 100 grams of wort). (See calculating boil evaporation rate, page 351.)

Q **After the protein break, is it okay to turn down the flame on my boil and put a lid on the brew kettle? It seems like a waste of liquid as I usually lose about 1 gallon during the boil.**

A The truth comes out. Wort boiling can waste energy and reduce wort volume! If you are losing about a gallon during a 5-gallon (19 L) boil, or 20 percent evaporation, you're about on track with most other homebrewers. The reason for your high evaporation rate is the large surface-to-volume ratio of a 5-gallon (19 L) brew kettle. In commercial breweries, the targeted evaporation rate is about 8 percent. You can reduce your evaporative losses by either using a lid, as you suggest, or simply turning down the intensity of the boil. I would recommend the latter and not a lid.

The problem with lids is that they trap many volatiles, especially dimethyl sulfide (DMS), which smells like cooked corn, in the wort. Most of the volatiles lost during the boil are lost by design, so that they don't contribute undesirable flavors to beer. Hop oils, on the other hand, contribute hoppy aroma to beer. Although volatile, hop oils survive into the finished beer if the aroma additions are made late in the boil and if the evaporation rate is reduced after the aroma addition. At home, I would recommend boiling without a lid and controlling the evaporation rate by adjusting the flame on the stove. After the last hops are added, placing a lid on the pot will help keep the valuable oils in the wort. At this stage, almost all of the DMS will have been driven off and closing the kettle should have few negative effects provided that the wort is rapidly cooled (within 45 minutes) after the boil. (See calculating boil evaporation rate, page 351.)

■ ══════ ■

Q **How do you change the pH of your sparge water? The pH of my water is too high.**

A The term pH is used to describe the concentration of hydrogen ions in a solution. As the concentration of hydrogen ions increase, a solution becomes more acidic — and since pH is a negative, logarithmic scale, the pH decreases as a solution becomes more acidic. The simple answer to this question is that you want to increase the concentration of hydrogen ions to reduce the pH of your sparge water. You can do this by adding an acid, such as phosphoric or lactic acid, to your sparge water.

Changing the pH of water is usually not so straightforward because most water contains compounds that resist pH changes. These buffers include the very common carbonate ion. Water high in carbonate typically results in a mash pH higher than ideal (pH 5.2–5.4 is in the ideal range) and also results in a faster increase in the wort pH during sparging compared to waters with little or no carbonate. Compared to the mash, water has a relatively weak buffering capacity.

Water chemistry can be a very confusing topic, but in practice you really need to pay attention to a few key points.

Check your mash pH. If it is between 5.2 and 5.4, you are doing well. If it is out of this range, mash pH can be adjusted after mash-in by adding calcium salts (from calcium sulfate or calcium chloride) or carbonate (from calcium carbonate or sodium bicarbonate). Calcium reacts with phosphates, proteins, and amino acids from malt and reduces mash pH. Carbonates, on the other hand, increase mash pH. You can also add acids to the mash to decrease mash pH. Organic acids, like phosphoric and lactic, are usually used because they act as buffers and are easier to use than strong acids like hydrochloric. Strong acids result in more rapid pH changes, and a little bit goes a long way.

I don't pay much attention to the pH of the sparge water, because a high water pH does not always result in a rapid increase of mash or wort pH. Water has a much lower buffering capacity than does a mash. Furthermore, most municipalities intentionally adjust water pH to around 8 to 9 to prevent corrosion in water lines. Strong bases, like sodium hydroxide, are usually used to adjust the pH — and strong bases, like strong acids, do not act as pH buffers. In other words, sparge water with a high pH and a low buffering capacity has little impact on mash or wort pH.

The thing to monitor during sparging is the pH of the wort. As a general rule, wort pH increases as the wort gravity decreases. This is due to the fact that the buffering capacity of the wort decreases as the wort gravity decreases. If you track your wort pH during sparging and find that it is too high, you can add a phosphoric or lactic acid to your sparge water so that the sparge water pH is in the low 5s.

Q I want to make a 1.120 original gravity all-grain barleywine, but my system seems to have a tough time getting above 1.090, even when I load it up with plenty of grain. Any ideas for successfully brewing a huge beer on an all-grain system?

A The key to obtaining a very high-gravity wort after boiling is to begin with a high-gravity wort running from the mash. This means that the mash has to be on the thick side. A thinner mash has more water per pound of grain, and the first-wort gravity will decrease as mash thickness decreases. You will have to determine your mash thickness empirically, since the malt you are using and the size of the grist after milling will have an impact on the gravity of the first wort. But a good starting point for a high-gravity wort is to use 74 fluid ounces (4.6 pints) of mash water per pound of malt. (For you metric brewers, this translates to 4.8 L water per kilogram of malt.)

Another key point to brewing high-gravity beers is to sacrifice your efficiency. You can do this by either not sparging at all or by sparging very little. You can sparge and get good extract efficiency, but you have to use a much longer boil to evaporate the sparge water needed to improve your efficiency. Most commercial brewers take a compromise approach. They sparge a little bit to improve their efficiency over not sparging at all, then use a longer boil — up to 3 hours — to hit their target gravity.

When using very long boils, you still want to add the hops at about the same times you do for a normal-length boil.

For example, boil your bittering hops for 60 to 90 minutes, your middle addition for 30 to 40 minutes, and your aroma addition for 0 to 10 minutes. Boiling hops for extremely long times can lead to unpleasant bitter flavors caused by the thermal decomposition of isomerized alpha acids.

Q What does the term *vorlauf* mean?

A Vorlauf is the first step of wort collection (one translation of vorlauf into English is "forerun"). The vorlauf removes weak wort from the underplate area of a lauter tun and returns this weak wort to the top of the grain bed. Strictly speaking, a lauter tun is only used for wort separation and is filled with mash after mashing has occurred. The false bottom of a lauter tun is covered with water before filling, and that is why weak wort exists in the underplate area. The vorlauf also helps clarify the wort before sending it off to the kettle. Most commercial brewers vorlauf for about 20 minutes; this time permits about 40 percent of the liquid in the mash to be recirculated.

GLOSSARY: FROM ADJUNCT TO ZAPAP

Adjunct. any substitute unmalted grain or fermentable ingredient added to a mash. Usually reduces cost and produces lighter-bodied, paler, and less malty beers.

Aeration. exposing a substance to air, performed at various stages of the brewing process.

Airlock (or fermentation lock). a one-way valve that allows carbon dioxide gas to escape while preventing the entry of contaminants.

Ale. a generic term for beers produced by top fermentation (for example, using ale yeast strains) at temperatures higher than lager fermentation temperatures; wort usually made by infusion mashing.

Alpha-acetolactate. a compound produced by yeast cells and a precursor to diacetyl.

Alpha acid. the soft, bitter hop resin responsible for most of beer's bitterness. Alpha acids must be boiled to convert alpha acids to iso-alpha acids. Measured as a percentage of the total weight of the hop cone.

Alpha acid units (AAU). percentage of alpha acids in a sample of hops multiplied by the weight in ounces of the entire sample. (One ounce of hops with an alpha-acid content of 5 percent contains 5 AAUs.) AAU values are used in the calculation of bitterness units.

All-grain beer. a beer made entirely from malted and unmalted grains, as opposed to beers made from malt extract.

Amylase. generic name for enzymes that break the bonds holding starch molecules together.

Apparent degree of fermentation (ADF). the most common method of measuring attenuation.

Attenuation. the drop in specific gravity that occurs as a wort goes through fermentation.

Bacteria. one-celled organisms that reproduce rapidly under strict temperature, pH, and other conditions. (Bacteria can be killed with disinfectants.)

Barley, 2-row and 6-row. the variety of barley that grows six rows of grains has more husk material by proportion than the 2-row variety. 6-row grain, which is usually smaller than 2-row grain, typically yields less in the way of extract yet contains more enzymes.

Beer stone (or beer scale). a hard film created by the combination of calcium oxalate, protein, and sugar that is formed when the same vessel is used repeatedly.

Body (or mouthfeel). the consistency, thickness, and sensation of fullness created by beer in the mouth.

Boil. the step in brewing when the sweet wort is transferred to a brew kettle and boiled with hops to produce a bitter wort.

Bottle-conditioned. beer carbonated naturally in the bottle by priming or re-yeasting.

Break the clumping and separation of protein matter during the boiling stage (hot break) and cooling stage (cold break).

Brewhouse yield. the calculation of extract yield from raw materials, as compared to theoretical laboratory yield.

Buttery. having a taste like butter or butterscotch, signifying the presence of diacetyl.

Calandria. a boiling unit, either internal or external to a kettle, used to increase surface area. Most are steamheated.

Caramel malt. a malt that is prepared by "stewing" (kilning in a moist environment) to produce sugars from starch (the sugars caramelize when the malt is dried to yield color and flavor compounds). Also called crystal malt.

Carbonation. injecting or dissolving carbon dioxide gas in a liquid to create a bubbly taste and texture.

Carboy. a large glass or plastic vessel with a narrow neck.

Chill haze. a haziness in beer caused by the precipitate formed when a beer is refrigerated.

Chlorophenol. a potently aromatic compound formed when phenols, which are present in malt, wort, and beer, react with chlorine.

Clarification. removing suspended particles from the wort or finished beer through mechanical or chemical means.

Conditioning. the process of carbonating beer in a bottle or keg.

Cross-contamination. the unwanted process of carrying bacteria from one ingredient, surface, or brew to another.

Crystal malt. another name for caramel malt.

Decoction mashing. the method of removing some of the mash, boiling it, then returning it to the main kettle to boost the mash temperature (this process is used in all-grain brewing).

Dextrose (or glucose). a monosaccharide used to prime bottle-conditions beers.

Diacetyl. a powerful aroma compound derived from yeast that can impart a butterscotch or buttery flavor to beer.

Draft (or draught). beer drawn from kegs or casks instead of being bottled.

Dry hopping. the practice of adding hops to the primary or secondary fermenter (or to finished beer) to increase the aroma and hop flavor of the beer without increasing its bitterness.

Dry malt. malt extract in a dried powder form (often called DME).

Enzyme. a protein that acts as a biological catalyst for chemical reactions, such as alpha-amylase, beta-amylase, and beta-glucanase.

Esterases. enzymes that break down esters.

Esters. powerful aroma compounds formed by the combination of organic acids and alcohols during fermentation. They contribute fruity aroma to beer.

Extract. the sugar left after mashing and lautering malted barley. By removing the liquid, sweet wort is reduced to a syrup or powder and packaged in cans for homebrewing.

Extract brewing. making beer from malt extract syrup or powder as opposed to milled malt (which is used in all-grain brewing).

Fermentation. the process by which yeast produces energy in the absence of oxygen by breaking sugar into carbon dioxide and alcohol.

Filler. a machine that pours liquid into bottles or other containers.

Filtration. the process of removing suspended solids, primarily yeast and proteins, to produce a brilliant beer (usually performed just before bottling).

First generation yeast. the first yeast in any particular strain grown in a lab.

Gelatin. a colorless and tasteless protein used as a fining agent.

Gelatinization. the transformation of starch from a solid, crystalline form to a liquid, soluble form, occuring when starch is heated in water. Gelatinized starch can be attacked by mashing enzymes whereas ungelatinized starch cannot.

Generation. a term describing each time yeasts are used in the brewing process.

Glucose. see dextrose.

Grist. crushed malt and adjuncts mixed with hot water for mashing.

Gypsum. hydrated calcium sulfate used to treat soft or neutral water making it hard.

Head. the foam at the top of a poured beer.

Heat exchanger. equipment used to heat or cool the wort rapidly.

High gravity. an original wort gravity of 1.060 or greater.

Hops. the cones or fruit (sometimes incorrectly called flowers) of the female hop plant used in brewing to impart flavor and bitterness. These can be used whole, or in form of pellets or plugs.

Hop sock. a simple device to remove hops from the wort before cooling.

Hop extract. resins and oils extracted from hops by using organic solvents or liquid carbon dioxide.

Hydrometer. a glass instrument used to measure the specific gravity of beer by comparing it to that of water.

IBU (International Bitterness Unit). unit of measurement used to express a beer's bitterness as milligrams of iso-alpha-acid (a compound created when alpha acids are boiled) per liter of beer.

Infusion mashing. the traditional British method of mashing, primarily used in ale brewing. It occurs at a single temperature and is carried out in a combination mash-lauter vessel called an infusion mash tun.

Invert sugar. a mixture of fructose and glucose produced by chemically breaking down sucrose; used for priming.

Irish moss. a red seaweed added at the end of the boiling process as a fining agent.

Iron. an ion that causes haze and oxidation and hinders yeast.

Isinglass. a very pure form of collagen derived from the swimming bladder of fish, used as a fining agent.

Jockey box. a beverage-dispensing system, often used to serve beer, consisting of a picnic cooler with an internal cooling coil and one or more externally mounted taps. The cooler is filled with ice, and the beverage is chilled as it passes through the coil to the tap.

Kegging. drawing beer from the fermenter to the keg.

Keggle. nickname for a commercial beer keg that has been converted into a homebrewing beer kettle.

Kettle. a large vessel used to heat wort.

Krausen. the fluffy head of foam that forms on the surface of wort during the first few days of fermentation. At its peak it is called "high krausen."

Krausening. adding a small amount of wort at high krausen to fully fermented lager to create a secondary fermentation and natural carbonation.

Lactic acid. an acid produced by bacteria during mashing or (more frequently) during fermentation and aging via contamination.

Lager. (n.) any beer produced by bottom fermentation; (v.) aging beer at cold-storage temperatures.

Lambic. a Belgian wheat beer traditionally brewed in winter that uses wild airborne yeast and bacteria to ferment the wort.

Lauter. to separate the wort produced during mashing from the spent grains (husks and coagulated protein).

Lauter tun. a large, perforated, false-bottomed vessel used to strain the sweet wort from the spent grains after mashing. Sometimes the mash tun is used for both mashing and lautering.

Lovibond. a scale often used to evaluate malt, wort and beer color.

Malt. barley or other grain steeped in water and germinated to create enzymes to be used in mashing, then kilned to stop the growth of the grain and to reduce moisture.

Malt extract. wort concentrated into a syrup or powder by removing all or most of the water.

Mash. (n.) a mixture of milled malted grains and hot water used to produce the sweet wort needed in brewing; (v.) mixing ground malt with hot water in the mash tun to extract the malt starch and convert it to grain starches and fermentable sugars.

Mashing-in. mixing ground malt with water, the first step in all-grain brewing.

Mash tun. a vessel used to hold the mash in infusion brewing. May be fitted with a perforated false bottom to remove the sweet wort produced during mashing from spent grains.

Milling. grinding the malt into grist before extracting sugars during mashing.

Modification. the net physical changes that occur within the barley kernel as it is converted from barley to malt.

Mouthfeel. see body.

Noble hops. a group of hops traditionally grown in Europe and now grown in North America as well. They are renowned for their flavor and aroma.

Nonhopped. any style beer or malt extract that has not had contact with hops.

Nose. a term used in tastings to describe the overall aroma of a beer or wine.

Nutrients. like any living creature, yeasts require nutrients to remain healthy while performing their duty (fermentation). Essential nutrients like nitrogen and phosphorous, are sold as "yeast nutrients" to add right after pitching your yeast.

Off-flavor. a term used to describe any taste in a brew that is inconsistent with the style or is just offensive. These flavors are often caused by poor sanitation, excessive aging and oxidation.

Original gravity (OG). this is the specific gravity of a wort before it goes through any fermentation. The measurement tells you the amount of solids that are in a wort in reference to that of pure water at a certain temperature (which is given the value of 1.000 SG).

Oxidized. a brewing fault where a brew is exposed to excessive oxygen, causing flavor problems and spoilage. This can be caused by poor bottling procedure, or excessive headspace.

Pale ale. an amber-colored beer brewed with pale malt. This ale originated in England and is known for its light color, hoppiness and drinkability with its typical alcohol content of 3.5 percent by volume.

Pasteurization. a stabilizing technique that uses high heat in packaged materials or brew to kill microorganisms. This process also prevents post packaging fermentation in brews and lengthens shelf life.

PH. this measurement is given a number between 1-14, representing the acidity or alkalinity in a solution. A solution below pH 7 is considered acidic; a solution above 7 is alkaline.

Pilsner. a style of beer that is light colored and hoppy. These brews originated in the city of Plzen, Czechoslovakia. Typically, this brew contains approximately 5 percent alcohol by volume.

Porter. an extremely dark brew that is mild in alcohol. It originated in London, supposedly by blending various draft ales. It gets its dark color and rich flavor from roasted, unmalted barley.

Primary fermentation. the first phase of fermentation where sugars are converted into ethyl alcohol and carbon dioxide.

Priming. the practice of adding sugar to fermented brew before bottling to reintroduce fermentation and carbonate the brew in bottle.

Proteases. enzymes that act upon proteins.

Quaternary ammonium compounds. effective no-rinse sanitizers used in the food industry; also called quats or QACs or Quats.

Rack. to move beer from one container to another, typically from a primary to secondary fermenter in order to separate beer from the solids that fall out of solution during the initial fermentation period.

Racking cane. a plastic tube with an arced end that is attached to a hose and used to siphon brew. The arced end stays above the solids when lowered to the bottom of a fermenter and helps to leave sediment behind.

Rauchbier. An amber colored brew from Germany that is noted for its smoked flavor that derives from roasting and drying malts over an open fire.

Rest. during the mash, brewers hold the mash at a predetermined temperature in order to draw out certain enzymes from the grain.

RIMS. an acronym for recirculating infusion mash system, a type of brewing system that many homebrewers use.

Roasted barley. an unmalted barley that is roasted in a kiln to give it a dark color and a bit of a bitter flavor.

Ropiness. the development of a complex polysaccharide slime in beer produced by certain bacteria.

Rouse. a technique used to keep fermentation on track.

Runoff. is synonymous with wort collection.

Saccharification. the process of converting starches contained in malt into fermentable sugars.

Saison. a Belgian beer typically amber in color and top-fermented. At least 90 days of bottle conditioning is called for in this beer, which has a noticeable fruity flavor and alcohol percentage of about 5 percent by volume.

Secondary fermentation. the second, slower stage of fermentation that takes place after primary fermentation has forced solids out of solution and the brew is racked to a closed bin (the "secondary fermenter").

Sediment. the solid material that falls out of solution during fermentation (more so in the primary fermentation, but also in the secondary for certain brews).

Skimming. the process of removing the top layer of yeast that forms on the head of the brew during primary fermentation (with a tool known as a skimming oar). Brewers can utilize this process to save the yeast for later use.

Smoked malt. a smoky flavored malt that gains its flavor through drying over open fire.

Soft water. water that is free of calcium, magnesium, cholorine, iron, and other elements that otherwise contribute to "hard water."

Sparge. as a verb, to rinse grains with hot water as the last step in mashing. Also used as an adjective to describe the water used in the process.

Sparging. a process that brewers conduct during wort collection, in which spent grains are sprayed with hot water in order to extract the remaining sugars from the husks.

Specific gravity (SG). a measurement that represents the density of a liquid at a specified temperature. Pure water is given a value of 1.000 SG at 39°F (4°C). This measurement is highly used in brewing in order to monitor various processes from boiling throughout fermentation.

Specific gravity points. the digits behind the decimal place of specifc gravity numbers. For example, 48 gravity points is the same as 1.048.

Stewing. see saccharification.

Sugaring. a black, granular oxide that forms inside a tube or pipe.

Tap. a device that is attached to a keg or cask in order to control the flow of the beer.

Terminal gravity. a term used to define the specific gravity after a beer has fermented and aged appropriately. A synonym is final gravity.

Thermometer. a tool for measuring temperature. Thermometers specifically made for brewing use alternative materials to mercury (such as alcohol) as a precautionary measure, so that if the thermometers break, no poisonous chemicals will taint the beer.

Toasted malt. a pale malt that is kilned for varying amounts of time, at different temperatures in order to produce certain "toasty" flavor characteristics.

Top fermentation. a fermentation method that utilizes yeast that rises to the surface as opposed to sinking to the bottom. Ales are "top fermented" beers while lagers are bottom fermented.

Topping up. a term used to define the addition of water after boiling a concentrated wort or extract; or the practice of adding water after primary fermentation in order to decrease the head space and prevent air contamination.

Trappist beer. beer brewed from any of the seven monasteries in Belgium and the Netherlands. These beers are all top-fermented, bottle conditioned and range in alcohol content from 4–12 percent by volume. They are renowned for their complex flavors and wonderful foam producing the delicate Belgian lace when consumed.

Uni-tanks. a type of fermenter that is used for both primary fermentation and conditioning.

Unload. the process of emptying the steeped malts from the steeping vessel.

Undermodified malt. malt containing cell wall constituents, such as beta-glucans and large protein molecules that contribute barley-like properties to malt.

Underoxygenated. a term used to describe worts that have not been sufficiently aerated for fermentation. Yeasts need an adequate amount of oxygen to effectively convert sugar to alcohol (and CO_2).

Viscosity. as an adjective, viscous describes body and mouthfeel, but viscosity refers to the resistance of liquid (beer) to flow — its thickness.

Vorlauf. German word referring to the process of recirculating wort through the grain bed.

Weissbier. the German term for wheat beer. Weiss literally means white, and wheat beers are very pale in color.

Weizen. the German term for top-fermented wheat beers.

Wild yeast. yeast that is naturally airborne. Originally, all beers were fermented with wild yeast.

Wort. the sweet solution created by boiling malt, hops and water. It is high in sugar and ferments when yeast is added.

Yeast. a single-celled organism belonging to the Fungi family. During fermentation, yeast convert sugar into alcohol and carbon dioxide.

Yeast nutrients. elements that can be added to a fermentation to promote yeast health and vitality. Homebrew supply shops sell premeasured packages of yeast nutrients for small batches.

Zapap. a simple and inexpensive lauter tun that consists of two buckets, one inside the other. The inner bucket is drilled with dozens of small (1/16-inch) holes so that the liquor drains from the grain bed into the other bucket.

INDEX

Page numbers in *italic* indicate illustrations; those in **bold** indicate tables.

A

acetaldehyde, 319–20
Acetobacter, 305
acid cleaners, 85, 87, 88
acidulated malt, 397–99
acid washing yeast, 199–201
adjunct, 18, 118–20, 203, 308–9
aeration
  banana aroma and, 316
  brewing basics, 20
  equipment, 51, *51*
  fermentation and, 224, 225, 226, 237–38
  hot-side aeration (HSA), 384–86
  oxidation and, 206, 386
  timing of, 205–6
  yeast, choosing, 172
aggressively bitter beer, 145–49
aging
  brewing basics, 16, 20, 21
  oak chips and, 157–61
  secondary fermenter, 235–37
  time for, 279–81
airlock
  brewing basics, 15
  equipment, 44, *44*

  foam through, 184, 217–18
  hopping techniques, 143, 149
alcohol
  attenuation and, 209, 212
  sanitizer, 88–89
  weight vs. volume, 38–39
alcohol lamp, 194, *194*
ales
  brewing basics, 22
  carbonation, 273
  equipment, 50
  fermentation, 217, 231
  ingredients, 122
  lagers vs., 24, 170–71, 237–38, 252
  yeast, choosing, 174
alkaline cleaners, 85, 87, 88
all-grain brewing, 357–406
  brewing basics, 13, 357–406
  equipment, 48–49, 57
  flavoring, 165–66
  foam (head), 308
alpha-acetolactate, 240, 241
alpha acids, 22, 131–32, 136, 406
alpha-amylase ("liquefaction"), 359, 378, 379, 380, 381, 391, 393
aluminum pots, 47

American double mash, 118–19, 382

amylase enzymes, 112, 343, 394

amylopectin, 378–79, 381

amylose, 378, 379

Anbesol flavor, 320–22

apparent attenuation (apparent degree of fermentation, ADF), 209–12

apparent gravity, 54

aromas of beer, 22, 34, 35–36, 219

attenuation, 169, 209–11, 243

autoclaves (pressure cookers), 106–8, 195, *195*

B

bacteria. *See also* cleaning, sanitizing
  brewing basics, 17
  cask beers, 305
  equipment and, 78–79
  freshness and, 296
  off-flavors and, 319, 327, 331, 393
  ropiness, 328–29
  scratches in vessels, 64–65, 68, 79, 85, 94, 104

baking vs. brewing yeast, 207

Balling scale, 61

banana aroma, 316

barley, 14, 22, 110, 114–15, *115,* 119

barleywines, 267–68, 281

batch sparging, 391, 396–97

bathtub ring, 189, 233, 234–35

beechwood chips for aging, 21

beer stone, 87, 88, 95

beta-amylase ("fermentability"), 359, 378, 379, 380–81, 393

beta-glucanase activity, 376

biological acidification, 398

bittering, 135–37, 138, 139–42, 145–49

black malts, 117, 121, 349

bleach, 84, 87, 88, 90–92, 94, 95, 103

blending, 333–34

blowing over, 235

blowoff, 187–89, 217–18, 262

boiling
  brewing basics, 14–15, 23, 25
  commercial beer, 19
  equipment, 46
  extracts and, 350–53
  sterilization, 25, 105–6, *106*
  wort volume, 400–401, 402

bottle capper and caps, 44, 259, *259,* 260, 291

bottle conditioning
  aging, 279, 282
  carbonation, 265–66
  filtering, 299–300, 311–12
  high-gravity beers, 208
  secondary fermentation, 214, 254–56
  sediment, 268–70

stability of beer, 268–72
storing, 263–64
terminal (final) gravity, 59
time for, 28–29
yeast, using from, *175,*
175–76
yeast autolysis, 280
bottles, 45, 63–64, 258
bottle trees, 98, 101, 258, *258*
bottling, kegging,
carbonation, 257–306
bourbon barrels, aging,
159–61
brass and fermentation,
74–76
braun hefe, 189, 233, 234–35
break, 25, 26, 53, 189
breaking bottles, 286–87
Brettanomyces, 51, 78
brewhouse yield, 367, 369
brewing basics, 12–40
Brew Your Own (magazine), 10
Brix scale, 61, 62
brown malts, 122
bubbles, watching, 232
buffering the pH of mash,
398
bug contamination, 329–30

C

calandrias (heat exchangers),
19, 52, 107
calibrating
hydrometer, 54, 58–59
thermometer, 71
Campden tablets, 152–53

canning pots, 46–47
cans, getting extract out,
339–40
caramel (crystal) malts, 22,
110, 111–12, 337, 348,
349–50
carbonation, 261–82
bottles and, 292
brewing basics, 16, 17–18,
24
carbon dioxide and, 262–63,
272–74, 278
conditioning and, 300
kegs and, 294, 305–6
nitrogenated beers, 40, 50,
275–79
overcarbonation, 281–82,
305–6
plastic bottles, 63–64
priming sugars, 261–62,
266–67, 271–72, 300
secondary fermentation,
254
stuck, 265–66, 288–89
carbonation stone, 278
carboy, 43, *43*
cask conditioning, 255, 304–
5, 310, 311
caustic cleaners, 104
ceramic canning vessels,
46–47
cereal mash, 119
chemical cleaners, 96–97, 104
chemical off-flavors, 302–3
cherry beer, 165–66
chewing grain, 110–11

chill haze, 118, 269, 270, 298, 312–14
chilling the wort
  brewing basics, 15, *15,* 20, 25–26
  cool dilution water, 354–55
  equipment, 42–43, *43,* 52–53
chlorinated polyvinyl chloride (CPVC), 77
chlorophenols, 90, 152–53, 302
chocolate malt, 117, 121, 349
clarification, 239, 269, 270, 298–300
clarity, 35
cleaning, sanitizing, 13, 45, 47, 68, 69, 83–108
Clerck, Jean De, 328
Clostridium botulinum, 107
cloudy wort, 388–89
clove flavor, 326–27
cold filtration, 313–14
cold storage, clarification, 298
color, 35, 112, 353
commercial beer, 17–21, 27, 122–23, 124, 214
compressed cones, 28, *127,* 127–28, 134, 146, 148, 232
conditioning. *See* carbonation
conical fermenters, 51, 65–68
conversions
  degrees Plato to specific gravity, 60
  honey to corn sugar, 162
copper and fermentation, 75, 76

copper kettles, 47–48
copper wort chillers, 105–8, *106*
corks, 289–90
corn, 14, 110, 118, 120
Cornelius kegs, 50, 278, 306
corn sugar (glucose), 186–87, 262, 267
counterflow wort chillers, 43, 51, *51, 52,* 106–8
counterpressure fillers, 259, *259,* 282–85, 287
cracking dark grains, 117, 349
creaminess, 40
cross-contamination, 78–79
cross-flow membrane filtration, 21
crushed grain, storing, 115–16
crystal (caramel) malts, 22, 110, 111–12, 337, 348, 349–50
culturing yeast, *175,* 175–76, *194–95,* 194–97

D

dark grains, 117, 121–22, 348–49
dechlorination, 152–53
decoction mashing, 118, 359, 366–67, 382
degassing beer, 281–82
degrees Plato, 60–62
denature, 393–95
density, 16, 54–55, *55. See also* gravity

detective (beer), 35–36, 37
diacetyl
  aeration and, 226
  brewing basics, 22
  lagers, 249–51, 331–32
  spoilage and, 296
  yeast, choosing, 169
diacetyl rest, 231, 240–42,
  255–56
difficulty of homebrewing, 13
dimethyl sulfide (DMS), 19,
  25, 34, 46, 316–19, 327,
  402
double IPA, 333–34
doubling recipes, 149
draft beers, 21, 272
dry beers, 223
dry beer/sweet beer, 378–82
dry heat for sanitizing, 94–95
dry hopping, 143–45, 148–49,
  232–34, 336
dry ice to evacuate air, 44
drying homegrown hops, 131
dry malt extract (DME)
  carbon dioxide, 262
  extract brewing and, 341
  liquid malt extract (LME)
    vs., 113–14, 168, 309, 337,
    339–40
  priming sugars, 266–67
  yeast starter, 185–87
dry vs. liquid yeast, 168–69,
  169, 173, 187–89, 220

E

enzymes and mashing, 364,

  378–82, 391–95
equipment
  bottling, 258–59, *258–59*
  choosing and using, 41–82
  cleaning, 47, 68, 69
  costs of, 45
  kegs, 48, 50, 76, *293,* 293–94
essences, flavoring beers, 166
esters, 22, 169, 219, 269, 316
ethanol, 89, 212
evaporation rate, 351, 400,
  402
extract brewing, 23, 223, 308–
  9, 335–56
extracts, 13, 14–15, 365–66,
  368–70

F

fast brewing, 28–29
fast fermentation, 228, 231
fermentation, 213–56. *See also*
  lagers; yeast
  brewing basics, 15–16, 18,
    20, 22, 24
  equipment, 43, 50, 54
  harvesting yeast, 191–93
  hops and, 138, 232–34
  krausening, 208, 214, 250–
    51, 254–55
  primary, 43, *43,* 143, 163,
    214
  refermentation, 16, 17–18
  secondary, 16, 44, 50, 192,
    214, 225, 254–56
  stuck, 217–18, 220, 225
  yeast off-flavors, 172, 173

ferrules, 49

filtration, 17, 19, 21, 72–73, 253, 269, 299, 315

final gravity (FG). *See* terminal (final) gravity

fining, 269, 298–99, 309–14, 315

first-wort hopping, 382–83

flavor, 22
 aging and, 280
 brewing basics, 25–26, 36
 carbonation and, 273
 chewing grains, 110–11
 essences for, 165–66
 metals and, 75–76
 yeast, choosing, 169, 170

Fleischmann's yeast, 207

flocculation, 169, 170, 270

foam. *See* head

foam-over, 217–18

force-carbonation of kegs, 294

forced fermentation, 223–24, 229–30

freshness of beer, 295–97

freshness of hops, 133

friability of grain, 110

frosted mugs, 33

fruity beers, 163–66, 219, 273

Fusarium, 355

G

gadgets, 49–52, *51,* 259

Garetz, Mark, 139, 140

gelatinization, 119

generations (yeast), 169, **169,** 174, 178–79

German ales, 24

glass vessels, 63, 64–65, 286–87

glassware, 32

glucanases, 377

grain bag method, 395–96

grain mill rollers, gap, 70–71

grains. *See* malt

gravity, 16. *See also* apparent gravity; density; hydrometer; original gravity (OG); terminal (final) gravity; specific gravity

gravity points per pound, 373

"green" aroma, 319–20

green-hop beer, 130–31

grist, 22, 118

growing
 hops, 129, 131, 132
 yeast, *175,* 175–76, 179–87, *194–95,* 194–97

gushing, 356

H

hard water, 154, 155–57

head, 304. *See also* krausen
 hop bittering acids, 325–26
 improving, *308,* 308–9
 mash profiles, 375–77
 pouring methods, 31–33, 326
 quats and, 102
 sensory evaluation, 35

headspace, 184, 187–89, 260

heat energy, fermentation, 230

heat exchangers (calandrias), 19, 52, 107
heat for sterilizing, 94–95
heat loss and sparging, 389–91
hefe-weizens, 22, 34, 170, 273
high fermentation temperature, 219
high-gravity beers, 20–21, 42, 208–9, 237, 405–6
high performance liquid chromatography (HPLC), 132
homebrew clubs or shops, 13
homebrewing. *See also* equipment; fermentation; yeast
  all-grain brewing, 357–406
  bottling, kegging, carbonation, 257–306
  brewing basics, 12–40
  cleaning, sanitizing, 13, 45, 47, 68, 69, 83–108
  extract brewing, 335–56
  glossary, 407–18
  ingredients, 109–66
  troubleshooting, 307–34
honey to corn sugar, 162
hop charge, calculating, 142
hop pellets, 27–28, 127, *127,* 133–34, 138, 146, 232
hop plugs, *127,* 127–28
hops
  brewing basics, 13, 14, 15, 20, 22, 27, 146–48

dry hopping, 143–45, 148–49, 232–34, 336
fermentation and, 232–34
first-wort hopping, 382–83
growing, 129, 131, 132
iced-tea flavor, 323–25
ingredient, 126–49
prehopped extract kits, 336–38
removal of, 253
whirlpooling, 20, 28, 138, 146, 353–54
hop socks, 137–38
hoses, 45, 69–70, 258–59
hot-side aeration (HSA), 384–86
hot water for cleaning, 84, 87, 88, 97, 98, 103, 106–8
hydrometer, 44, 54–59, *55,* 222, 223, 232, 369

I

iced-tea flavor, 323–25
immersion chillers, 42–43, *43,* 105–6, *106*
Imperial Stouts, 235–37
India Pale Ales (IPAs), 126, 323–25
infusion mashing, *79,* 80–81, 358–61, 365–66, 374
infusion mash tun, 19
ingredients, 109–66
inoculation loop, 194, *194*
insects in malt, 329–30
International Bitterness Unit (IBU), 142

invert sugar, 262, 267
iodophors, 87, 88, 98, 100–101, 103, 106
Irish moss, 310, 312–13
iron and fermentation, 75
isinglass fining, 269, 298–99, 310–11, 312, 315
iso-alpha acids, 314

K

Keep It Simple, Stupid (KISS), 154–55, 309
kegs, 293–306
  brewing basics, 21
  equipment, 48, 50, 76, *293,* 293–94
kettles, 14, 19, 42, *42,* 46–48, 49
kits, 13, 336–37
Kölsch, 316–19, 399
krausen
  airlock spills, 183–84
  removal, 234–35
  volume, 217–18
krausening, 208, 214, 250–51, 254–55

L

lactic acid, 398, 399
Lactobacillus, 78, 296, 393
lagering, 237–57
lagers. *See also* fermentation
  ales vs., 24, 170–71, 237–38, 252
  brewing basics, 17
  carbonation, 222, 272–75

diacetyl, 249–51, 331–32
  equipment, 50
  mashing, 398
  yeast and, 169, 174, 184–85, 189–91, 217, 246–47
  yeast at bottling, 274–75
lambics, 78–79, 166, 273, 331
late extract method, 350–52
lautering, 14, 71, 205, 345–46, 395–96
lauter tun, 19, 366, 372, 374
lead conductance valve (LCV), 132
Leuconostoc oenos, 241
lids for boiling wort, 402–3
light-struck (skunky) beer, 314
liquid malt extract (LME), 113–14, 168, 309, 337, 339–40
liquid vs. dry yeast, 168–69, **169,** 173, 187–89, 220

M

Maillard reaction products (MRPs), 111–12
malt
  acidulated malt, 397–99
  adjunct vs. all-malt brewing, 118–20
  brewing basics, 14, 15, 22
  cracking dark grains, 117, 349
  crystal (caramel), 22, 110, 111–12, 337, 348, 349–50

dark grains, 117, 121–22,
348–49
evaluating by chewing,
110–11
extract vs. grain, 23
insects in, 329–30
moldy, 355–56
roasted, 70, 110, 117,
121–22
specifications (specs),
122–24
storing, 115–16, 133–35,
356
malt coffee, 117
malt mill, 51, *51*, 70–71
mash
cereal mash, 119
consistency of, 363
fermentability and, 223
mash filters, 19
mashing. *See also* all-grain
brewing
aeration, 205
brewing basics, 14, 18–19,
23, 358–59
profiles, 375–77
protein and, 115
sanitation during, 93
sparging vs., 93
steeping vs., 343–46
stuck mash, 371–72
yields, 365–70, 373–74
mashing-off, 374
mash tun, 19, 48, *363*
maturation, 16
medicinal aromas, 302–3

microbrewed beers, 29, 274
milling
brewing basics, 18
cracking dark grains, 117,
349
evaluating grain, 110
stuck mash and, 371
yields (low) and, 365,
366–68
mineral deposits, 85, 88
moldy malt, malt extract,
355–56
mouthfeel, 32, 112, 120, 276,
304

N

natural gas ring burner, 81–82
nitrogenated beers, 40, 50,
275–79
noble hops, 136
"no-boil" extracts, 25
nonhopped extract, 336–37
"no-rinse" sanitizers, 87, 97,
100, 101–3
nutrients, yeast, 201–2

O

oak and aging, 157–61
oatmeal, 120
Obesumbacterium proteus, 327
off-flavors
chemical, 302–3
clarification, 298–300
mashing and, 393
reducing, 172–73, 315
sanitation and, 87, 97, 100

off-flavors *(continued)*
   trichloroanisole (TCA), 290
   wild yeast and, 296
   yeast, 65–66, 172–73, 192–
     93, 269, 279, 280, 315
one-way bottles, 291, 292
orifice plate, 40
original gravity (OG)
   brewing basics, 141
   esters and, 316
   fermentation and, 221
   low yields and, 366–68
   specific gravity and, 53
oven heat for sanitizing,
   94–95
overcarbonation, 281–82,
   305–6
overpitching, 315
oxidation and
   aeration, 206, 386
   aging, 279–80, 282, 283,
     301
   diacetyl, 241
oxygen
   adding, fermentation, 226
   growing yeast and, 181–82
   primary fermentation,
     203–5

P

packaging, 16, 21
pain beers, 273
Papazian, Charlie, 48, 139
passivation, 104–5
pasteurization, 21, 126, 240
peated malt, 125

pectin in recipes, 163–65
Pediococcus, 78, 296, 328–29,
   331
pelletized hops, 27–28, 127,
   127, 133–34, 138, 146, 232
peroxyacetic acid (PAA), 87,
   88, 90, 97–98, 102, 103
phenolic flavor, 320–23,
   326–27
pH of water, 397–99, 403–4
photolysis, 314
Pilsners, 316–20, 398
pitching yeast
   brewing basics, 20
   equipment, 57
   forced fermentation, 224
   off-flavors and, 172
   overpitching, 315
   rate, 183–84, 217
   underpitching, 220, 225, 228
plastic bottles, 63–64
plastic buckets, 44, 373–74
plastic fermenters, 64–65,
   93–94
Plato, degrees Plato, 60–62
points per pound, 373
polyvinylpolypyrrolidone
   (PVPP), 313
porters, 29, 122
pots, 42, *42,* 46–48, 49
pouring methods, 31–34, 326
powder brewery wash (PBW),
   104
prehopped extract kits,
   336–38
prerinsing of bottles, 98–100

pressure cookers (autoclaves), 106–8, 195, *195*

pressure loss, kegs, 295

primary fermentation, 43, *43*, 143, 163, 214

priming sugars, 16, 261–63, 265–67, 271–72, 300

propagation wort, 180–81

proteases, 269, 377

Q

quaternary ammonium compounds (quats, QACs), 87, 88, 101–3, 106

R

racking beers
brewing basics, 16
fermentation and, 221–22, 227–28
yeast off-flavors, 172, 173

racking cane, 44, 204, 215–16, *216*, 258–59

Rager, Jackie, 139, 140

rauchbier beer, 125

real degree of fermentation (RDF), 211, 212

recipes, adjusting, 149, 150–51

recirculated infusion mash system (RIMS), *79*, 80–81

recontamination, 101

recovering yeast, 199–201

reducing sugars, 111–12

refermentation, 16, 17–18

refractometer, 62–63

rehydrating dried yeast, 188–89

Reinheitsgebot, 267, 397

removing hops and trub, 253

rest, 199

retronasal, 36

returnable bottles, 291, 292

reusing yeast, 176–79

rice, 14, 110, 118, 120

rinsing after cleaning, 87, 97, 100, 101–3

roasted malts, 70, 110, 117, 121–22

ropiness, 328–29

rubbing (isopropyl) alcohol, 88–89

runoff, 62–63, 117

S

saccharification (stewing), 111–12

Saccharomyces cerevisiae, 207

safety, 81–82, 104, 282

sampling wort, 56–58

sanitizers vs. cleaners, 84, 85, 86, 87, 88, 92, 98–99

sanitizing bottle caps, 260

scratches and bacteria, 64–65, 68, 79, 85, 94, 104

sealing kegs, 295

secondary fermentation, 16, 44, 50, 192, 214, 225, 254–56. *See also* bottle conditioning; cask conditioning; krausening; lagers

sediment
  bottle conditioning, 268–70
  brewing basics, 16
  pouring beer, 33–34
  siphoning and, 215–16
sensory evaluation basics,
  35–37
separation, 20, 27
septic systems, 96–98
serving temperatures, 29–31
Servomyces, 202, 203
sherry casks for aging, 159–61
siphoning beer, 215–16, *216*
skimming, 234
skunky (light-struck) beer,
  314
S-methylmethionine (SMM),
  317, 318, 319
smoked beers, 125, 322–23
sodium hydroxide, 47, 84, 85,
  86, 88, 104
sodium hypochlorite, 84, 87,
  88, 90–92, 94, 95, 103
sodium metasilicate, 85, 88
soft water, 153–55
sour beers, 17
space for brewing, 51–52
sparge water, 14, 49
sparging
  batch sparging, 391, 396–97
  equipment, 49, 62–63
  mashing vs., 93
  pH and, 403–4
  specific gravity and, 346
  techniques, 389–90
specialty grains, 23, 337

specific gravity. *See also*
  hydrometer
  brewing basics, 38
  dry solids and, 162
  original gravity and, 53
  scales, 60–62
spigot, adding to kettle, 72–73
spunding, 245
stability of beer
  bottle conditioning, 268–72
  counterpressure filler,
    282–83
  kegs, 295–96
stainless steel vessels, 46, 64–
  65, 66–68, 103–5
steeping, 23, 343–48
step mashing, 359–61
sterilizing vs. sanitizing, 92
stewing (saccharification),
  111–12
storage of
  beers, 300–301
  grains, 115–16, 133–35, 356
stout faucets, 40, 278
stouts, 120
straining hops, 27
streaking for isolation, 196
stuck
  carbonation, 288–89
  fermentation, 217–18, 220,
    225
  mash, 371–72
styles of beer, 17–18, 272–74
submersion chillers, 52–53
sucrose (table sugar), 262
sugaring, 67

sulfur smell, lagers, 247–49, 252

sweet beer/dry beer, 378–82

T

tap system, 50

tap water for extract beers, 342

taste, 36

temperature
  carbonation, 263–64, 288–89
  esters, 316
  fermentation, 219, 230, 238
  mashing, 375–82, 386–88, 391–93
  serving beers, 29–31
  storage of beers, 300–301
  wort and adding yeast, 214

temperature stratification, 57

terminal (final) gravity
  determining, 59–60, 141
  fermentation, 242–47
  forced fermentation, 229
  racking and, 222

Textbook of Brewing (Clerck), 328

thermometer, 44, *45*, 59, 71

thick, syrupy beer, 328–29

thief, 51, 56, 60, *60*

Tinseth, Glenn, 139, 140

toasty flavor, 349–50

tourist (beer), 35, 36–37

trichloroanisole (TCA), 290

trisodium phosphate (TSP), 86

troubleshooting, 307–34

trub, 15, 28, 138, 189, 191–92, 233, 253, 353

turbo conditioning, 263–64

twist-off style bottles, 291–92

2-row vs. 6-row barley, 114–15, *115*, 119

U

underpitching, 220, 225, 228

uni-tank, 66, 227, 235

utilization, estimating, 139–42

V

viscosity of wort, 361, 374

vorlauf, 406

W

warm conditioning, 263–64

water cooler, 49

water for brewing, 358
  hard water, 154, 155–57
  pH of, 397–99
  soft water, 153–55
  tap water, 342

weizen yeast strains, 170

welded fitting for spigot, 73, 74

welded kettles, 66–68

wheat, 14, 22

wheat beers, 273, 305–6

whirlpooling, 20, 28, 138, 146, 353–54

whole hops, 28, *127,* 127–28, 134, 146, 148, 232

wild yeast, 96, 296, 302–3, 321, 327
wooden barrels for aging, 51
wort. *See also* boiling
  brewing basics, 13, 14, 15, *15,* 18
  cloudy, 388–89
  fermentability, 222–24
  gravity, 204–5
  growing yeast, 180–81, 187
  priming with, 267–68
  sampling, 56–58
  temperature and adding yeast, 215
  volume, 400–401, 402
  yeast nutrient, 202
wort chillers, 42–43, *43,* 52–53, 105–8, *106*

Y

yeast. *See also* fermentation; pitching yeast
  adding, 215

autolysis, 65–66, 192–93, 269, 279, 280, 299, 301
bottling time and, 274–75
brewing basics, 13, 16, 17, 22
choosing and using, 167–212
conditioning, 266
growing, *175,* 175–76, 179–87, *194–95,* 194–97
off-flavors, 172–73, 192–93, 269, 279, 280, 315
pouring beer, 33–34
removal, 298–300
strains, 24
washing, 198–99
wild yeast, 96, 296, 302–3, 321, 327
Yorkshire stone squares, 226

Z

zinc, 75, 202, 203